Bloom's Modern Critical Views

African American
  Poets:
    Wheatley–Tolson
African American
  Poets:
    Hayden–Dove
Edward Albee
Dante Alighieri
Isabel Allende
American and
  Canadian Women
  Poets,
  1930–present
American Women
  Poets, 1650–1950
Hans Christian
  Andersen
Maya Angelou
Asian-American
  Writers
Margaret Atwood
Jane Austen
Paul Auster
James Baldwin
Honoré de Balzac
Samuel Beckett
The Bible
William Blake
Jorge Luis Borges
Ray Bradbury
The Brontës
Gwendolyn Brooks
Elizabeth Barrett
  Browning
Robert Browning
Italo Calvino
Albert Camus
Truman Capote
Lewis Carroll
Miguel de Cervantes
Geoffrey Chaucer

Anton Chekhov
G.K. Chesterton
Kate Chopin
Agatha Christie
Samuel Taylor
  Coleridge
Joseph Conrad
Contemporary Poets
Julio Cortázar
Stephen Crane
Daniel Defoe
Don DeLillo
Charles Dickens
Emily Dickinson
E.L. Doctorow
John Donne and the
  17th-Century Poets
Fyodor Dostoevsky
W.E.B. DuBois
George Eliot
T.S. Eliot
Ralph Ellison
Ralph Waldo Emerson
William Faulkner
F. Scott Fitzgerald
Sigmund Freud
Robert Frost
William Gaddis
Johann Wolfgang
  von Goethe
George Gordon,
  Lord Byron
Graham Greene
Thomas Hardy
Nathaniel Hawthorne
Robert Hayden
Ernest Hemingway
Hermann Hesse
Hispanic-American
  Writers
Homer

Langston Hughes
Zora Neale Hurston
Aldous Huxley
Henrik Ibsen
John Irving
Henry James
James Joyce
Franz Kafka
John Keats
Jamaica Kincaid
Stephen King
Rudyard Kipling
Milan Kundera
Tony Kushner
Ursula K. Le Guin
Doris Lessing
C.S. Lewis
Sinclair Lewis
Norman Mailer
Bernard Malamud
David Mamet
Christopher Marlowe
Gabriel García
  Márquez
Cormac McCarthy
Carson McCullers
Herman Melville
Arthur Miller
John Milton
Molière
Toni Morrison
Native-American
  Writers
Joyce Carol Oates
Flannery O'Connor
George Orwell
Octavio Paz
Sylvia Plath
Edgar Allan Poe
Katherine Anne
  Porter

Bloom's Modern Critical Views

Marcel Proust
Thomas Pynchon
Philip Roth
Salman Rushdie
J. D. Salinger
José Saramago
Jean-Paul Sartre
William Shakespeare
William Shakespeare's
   Romances
George Bernard Shaw
Mary Wollstonecraft
   Shelley
Alexander Solzhenitsyn

John Steinbeck
Jonathan Swift
Amy Tan
Alfred, Lord Tennyson
Henry David Thoreau
J.R.R. Tolkien
Leo Tolstoy
Ivan Turgenev
Mark Twain
John Updike
Kurt Vonnegut
Derek Walcott
Alice Walker
Robert Penn Warren

H.G. Wells
Eudora Welty
Edith Wharton
Walt Whitman
Oscar Wilde
Tennessee Williams
Tom Wolfe
Virginia Woolf
William Wordsworth
Jay Wright
Richard Wright
William Butler Yeats
Émile Zola

Bloom's Modern Critical Views

GABRIEL GARCÍA MÁRQUEZ
Updated Edition

Edited and with an introduction by
Harold Bloom
Sterling Professor of the Humanities
Yale University

CHELSEA HOUSE
PUBLISHERS
An imprint of Infobase Publishing

Bloom's Modern Critical Views: Gabriel García Márquez—Updated Edition

Copyright ©2007 by Infobase Publishing

Introduction ©2007 by Harold Bloom

Chelsea House
An imprint of Infobase Publishing
132 West 31st Street
New York NY 10001

Library of Congress Cataloging-in-Publication Data

Gabriel García Márquez / Harold Bloom, editor. — Updated ed.
    p. cm. — (Bloom's modern criticial views)
  Includes bibliographical refereences and index.
  IBN 0-7910-9312-3 (hardcover)
  1. García Márquez, Gabriel, 1928—Criticism and interpretation. I. Bloom Harold.
  PQ8180.17.A73Z673 2006
  863'.64—dc22   2006020462

Chelsea House books are available at special discounts when purchased in bulk quantities for businesses, associations, institutions, or sales promotions. Please call our Special Sales Department in New York at (212) 967-8800 or (800) 322-8755.

You can find Chelsea House on the World Wide Web at http://www.chelseahouse.com.

Contributing Editor: Amy Sickels
Cover designed by Takeshi Takahashi
Cover photo © Piero Pomponi/Liaison/Getty Images

Printed in the United States of America

Bang EJB 10 9 8 7 6 5 4 3 2 1

This book is printed on acid-free paper.

All links and web addresses were checked and verified to be correct at the time of publication. Because of the dynamic nature of the web, some addresses and links may have changed since publication and may no longer be valid.

Contents

Editor's Note

My introduction suffers some doubt as to the permanence of *One Hundred Years of Solitude* (where all is hyperbole), while giving the preference to *Love in the Time of Cholera*, where erotic vitalism seems to me more appropriate in its extravagance.

An interview with the novelist opens the selection of essays, after which Gene H. Bell-Villada describes the principal events, so far, of the life of García Márquez.

The influence of Hemingway is traced by Harley Oberhelman, while Vera Kutzinski learnedly relates García Márquez to the poetry of Robert Hayden.

One wonders if Stephen Hart enhances *One Hundred Years of Solitude* by juxtaposing it with Isabel Allende's *The House of the Spirits* and Toni Morrison's *Beloved*, both of which essentially are ideological rather than literary texts, in my own judgment, but then I am an aesthete, always.

Steven Boldy seconds García Márquez's compassion for the characters of *One Hundred Years*.

The escape from sexual slavery by Eréndira in his famous tale of child prostitution is seen as an instance of García Márquez's transcendental irony by Diane E. Marting, while Raymond L. Williams commends *The Autumn of the Patriarch* as a worthy companion to the *Hundred Years*.

Jo Labanyi agrees with that judgment, though she sees *The Autumn of the Patriarch* as more modest in its style, after which Isabel Alvarez-Borland stresses parodistic elements in *Chronicle of a Death Foretold*.

Love in the Time of Cholera, perhaps García Márquez's masterwork, is seen as open-ended to interpretation by Robin Fiddian, while Lois Parkinson Zamora concludes this volume by highnoting the optimistic Nobel speech of the novelist, with its utopian hope.

HAROLD BLOOM

Introduction

I

Macondo, according to Carlos Fuentes, "begins to proliferate with the richness of a Columbian Yoknapatawpha." Faulkner, crossed by Kafka, is the literary origins of Gabriel García Márquez. So pervasive is the Faulknerian influence that at times one hears Joyce and Conrad, Faulkner's masters, echoed in García Márquez, yet almost always as mediated by Faulkner. *The Autumn of the Patriarch* may be too pervaded by Faulkner, but *One Hundred Years of Solitude* absorbs Faulkner, as it does all other influences, into a phantasmagoria so powerful and self-consistent that the reader never questions the authority of García Márquez. Perhaps, as Reinard Argas suggested, Faulkner is replaced by Carpentier and Kafka by Borges in *One Hundred Years of Solitude*, so that the imagination of García Márquez domesticates itself within its own language. Macondo, visionary realm, is an Indian and Hispanic act of consciousness, very remote from Oxford, Mississippi, and from the Jewish cemetery in Prague. In his subsequent work, García Márquez went back to Faulkner and Kafka, but then *One Hundred Years of Solitude* is a miracle and could only happen once, if only because it is less a novel than it is a Scripture, the Bible of Macondo; Melquíades the Magus, who writes in Sanskrit, may be more a mask for Borges than for the

1

author himself, and yet the Gypsy storyteller also connects García Márquez to the archaic Hebrew storyteller, the Yahwist, at once the greatest of realists and the greatest of fantasists but above all the only true rival of Homer and Tolstoy as a storyteller.

My primary impression, in the act of rereading *One Hundred Years of Solitude*, is a kind of aesthetic battle fatigue, since every page is rammed full of life beyond the capacity of any single reader to absorb. Whether the impacted quality of this novel's texture is finally a virtue I am not sure, since sometimes I feel like a man invited to dinner who has been served nothing but an enormous platter of Turkish Delight. Yet it is all story, where everything conceivable and inconceivable is happening at once, from creation to apocalypse, birth to death. Roberto González Echevarría has gone so far as to surmise that in some sense it is the reader who must die at the end of the story, and perhaps it is the sheer richness of the text that serves to destroy us. Joyce half-seriously envisioned an ideal reader cursed with insomnia who would spend her life in unpacking *Finnegans Wake*. The reader need not translate *One Hundred Years of Solitude*, a novel that deserves its popularity as it has no surface difficulties whatsoever. And yet, a new dimension is added to reading by this book. Its ideal reader has to be like its most memorable personage, the sublimely outrageous Colonel Aureliano Buendía, who "had wept in his mother's womb and been born with his eyes open." There are no wasted sentences, no mere transitions, in this novel, and you must notice everything at the moment you read it. It will all cohere, at least as myth and metaphor if not always as literary meaning.

In the presence of an extraordinary actuality, consciousness takes the place of imagination. That Emersonian maxim is Wallace Stevens's and is worthy of the visionary of *Notes toward a Supreme Fiction* and *An Ordinary Evening in New Haven*. Macondo is a supreme fiction, and there are no ordinary evenings within its boundaries. Satire, even parody, and most fantasy—these are now scarcely possible in the United States. How can you satirize Ronald Reagan or Jerry Falwell? Pynchon's *The Crying of Lot 49* ceases to seem fantasy whenever I visit Southern California, and a ride on the New York City subway tends to reduce all literary realism to an idealizing projection. Some aspects of Latin American existence transcend even the inventions of García Márquez. I am informed, on good authority, that the older of the Duvalier dictators of Haiti, the illustrious Papa Doc, commanded that all black dogs in his nation be destroyed when he came to believe that a principal enemy had transformed himself into a black dog. Much that is fantastic in *One Hundred Years of Solitude* would be fantastic anywhere, but much that seems unlikely to a North American critic may well be a representation of reality.

Emir Monegal emphasized that García Márquez's masterwork was unique among Latin American novels, being radically different from the diverse achievements of Julio Cortázar, Carlos Fuentes, Lezama Lima, Mario Vargas Llosa, Miguel Angel Asturias, Manuel Puig, Guillermo Cabrera Infante, and so many more. The affinities to Borges and to Carpentier were noted by Monegal as by Arenas, but Monegal's dialectical point seemed to be that García Márquez was representative only by joining all his colleagues in not being representative. Yet it is now true that, for most North American readers, *One Hundred Years of Solitude* comes first to mind when they think of the Hispanic novel in America. Alejo Carpentier's *Explosion in a Cathedral* may be an even stronger book, but only Borges has dominated the North American literary imagination as García Márquez has with his grand fantasy. It is inevitable that we are fated to identify *One Hundred Years of Solitude* with an entire culture, almost as though it were a new *Don Quixote*, which it most definitely is not. Comparisons to Balzac and even to Faulkner are also not very fair to García Márquez. The titanic inventiveness of Balzac dwarfs the later visionary, and nothing even in Macondo is as much a negative Sublime as the fearsome quest of the Bundrens in *As I Lay Dying*. *One Hundred Years of Solitude* is more of the stature of Nabokov's *Pale Fire* and Pynchon's *Gravity's Rainbow*, latecomers' fantasies, strong inheritors of waning traditions.

Whatever its limitations may or may not be, García Márquez's major narrative now enjoys canonical status as well as a representative function. Its cultural status continues to be enhanced, and it would be foolish to quarrel with so large a phenomenon. I wish to address myself only to the question of how seriously, as readers, we need to receive the book's scriptural aspect. The novel's third sentence is: "The world was so recent that things lacked names, and in order to indicate them it was necessary to point," and the third sentence from the end is long and beautiful:

Macondo was already a fearful whirlwind of dust and rubble being spun about by the wrath of the biblical hurricane when Aureliano skipped eleven pages so as not to lose time with facts he knew only too well, and he began to decipher the instant that he was living, deciphering it as he lived it, prophesying himself in the act of deciphering the last page of the parchment, as if he were looking into a speaking mirror.

The time span between this Genesis and this Apocalypse is six generations, so that José Arcadio Buendía, the line's founder, is the grandfather of the last Aureliano's grandfather. The grandfather of Dante's grandfather, the crusader Cassaguida, tells his descendant Dante that the poet perceives the truth because he gazes into that mirror in which the great and small of this life, before they think, behold their thought. Aureliano, at the end, reads the Sanskrit parchment of the gypsy, Borges-like Magus, and looks into a speaking mirror, beholding his thought before he thinks it. But does he, like Dante, behold the truth? Was Florence, like Macondo, a city of mirrors (or mirages) in contrast to the realities of the Inferno, the Purgatorio, the Paradiso? Is *One Hundred Years of Solitude* only a speaking mirror? Or does it contain, somehow within it, an Inferno, a Purgatorio, a Paradiso?

Only the experience and disciplined reflections of a great many more strong readers will serve to answer those questions with any conclusiveness. The final eminence of *One Hundred Years of Solitude* for now remains undecided. What is clear to the book's contemporaries is that García Márquez has given contemporary culture, in North America and Europe, as much as in Latin America, one of its double handful of necessary narratives, without which we will understand neither one another nor our own selves.

II

The aesthetic principle of *Love in the Time of Cholera* is only a slightly chastened version of what might be the motto of *One Hundred Years of Solitude*: "Anything goes," or even "Everything goes." Anything and everything goes into the mix: Faulkner, Kafka Borges, Carpentier, Conrad, Joyce. Both novels are Scriptures: *Solitude* is an Old Testament, and *Cholera* a New Testament, at least for García Márquez and the most devoted of his readers and critics. I myself have come to value *Cholera* over *Solitude*, but that is a choice of riches.

What Faulkner—who most valued the Bible (as literature only), Shakespeare, Melville, Conrad, and Joyce—would have made of these New World Hispanic masterpieces, I cannot surmise. The verbal cascades he would have recognized as akin to his own, and the heroic individualism surely would have moved him. Yet he went about while waiting for his doom to lift, and his greatest figures—Darl Bundren, Quentin Compson, Sutpen, Joe Christmas, Popeye—are damned beyond damnation. Though Faulkner could be as grandly comic as Dickens, as is witnessed by the Snopes family, who now constitute the Texan Republican party, led by Tom De Lay Snopes, while our nation has chosen Benito Bush as Il Duce. Oscar Wilde was always right: life has no choice but to imitate art.

The antic joy of García Márquez might have been shrugged away by Faulkner, at least in his tragic mode, but he would have approved the last-ditch humanism affirmed both by precursor and latecomer. Decadence, the obsessive fear of incest, the drowning out of creative solitude by an ocean of information: these are common themes and apprehensions. What then is the saving difference, besides amazing high spirits in García Márquez, that distinguishes the two?

Faulkner's hopes rarely are persuasive: his greatest characters are as nihilistic as Shakespeare's. The immense popularity of García Márquez was earned by his exuberance, which veils his own apocalyptic forebodings. What Shakespeare was to Faulkner, Cervantes necessarily is to García Márquez: the truest ancestor. Cervantes, in his dark wisdom, is not less nihilistic than Shakespeare, and I do not believe that either ultimately was a Christian believer, any more than Faulkner or García Márquez can be said to be.

García Márquez's difference from all three is more evident in *Cholera* than in *Solitude*: he really does have a High Romantic faith in Eros, though he knows the Freudian truth that love too frequently is a mask for the Death Drive. Yet I prefer *Cholera* to *Solitude* finally because Florentine Ariza is dauntless, as here in the novel's closing passage:

> "Let us keep going, going, going, back to La Dorada."
>
> Fermina Daza shuddered because she recognized his former voice, illuminated by the grace of the Holy Spirit, and she looked at the Captain: he was their destiny. But the Captain did not see her because he was stupefied by Florentino Ariza's tremendous powers of inspiration.
>
> "Do you mean what you say?" he asked.
>
> "From the moment I was born," said Florentino Ariza, "I have never said anything I did not mean."
>
> The Captain looked at Fermina Daza and saw on her eyelashes the first glimmer of wintry frost. Then he looked at Florentino Ariza, his invincible power, his intrepid love, and he was overwhelmed by the belated suspicion that it is life, more than death, that has no limit.
>
> "And how long do you think we can keep up this goddamn coming and going?" he asked.
>
> Florentino Ariza had kept his answer ready for fifty-three years, seven months, and eleven days and nights.
>
> "Forever," he said.

Interview with
Gabriel García Márquez

New York City   June 3, 1971

The fact of the matter is that my pursuit of García Márquez—a special trip from Paris to Barcelona, a two-week wait in a Catalonian hotel, long-distance calls and cables and letters from New York to Spain—actually started only after I handed over to him, during our second and last meeting in the Barcelona Ritz, the questionnaire I had prepared at his own suggestion. You see, García Márquez is well known for his resistance to reporters, and he was at that time only willing to grant a written interview. Over a cup of tea he promised to have his answers ready in a couple of days, suggesting that if I wait there I could follow through my interview with new questions based on his written statements. But from then on I was unable to reach García Márquez, although before I left, he did get word to me through his wife that he would mail me the manuscript which I never received.

Six months later, when García Márquez came to New York to receive the honorary degree given to him by Columbia University, he answered my telephone call without delay. The following morning we met at his hotel, the Plaza, where we had an early breakfast after persuading the maître d' to let us in—not because of García Márquez's mafioso mustache, but because he was tieless. Then we borrowed the deserted Persian Room, and this time,

From *Seven Voices: Seven Latin American Writers Talk to Rita Guibert*. © 1973 by Alfred A. Knopf, Inc.

with a whirling tape, we finished in less than three hours the long-awaited interview.

Gabriel García Márquez (Gabo to his friends) was born in 1928 in Aracataca, a very small Colombian town close to a banana plantation in a place called Macondo, an even tinier town in the middle of nowhere, which García Márquez used to explore when he was a child.

Years later, he named the mythical land where some of his stories take place after Macondo, and closed the cycle with *One Hundred Years of Solitude*, the novel he began when he was eighteen. But as a young writer he had "neither the vital experience nor the literary means" to complete such a work (then called "The House") and decided instead to write Leaf Storm, his first book. Only in 1967, after many years of struggle and frustration in writing it, *One Hundred Years of Solitude* (his fifth book) was published in Buenos Aires, provoking—as the Peruvian novelist Mario Vargas Llosa wrote—"a literary earthquake throughout Latin America. The critics recognized the book as a masterpiece of the art of fiction and the public endorsed this opinion, systematically exhausting new editions.... Overnight, García Márquez became almost as famous as a great soccer player or an eminent singer of boleros." In 1969, the book's translation was selected by the Académie Française as the best foreign book of the year and other translations earned an equally enthusiastic response. But, according to the author, the best reviews he received came from the United States; "They are professional readers ... some are progressive, others so reactionary, as they are supposed to be; but as readers, they are wonderful."

García Márquez doesn't consider himself an intellectual but "a writer who rushes into the arena like a bull and then attacks." For him, literature is a very simple game and "in a literary panorama dominated by Julio Cortázar's *Hopscotch*, Lezama Lima's *Paradiso*, Carlos Fuentes's *A Change of Skin*, and Guillermo Cabrera Infante's *Three Trapped Tigers*," writes Emir Rodriguez Monegal, "all experimental works to the limit of experimentation itself; all hard and demanding on their readers," García Márquez, in his *One Hundred Years of Solitude*, "with an olympian indifference to alien technique, sets himself free to narrate, with an incredible speed and apparent innocence, an absolutely lineal and chronological story ... with its beginning, middle and end." And, as García Márquez himself says, it is the "least mysterious" of his books because "I tried to lead the reader by the hand so as not to get him lost at any moment."

Similarly, in a way, García Márquez had been led to success by his friends—because it was his friends who took the manuscript of *Leaf Storm* (1955) to the printer when they found it on his desk after he has gone to Italy in 1954 as a reporter for the Colombian daily *El Espectador*. Then in Paris, in

1957, after the dictator Rojas Pinilla had shut down the newspaper, García Márquez, who was living on credit in a Latin Quarter hotel, finished *No One Writes to the Colonel*; but considering his work a failure, he buried the manuscript, "tied with a colored ribbon in the bottom of a suitcase." Subsequently, he returned to Colombia to marry his fiancée, Mercedes—the same Mercedes of the "sleepy eyes" engaged to Gabriel in *One Hundred Years of Solitude*—and moved for a couple of years to Venezuela where, while working as a journalist, he wrote *Los funerales de Mamá grande*. From Caracas he went to New York as the correspondent for Prensa Latina—revolutionary Cuba's news agency. Resigning after several months, and traveling by land through the south of the United States, he arrived in Mexico in 1961, where he settled for several years. And there, again, it was García Márquez's friends who arranged for his two recent books to be published in 1961–2, the same period in which his novel *La mala hora*, written in Mexico, was published after winning a Colombian literary contest. His friends had forced him to submit the manuscript to the competition after persuading him to change the original title, "Este pueblo de mierda." "The truth is," says Mario Vargas Llosa, "that without the obstinacy of his friends, García Márquez would perhaps still today be an unknown writer."

Today García Márquez can allow himself to live as a "professional writer" on the success earned mainly from *One Hundred Years of Solitude*—the saga of Macondo and the Buendías, which starts in a world "so recent many things lacked names and in order to indicate them it was necessary to point," a world where carpets fly; the dead are resuscitated; a rain lasts exactly four years, eleven months, and two days; the first Buendía spends his last years tied to a chestnut tree in his orchard muttering in Latin; tiny yellow flowers fall from the sky when he dies; Úrsula, his wife, lives through generations and generations; Aureliano discovers that literature is the best toy ever invented to mock the public ... and the chronicle ends when, after more than one hundred years of the family's struggles to avoid the fulfillment of an old prophecy, the line of the Buendías comes to an end when out of incestuous union a boy born with a pig's tail is devoured by an army of ants. And with this saga the author confirms what he said some time ago: "Everything is permitted to the writer, as long as he is capable of making it believable."

Postscript: Before leaving New York, García Márquez, who after our interview moved from his previous hotel to an undisclosed address, called to send me "a kiss as a gesture of tenderness." I then asked him how he spent the days in the city. "Great, Mercedes and I spent three delicious days shopping in New York." "Did you visit the museums? Did you go to the country?" "Of course not, and you can add to everything I told you that I don't like either art or nature."

RG: Your resistance to journalists is well known, and in the present case a lot of persuasion and several months of waiting have been necessary to overcome it.

GGM: Look, I've got absolutely nothing against journalists. I've done the job myself and I know what it's like. But if at this stage of my life I were to answer all the questions they want to ask me, I shouldn't be able to work. Besides, I should also be left with nothing to say. You see I realize that just because I have a fellow feeling for journalists, interviews have in the end become a form of fiction for me. I want the reporter to go away with something new, so I try to find a different answer to the same old questions. One no longer tells the truth, and the interview becomes a novel instead of journalism. It's literary creation, pure fiction.

RG: I don't object to fiction as a part of reality.

GGM: That could make a good interview!

RG: In *Relato de un náufrago* (*The Story of a Castaway*)—a journalistic report written in 1955 for Bogotá's newspaper *El Espectador* and published as a book in Barcelona in 1970—you narrate the odyssey of a sailor who lived for ten days adrift on a raft. Is there any element of fiction in that story?

GGM: There's not a single invented detail in the whole account. That's what's so astonishing. If I had invented that story I would have said so, and been very proud of it too. I interviewed that boy from the Colombian navy—as I explain in my introduction to the book—and he told me his story in minute detail. As his cultural level was only fair he didn't realize the extreme importance of many of the details he told me spontaneously, and was surprised at my being so struck by them. By carrying out a form of psychoanalysis I helped him remember things—for instance, a seagull he saw flying over his raft—and in that way we succeeded in reconstructing his whole adventure. It went like a bomb! The idea had been to publish the story in five or six installments in *El Espectador* but by about the third there was such enthusiasm among the readers, and the circulation of the paper had increased so enormously, that the editor said to me, "I don't know how you're going to manage, but you must get at least twenty installments out of this." So then I set about enriching every detail.

RG: As good a journalist as a writer ...

GGM: It was my bread and butter for many years, wasn't it? ... and now as a writer. I've earned my living at both professions.

RG: Do you miss journalism?

GGM: Well, I do feel a great nostalgia for my journalist days. As things have turned out I couldn't be a hard-nosed reporter now, which was what I used to prefer ... going wherever the news was, whether it was a war, a fight, or a beauty contest, landing by parachute if necessary. Although my work as a writer, particularly as I do it now, derives from the same source as my journalism, the elaboration is purely theoretical, whereas the other was done on the spot. Today, when I read some of the things I wrote as a journalist I'm full of admiration, much more than for my work as a novelist, although I can give all my time to that now. Journalism was different; I used to arrive at the newspaper office and the editor would say, "We've got just an hour before this piece of news must be handed in." I think I should be incapable of writing one of those pages nowadays, even in a month.

RG: Why? Have you become more conscious of language?

GGM: I think one needs a certain degree of irresponsibility to be a writer. I was about twenty at that time and I was hardly aware what dynamite I held between my hands and in every page I produced. Now, particularly since *One Hundred Years of Solitude*, I've become very conscious of it because of the enormous interest the book has aroused ... a boom of readers. I no longer think of what I write as if it would only be read by my wife and my friends, I know that a lot of people are waiting for it. Every letter I write weighs me down, you can't imagine how much! Then I nearly die of envy of my old journalist self, and the days when I used to dispatch the business so easily. It was terrific to be able to do that....

RG: How has the success of *One Hundred Years of Solitude* affected your life? I remember your saying in Barcelona, "I'm tired of being García Márquez."

GGM: It's changed my whole life. I was once asked, I can't remember where, how my life differed before and after that book, and I said that after it "there are four hundred more people." That's to say before the book I had my friends, but now there are enormous numbers of people who want to see me and talk to me—journalists, academics, readers. It's strange ... most of my readers aren't interested in asking questions, they only want to talk about the book. That's very flattering if you consider case by case, but added up they begin to be a problem in one's life. I would like to please them all, but as that's impossible I have to act meanly ... you see? For instance, by saying I'm leaving a town when all I'm really doing is changing my hotel. That's how vedettes behave, something I always hated, and I don't want to play the vedette. There is, besides, a problem of conscience when deceiving people and dodging them. All the same I have to lead my own life, so the moment comes when I tell lies. Well, that can be boiled down to a cruder phrase than the one you mentioned. I say, "I've had it to the balls with García Márquez!"

RG: Yes, but aren't you afraid that attitude may end by isolating you in an ivory tower, even against your will?

GGM: I'm always aware of that danger, and remind myself of it every day. That's why I went to the Caribbean coast of Colombia a few months ago, and from there explored the Lesser Antilles, island by island. I realized that by escaping from those contacts I was reducing myself to the four or five friends I make wherever I live. In Barcelona, for instance, we always mix with about four couples, people with whom we have everything in common. From the point of view of my private life and my character, that's marvelous—that's what I like, but a moment came when I realized that this life was affecting my novel. The culmination of my life—to be a professional writer—had been achieved in Barcelona, and I suddenly became aware that it was a terribly damaging thing to be. I was leading the life of the complete professional writer.

RG: Could you describe what the life of a professional writer is like?

GGM: Listen, I'll tell you what a typical day is like. I always wake very early, at about six in the morning. I read the paper in bed, get up, drink my coffee while I listen to music on the radio, and at about nine—after the boys have gone to school—I sit down to write. I write without any sort of interruption until half past two, which is when the boys come home and noise begins in the house. I haven't answered the telephone all morning ... my wife has been filtering calls. We lunch between half past two and three. If I've been to bed late the night before I have a siesta until four in the afternoon. From that time until six I read and listen to music—I always listen to music, except when I'm writing because I attend to it more than to what I'm writing. Then I go out and have a coffee with someone I have a date with and in the evening friends always come to the house. Well ... that seems to be an ideal state of things for a professional writer, the culmination of all he's been aiming at. But, as you find out once you get there, it's sterile. I realized that I'd become involved in a completely sterile existence—absolutely the opposite of the life I led when I was a reporter, what I wanted to be—and that this was having an effect on the novel I was writing—a novel based on cold experience (in the sense that it no longer interested me much), whereas my novels are usually based on old stories combined with fresh experiences. That's the reason I went to Barranquilla, the town where I was brought up and where all my oldest friends live. But ... I visit all the islands in the Caribbean, I take no notes, I do nothing, I spend two days here and then go on somewhere else ... I ask myself, "What did I come for?" I'm not very clear what I'm doing, but I know I'm trying to oil some machinery that has ground to a halt. Yes, there's a natural tendency—when you have solved a series of material problems—to become bourgeois and shut yourself in an ivory tower, but I have an urge, and also an instinct, to escape from that situation— a sort of tug-of-war is going on inside me. Even in Barranquilla—where I may be staying for a short period of time, which has a lot to do with not being isolated—I realize that I'm losing sight of a large area that interests me, out of my tendency to confine myself to a small group of friends. But this isn't me, it's imposed by the medium, and I must defend myself. Just another argument, as you see, which makes me say without dramatization but for the sake of my work—"I've had it to the balls with García Márquez."

RG: Your awareness of the problem should make it easier to deal with this crisis.

GGM: I feel as if the crisis had lasted longer than I thought it would, much longer than my publisher thought, much longer than the critics thought. I keep on meeting someone who is reading my book, someone who has the same reaction that readers had four years ago: Readers seem to emerge from caves like ants. It's really phenomenal....

RG: Which doesn't make it any less flattering.

GGM: Yes, I do think it's very flattering, but the difficulty is how to deal with this phenomenon in practice. It's not only the experience of meeting people who have read the book, and hearing what it meant to them (I've been told amazing things), it's the experience of being popular. Those books have brought me a popularity more like that of a singer or film star than a writer. All this has become quite fantastic, and strange things happen to me: since the time I was on night shift at the newspaper I have been very friendly with the taxi drivers of Barranquilla, because I used to go and drink coffee with those parked at the cab stand across the street. Many of them are still driving, and when I take their taxis today they don't want to be paid; but the other day one who obviously didn't know me took me home, and when I paid him he said to me confidentially: "Did you know that García Márquez lives here?" "How do you know?" I asked him. "Because I've often taken him in my cab," he replied. You notice that the phenomenon is being reversed, and the dog is biting its own tail ... the myth has caught up with me.

RG: Anecdotes for a novel ...

GGM: It would be a novel about a novel.

RG: The critics have written at length about your work. Which of them do you agree with most?

GGM: I don't want my answer to seem unappreciative, but the truth is—and I know it's difficult to believe—that I don't pay much attention to the critics. I don't know why, but I don't compare what I think with what they say. So I don't really know whether I agree with them or not....

RG: Aren't you interested in the critics' opinions?

GGM: They used to interest me a lot at first, but now rather less. They seem to have said very little that's new. There was a moment when I stopped reading them because they were conditioning me—in a way they were telling me what my next book ought to be like. As soon as the critics began rationalizing my work I kept on discovering things that were not convenient for me to discover. My work stopped being intuitive.

RG: Melvin Maddocks of *Life*, said of *One Hundred Years of Solitude*, "Is Macondo meant to be taken as a sort of surrealistic history of Latin America? Or does García Márquez intend it as a metaphor for all modern men and their ailing communities?"

GGM: Nothing of the sort. I merely wanted to tell the story of a family who for a hundred years did everything they could to prevent having a son with a pig's tail, and just because of their very efforts to avoid having one they ended by doing so. Synthetically, speaking, that's the plot of the book, but all that about symbolism ... not at all. Someone who isn't a critic said that the interest the novel had aroused was probably due to the fact that it was the first real description of the private life of a Latin American family ... we go into the bedroom, the bathroom, the kitchen, into every corner of the house. Of course I never said to myself, "I shall write a book that will be interesting for that reason," but now that it's written, and this has been said about it, I think it may be true. Anyway it's an interesting concept and not all that shit about a man's destiny, etc....

RG: I think the theme of solitude is a predominant one in your work.

GGM: It's the only subject I've written about, from my first book until the one I'm working on now, which is an apotheosis of the theme of solitude. Of absolute power, which I consider must be total solitude. I've been writing about that process from the first. The story of Colonel Aureliano Buendía—the wars he fought and his progress to power—is really a progress toward solitude. Not only is every member of his family solitary—as I've repeated often in the book, perhaps more than I ought—but there's also the anti-solidarity, even of people who sleep in the same bed.

I think the critics who most nearly hit the mark were those who concluded that the whole disaster of Macondo—which is a telluric disaster as well—comes from this lack of solidarity—the solitude which results when everyone is acting for himself alone. That's then a political concept, and interests me as such—to give solitude the political connotation I believe it should have.

RG: When you were writing it, were you consciously intending to convey a message?

GGM: I never think about conveying messages. My mental makeup is ideological and I can't get away from it—nor do I try or want to. Chesterton said that he could explain Catholicism starting from a pumpkin or a tramway. I think one could write *One Hundred Years of Solitude*, or a story about sailors, or the description of a football match, and still keep its ideological content. It's the ideological spectacles I wear that explain—not Catholicism in this case—but something else which I can't define. I have no preconceived intention to say this or the other thing in a book of mine. I'm solely interested in the behavior of the characters, not whether that behavior is exemplary or reprehensible.

RG: Are you interested in your characters from a psychoanalytical point of view?

GGM: No, because that would need a scientific training which I don't possess. The opposite happens. I develop my characters and work on them, in the belief that I'm only making use of their poetical aspects. When a character has been assembled, some of the experts tell me that this is a psychoanalytic analysis. And I'm confronted then with a series of scientific assumptions that I don't hold and have never even dreamed of. In Buenos Aires—a city of psychoanalysts, as you know—some of them held a meeting to analyze *One Hundred Years of Solitude*. They came to the conclusion that it represented a well-sublimated Oedipus complex, and goodness knows what else. They discovered that the characters were perfectly coherent from a psychoanalytic point of view, they almost seemed like case histories.

RG: And they talked about incest too.

GGM: What interested me was that the aunt should go to bed with her nephew, not the psychoanalytic origins of this event.

RG: It still seems strange that, although machismo is one of the typical features of Latin American society, it's the women in your books who have strong, stable characters—or, as you've said yourself, they are masculine.

GGM: This didn't happen consciously, the critics made me see it, and set me a problem by so doing, because I now find it more difficult to work on that material. But there's no doubt that it's the power of women in the home—in society as it's organized, particularly in Latin America—that enables men to launch out into every sort of chimerical and strange adventure, which is what makes our America. This idea came to me from one of the true stories my grandmother used to tell about the civil wars of the last century, which can be more or less equated with Colonel Aureliano Buendía's wars. She told me that a certain man went to the war and said to his wife, "You'll decide what to do with your children." And for a year or more the wife was the one who kept the family going. In terms of literature, I see that if it weren't for the women taking responsibility for the rearguard, the evil wars of the last century, which are so important in the history of our country, would never have taken place.

RG: That shows that you're not antifeminist.

GGM: What I most definitely am is antimachista. Machismo is cowardly, a lack of manliness.

RG: To return to the critics ... you know that some of them have insinuated that *One Hundred Years of Solitude* is a plagiarism of Balzac's *La Recherche de l'absolu*. Günther Lorenz suggested this at a writer's conference in Bonn in 1970. Luis Cova García published an article called "Coincidence or Plagiarism?" in the Honduran review *Ariel,* and in Paris a Balzac specialist, Professor Marcelle Bargas, made a study of the two novels and drew attention to the fact that the vices of one society and period, as depicted by Balzac, had been transferred to *One Hundred Years of Solitude.*

GGM: It's strange; someone who had heard these comments sent me Balzac's book, which I had never read. Balzac doesn't interest me now, although he's sensational enough and I read what I could of him at one time—however, I glanced through it. It struck me that to say one book derives from the other is pretty light and superficial. Also, even if I were prepared to accept the fact that I had read it before and decided to plagiarize it, only some five pages of my book could possibly have come from *La Recherche*, and in the final analysis a single character, the alchemist. Well ... I ask you, five pages and one character against three hundred pages and some two hundred characters that don't come from Balzac's book. I think the critics ought to have gone on and searched two hundred other books to see where the rest of the characters came from. Besides which, I'm not at all afraid of the idea of plagiarism. If I had to write *Romeo and Juliet* tomorrow I would do it, and would feel it was marvelous to have the chance to write it again. I've talked a lot about the *Oedipus Rex* of Sophocles, and I believe it has been the most important book in my life; ever since I first read it I've been astonished by its absolute perfection. Once, when I was at a place on the Colombian coast, I came across a very similar situation to that of the drama of *Oedipus Rex*, and I thought of writing something to be called *Oedipus the Mayor*. In this case I wouldn't have been charged with plagiarism because I should have begun by calling him Oedipus. I think the idea of plagiarism is already finished. I can myself say where I find Cervantes or Rabelais in *One Hundred Years of Solitude*—not as to quality but because of things I've taken from them and put there. But I can also take the book line by line—and this is a point the critics will never be able to reach—and say what event or memory from real life each comes from. It's a very curious experience to talk to my mother about such things; she remembers the origin of many of the episodes, and naturally describes them more faithfully than I do because she hasn't elaborated them as literature.

RG: When did you start writing?

GGM: As far back as I can remember. My earliest recollection is of drawing "comics" and I realize now that this may have been because I couldn't yet write. I've always tried to find ways of telling stories and I've stuck to literature as the most accessible. But I think my vocation is not so much to be a writer as a story-teller.

RG: Is that because you prefer the spoken word to writing?

GGM: Of course. The splendid thing is to tell a story and for that story to die there and then. What I should find ideal would be to tell you the story of the novel I'm now writing, and I'm sure it would produce the same effect I'm trying to get by writing it, but without so much effort. At home, at any time of day, I recount my dreams, what has happened to me or not happened to me. I don't tell my children make-believe stories, but about things that have happened, and they like that very much. Vargas Llosa, in the book he's doing on the literary vocation, *García Márquez, historia de un deicidio*, takes my work as an example and says I'm a seedbed of anecdotes. To be liked because I've told a good story: that's my true ambition.

RG: I've read that when you finish *El otoño del patriarca* (*The Autumn of the Patriarch*) you're going to write stories instead of novels.

GGM: I've got a notebook where I'm jotting down the stories that occur to me and making notes for them. I've already got about sixty, and I fancy I shall reach a hundred. What is curious is the process of internal elaboration. The story—which may arise from a phrase or an incident—

either occurs to me complete in a fraction of a second or not at all. It has no starting point; a character just arrives or goes away. I'll tell you an anecdote which may give you some idea how mysteriously I arrive at a story. One night in Barcelona when we had visitors, the lights suddenly went out. As the trouble was local we sent for an electrician. While he was putting the defect right and I was holding a candle for him to see by, I asked him, "What the devil's happened to the light?" "Light is like water," he said, "you turn a tap and out it comes, and the meter registers it as it comes through." In that fraction of a second, a complete story came to me:

In a city away from the sea—it might be Paris, Madrid, or Bogotá—there live on the fifth floor a young couple and their two children of ten and seven. One day the children ask their parents to give them a rowboat. "How can we give you a rowboat?" says the father. "What can you do with it in this town? When we go to the seaside in the summer we can hire one." The children obstinately persist that they want a rowboat, until their father says: "If you get the top places in school I'll give you one." They get the top places, their father buys the boat, and when they take it up to the fifth floor he asks them: "What are you going to do with it?" "Nothing," they reply, "we just wanted to have it. We'll put it in our room." One night when their parents are at the cinema, the children break an electric light bulb and the light begins to flow out—just like water—filling the whole house three feet deep. They take the boat and begin rowing through the bedrooms and the kitchen. When it's time for their parents to return they put it away in their room and pull up the plugs so that the light can drain away, put back the bulb, and ... nothing has happened. This becomes such a splendid game that they begin to let the light reach a greater depth, put on dark glasses and flippers, and swim under the beds and tables, practicing underwater fishing.... One night, passersby in the street notice light streaming out of the windows and flooding the street, and they send for the fire brigade. When the firemen open the door they find that the children had been so absorbed in their game that they had allowed the light to reach the ceiling, and are floating in the light, drowned.

Can you tell me how it was that this complete story, just as I've told you, occurred to me within a fraction of a second? Naturally, as I've told it often, I find a new angle every time—change one thing for another or add a detail—but the idea remains the same. There's nothing deliberate or predictable in all this, nor do I know when it's going to happen to me. I'm at the mercy of my imagination, and that's what says yes or no.

RG: Have you written that story yet?

GGM: I've merely made a note: #7 "Children drowning in light." That's all. But I carry that story in my head, like all the rest, and I revise it from time to time. For instance, I take a taxi and remember story #57—I completely revise it and realize that in an incident that had occurred to me the roses I visualized aren't roses at all but violets. I incorporate this change in my story and make a mental note of it.

RG: What a memory!
GGM: No, I only forget what has no literary value for me.

RG: Why don't you write it when you first think of it?
GGM: If I'm writing a novel I can't mix other things with it, I must work at that book only, even if it takes me more than ten years.

RG: Don't you unconsciously incorporate these stories in the novel you're writing?
GGM: These stories are in completely separate compartments and have nothing to do with the book about the dictator. That happened with *Big Mama's Funeral*, *La mala hora* (*Bad Times*) and *No One Writes to the Colonel*, because I was working on the lot of them at practically the same time.

RG: Have you never thought of becoming an actor?
GGM: I'm terribly inhibited in front of cameras or a microphone. But in any case I would be the author or director.

RG: On one occasion you said, "I've become a writer out of timidity. My real inclination is to be a conjuror, but I get so confused when I try to perform a trick that I've had to take refuge in the solitude of literature. In my case, being a writer is a stupendous task, because I'm a numbskull at writing."
GGM: What a good thing to read me! The bit about my real vocation being to be a conjuror corresponds exactly with what I've told you. It would delight me to have success telling stories in salons, like a conjuror pulling rabbits out of a hat.

RG: Is writing a great effort for you?
GGM: Terribly hard work, more so all the time. When I say I'm a writer out of timidity, it's because what I ought to do is fill this room, and go out and tell my story, but my timidity prevents me. I couldn't have carried on this conversation of ours if there had been two more people at this table; I should have felt I couldn't control my audience. Therefore when I want to tell a story I do it in writing, sitting alone in my room and working hard. It's agonizing work, but sensational. Conquering the problem of writing is so delightful and so thrilling that it makes up for all the work … it's like giving birth.

RG: Since you first made contact in 1954 with the Experimental Cinema in Rome, you've written scripts and directed films. Doesn't this expressive medium interest you any more?

GGM: No, because my work in the cinema showed me that what the writer succeeds in putting across is very little. So many interests, so many compromises are involved that in the end very little of the original story remains. Whereas if I shut myself in my room I can write exactly what I want to. I don't have to put up with an editor saying, "Get rid of that character or incident and put in another."

RG: Don't you think the visual impact of the cinema can be greater than that of literature?

GGM: I used to think so, but then I realized the limitations of the cinema. That very visual aspect puts it at a disadvantage compared to literature. It's so immediate, so forceful, that it's difficult for the viewer to go beyond it. In literature one can go much further and at the same time create an impact that is visual, auditory, or of any other sort.

RG: Don't you think the novel is a disappearing form?

GGM: If it disappears it'll be because those who write it are disappearing. It's difficult to imagine any period in the history of humanity when so many novels have been read as at present. Whole novels are published in all the magazines—both for men and for women—and in the newspapers, while for the almost illiterate there are comic strips which are the apotheosis of the novel. What we could begin to discuss is the quality of the novels that are being read, but that has nothing to do with the reading public, only with the cultural level the state has given them. To return to the phenomenon of *One Hundred Years of Solitude*—and I don't want to know what caused it, nor to analyze it, nor for others to analyze it at present—I know of readers, people without intellectual training, who have passed straight from "comics" to that book and have read it with the same interest as the other things they have been given, because they underestimated it intellectually. It's the publishers, who, underestimating the public, publish books of very low literary value; and the curious thing is that that level also consumes books like *One Hundred Years of Solitude*. That's why I think there's a boom in novel readers. Novels are read everywhere, at all times, all over the world. Story-telling will always be of interest. A man comes home and starts telling his wife what's happened to him ... or what hasn't happened so that his wife believes it.

RG: In your interview with Luis Harss you say: "I've got fixed political opinions ... but my literary ideas change with my digestion." What are your literary ideas today at eight o'clock in the morning?

GGM: I've said that anyone who doesn't contradict himself is a dogmatist, and every dogmatist is a reactionary. I contradict myself all the time and particularly on the subject of literature. My method of work is such that I would never reach the point of literary creation without constantly contradicting myself, correcting myself, and making mistakes. If I didn't I should be always writing the same book. I have no recipe....

RG: Have you a method for writing a novel?

GGM: Not always the same, nor do I have a method for looking for a novel. The act of writing is the least important problem. What's difficult is assembling the novel and solving it according to my view of it.

RG: Do you know whether analysis, experience, or imagination controls that process?

GGM: If I were to try and make such an analysis I think I should lose a great deal of spontaneity. When I want to write something it's because I feel that it's worth saying. Still more ... when I write a story it's because I should enjoy reading it. What happens is that I set about telling myself a story. That's my method of writing, but although I have a hunch which of these— intuition, experience, or analysis—plays the greater part, I avoid inquiring deeply into the question because either my character or my system of writing makes me try to prevent my work becoming mechanical.

RG: What is the starting point of your novels?

GGM: A completely visual image. I suppose that some writers begin with a phrase, an idea, or a concept. I always begin with an image. The starting point of *Leaf Storm* is an old man taking his grandson to a funeral, in *No One Writes to the Colonel* it's an old man waiting, and in *One Hundred Years*, an old man taking his grandson to the fair to find out what ice is.

RG: They all begin with an old man....

GGM: The guardian angel of my infancy was an old man—my grandfather. My parents didn't bring me up, they left me in my grandparents' house. My grandmother used to tell me stories and my grandfather took me to see things. Those were the circumstances in which my world was constructed. And now I'm aware that I always see the image of my grandfather showing me things.

RG: How does that first image develop?

GGM: I leave it to simmer ... it's not a very conscious process. All my books have been brooded over for a good many years. *One Hundred Years* for fifteen or seventeen, and I began thinking about the one I'm writing now a long while ago.

RG: How long do you take writing them?

GGM: That's rather quicker. I wrote *One Hundred Years of Solitude* in less than two years—which I think is pretty good. Before, I always used to write when I was tired, in my free time after my other work. Now that I'm not under economic pressure and I have nothing to do but write, I like indulging in the luxury of doing it when I want to, when I feel the impulse. I'm working differently on the book about the old dictator who lived for 250 years—I'm leaving it alone to see where it goes.

RG: Do you correct your writing much?

GGM: As to that, I keep on changing. I wrote my first things straight off without a break, and afterwards made a great many corrections on the manuscript, made copies, and corrected it again. And now I've acquired a habit which I think is a vice. I correct line by line as I work, so that by the time a page is finished it's practically ready for the publisher. If it has a blot or a slip it won't do for me.

RG: I can't believe you're so methodical.

GGM: Terribly! You can't imagine how clean those pages are. And I've got an electric typewriter. The only thing I am methodical about is my work, but it's an almost emotional question. The page that I've just finished looks so beautiful, so clean, that it would be a pity to spoil it with a correction. But within a week I don't care about it so much—I only care about what I'm actually working on—and then I can correct it.

RG: And the galley proofs?

GGM: In *One Hundred Years* I only changed one word, although Paco Porrúa, literary editor of *Sudamericana*, told me to change as many as I liked. I believe the ideal thing would be to write a book, have it printed, and correct it afterwards. When one sends something to the printers and then reads it in print one seems to have taken a step, whether forward or backward, of extreme importance.

RG: Do you read your books after they are published?

GGM: When the first copy arrives I cut everything I have to do, and sit down—at once—and read it straight through. It has already become a different book from the one I know because a distance has been established between author and book. This is the first time I'm reading it as a reader. Those letters before my eyes weren't made by my typewriter, they aren't my words, they are others that have gone out into the world and don't belong to me. After that first reading I've never again read *One Hundred Years of Solitude*.

RG: How and when do you decide on the title?

GGM: A book finds its title sooner or later. It's not a thing I consider very important.

RG: Do you talk to your friends about what you're writing?

GGM: When I tell them something it's because I'm not quite sure about it, and I generally don't let it remain in the novel. I know from the reaction of my listeners—by means of some strange electric current—whether it's going to work or not. Although they may say sincerely, "Marvelous, terrific," there's something in their eyes that tells me it won't do. When I'm working on a novel I'm more of a nuisance to my friends than you can possibly imagine. They have to put up with it all, and afterwards when they read the book they get a surprise—as happened to those who were with me when I was writing *One Hundred Years*—because they don't find in it any of the incidents I told them about. What I had talked about was rejected material.

RG: Do you think about your readers when you write?

GGM: I think of four or five particular people who make up my public when I'm writing. As I consider what would please or displease them, I add or subtract things, and so the book is put together.

RG: Do you generally keep the material that has accumulated while you are working?

GGM: I don't keep anything. When the publishers notified me that they had received my first manuscript of *One Hundred Years of Solitude*, Mercedes helped me throw away a drawerful of working notes, diagrams, sketches, and memoranda. I threw it out, not only so that the way the book was constructed shouldn't be known—that's something absolutely private—but in case that material should ever be sold. To sell it would be selling my soul, and I'm not going to let anyone do it, not even my children.

RG: Which of your writings do you like best?

GGM: *Leaf Storm*, the first book I ever wrote. I think a lot of what I've done since then springs from it. It's the most spontaneous, the one I wrote with most difficulty and with fewer technical resources. I knew fewer writers' tricks, fewer nasty tricks at that time. It seems to me a rather awkward, vulnerable book, but completely spontaneous, and it has a raw sincerity not to be found in the others. I know exactly how *Leaf Storm* went straight from my guts onto the paper. The others also came from my guts but I had served my apprenticeship.... I worked on them, I cooked them, I added salt and pepper.

RG: What influences have you been conscious of?

GGM: The notion of influence is a problem for the critics. I'm not very clear about it, I don't know exactly what they mean by it. I think the fundamental influence on my writing has been Kafka's *Metamorphosis*, although I don't know whether the critics who analyze my work discover any direct influence in the books themselves. I remember the moment when I bought the book, and how as I read it I began to long to write. My first stories date from that time—about 1946, when I had just gotten my baccalaureate. Probably as soon as I say this to the critics—they've got no detector, they have to get certain things from the author himself—they'll discover the influence. But what sort of influence? He made me want to write. A decisive influence, which is perhaps more obvious, is *Oedipus Rex*. It's a perfect structure, wherein the investigator discovers that he is himself the assassin ... an apotheosis of technical perfection. All the critics have mentioned Faulkner's influence. I accept that, but not in the sense they think when they see me as an author who read Faulkner, assimilated him, was impressed by him and, consciously or unconsciously, tries to write like him. That is more or less, roughly, what I understand by an influence. What I owe to Faulkner is something entirely different. I was born in Aracataca, the banana-growing country where the United Fruit Company was established. It was in this region, where the Fruit Company was building towns and hospitals and draining some zones, that I grew up and received my first impressions. Then, many years later, I read Faulkner and found that his whole world—the world of the southern United States which he writes about—was very like my world, that it was created by the same people. And also, when later I traveled in the southern states, I found evidence—on those hot, dusty roads, with the same vegetation, trees, and great houses—of the similarity between our two worlds. One mustn't forget that Faulkner is in a way a Latin American writer. His world is that of the Gulf of Mexico. What I found in him was affinities between our experiences, which were not as different as might appear at first sight. Well, this sort of influence of course exists, but it's very different from what the critics pointed out.

RG: Others speak of Borges and Carpentier, and think they see the same telluric and mythological approach as that of Rómulo Gallegos, Evaristo Carrera Campos, or Asturias....

GGM: Whether I follow the same telluric line or not I really don't know. It's the same world, the same Latin America, isn't it? Borges and Carpentier, no. I read them when I had already written quite a lot. That's to say I would have written what I did anyhow, without Borges and Carpentier, but not without Faulkner. And I also believe that after a certain moment—

by searching for my own language and refining my work—I have taken a course aimed at eliminating Faulkner's influence, which is much in evidence in *Leaf Storm* but not in *One Hundred Years*. But I don't like making this sort of analysis. My position is that of a creator, not of a critic. It's not my job, it's not my vocation, I don't think I'm good at it.

RG: What books do you read nowadays?

GGM: I scarcely read at all, it doesn't interest me. I read documentaries and memoirs—the lives of men who have held power, memoirs and revelations by secretaries, even if they aren't true—out of professional interest in the book I'm working on. My problem is that I am and have always been a very poor reader. As soon as a book bores me I give it up. As a boy I began reading *Don Quixote*, got bored and stopped in the middle. I've read it and reread it since, but only because I enjoy it, not because it's obligatory reading. That has been my method of reading and I have the same concept of reading while I'm writing. I'm always in terror lest at some page the reader may get bored and throw down the book. Therefore I try not to bore him, so that he shan't treat me as I treat others. The only novels I read now are those by my friends because I'm curious to know what they're doing, not out of literary interest. For many years I read, or devoured, quantities of novels, particularly adventure stories in which a lot happened. But I was never a methodical reader. Since I didn't have the money to buy books, I used to read what fell into my hands, books lent me by friends who were almost all teachers of literature or concerned with it. What I have always read, almost more than novels, is poetry. In fact I began with poetry, although I've never written poetry in verse, and I'm always trying to find poetical solutions. I think my last novel is really an extremely long poem about the loneliness of a dictator.

RG: Are you interested in concrete poetry?

GGM: I've lost sight of poetry altogether. I don't know precisely where poets are going, what they are doing, or even what they want to do. I suppose it's important for them to make experiments of every description and look for new ways of expressing themselves, but it's very difficult to judge something in the experimental stage. They don't interest me. I've solved the problem of my own means of expressing myself, and I can't now be involved in other things.

RG: You mentioned that you are always listening to music....

GGM: I enjoy it much more than any other manifestation of art, even than literature. With every day that passes I need it more, and I have the impression that it acts on me like a drug. When I travel I always take along a portable radio with headphones, and I measure the world by the concerts I can hear—from Madrid to San Juan in Puerto Rico one can hear Beethoven's nine symphonies. I remember that when I was traveling by train in Germany with Vargas Llosa—on an extremely hot day when I was in a very bad mood—how I suddenly, perhaps unconsciously, cut myself off and listened to music. Mario said to me afterwards, "It's incredible, your mood has changed, you've calmed down." In Barcelona, where I can have a fully equipped set, in times of great depression I have sometimes listened to music from two in the afternoon until four in the morning, without moving. My passion for music is like a secret vice, and I hardly ever talk about it. It's a part of my most profoundly private life. I'm not at all attached to objects—I don't consider the furniture and other things in my house as mine, but as belonging to my wife and children—and the only objects I'm fond of are my musical apparatuses. My typewriter is a necessity, otherwise I would get rid of it. Nor do I possess a library. When I've read a book I throw it out, or leave it somewhere.

RG: Let's come back to your statement that you "have fixed political opinions." Can you say exactly what they are?

GGM: I think the world ought to be socialist, that it will be, and that we should help this to happen as quickly as possible. But I'm greatly disillusioned by the socialism of the Soviet Union. They arrived at their brand of socialism through special experiences and conditions, and are trying to impose in other countries their own bureaucracy, their own authoritarianism, and their own lack of historical vision. That isn't socialism and it's the great problem of the present moment.

RG: When the Cuban poet Heberto Padilla was imprisoned and made a signed "confession," international intellectuals—who have always supported the Cuban Revolution—sent two letters of protest to Castro in the course of a month. After the first letter—which you also signed—Castro said in his May Day speech that the signatories were pseudo-revolutionary intellectuals who "gossip in Paris literary salons" and pass judgment on the Cuban revolution; Cuba, he said, does not need the support of "bourgeois intrigue-mongers." According to international commentaries this showed a rupture between intellectuals and the Cuban regime. What's your own position?

GGM: When all this came to light, international and Colombian news agencies naturally began to press me to give my opinion, because in a way I was involved in all this. I didn't want to do so until I had complete information and could read the shorthand reports of the speeches. I couldn't give an opinion on such an important matter merely on the versions put out by the information agencies. Besides, I knew at the time that I was going to receive a Doctorate of Letters at Columbia University. For anyone who didn't know that this decision had been made previously, it might lead them to believe that I was going to the United States because I had broken with Castro. I therefore made a statement to the press, completely clarifying my position toward Castro, my doctorate, and my return to the United States after twelve years, during which time I had been refused a visa:

(Summary of García Márquez's statement to the Colombian press, May 29, 1971)

Columbia University is not the government of the United States, but a stronghold of nonconformism, of intellectual integrity ... of those who will annihilate the decrepit system of their country. I understand that I am being granted this distinction principally as a writer, but those who grant it are not unaware that I am infinitely hostile to the prevailing order in the United States.... It is good for you to know that I only discuss these decisions with my friends, and especially with the taxi drivers of Barranquilla, who are champions of common sense.... The conflict between a group of Latin American writers and Fidel Castro is an ephemeral triumph for the news agencies. I have here the documents relevant to this matter, including the shorthand report of Fidel Castro's speech, and although it does in fact contain some very stern passages, none of them lend support to the sinister interpretations given them by the international news agencies. Certainly we have to do with a speech in which Fidel Castro makes fundamental proposals about cultural matters, but the foreign correspondents said nothing about these; instead they carefully extracted and put together again as they chose certain loose phrases so as to make it seem that Fidel Castro had said what in fact he had not said ... I didn't sign the letter of protest because I was not in favor of their sending it. The truth is that I believe such public messages are valueless as a means to the desired ends, but very useful for hostile propaganda.... However, I will at no time cast doubt on the intellectual integrity and revolutionary sincerity of those who signed the letter, who include some of my best friends.... When writers wish to take part in politics they are actually being moral rather than political, and those two terms aren't always compatible. Politicians, for their part, resist writers meddling in their affairs, and on the whole accept us when we support them and reject us when we are against them. But that's hardly a catastrophe. On the contrary, it's a very useful, very positive dialectic contradiction, which will continue until the end of mankind, even if politicians die of rage and writers are skinned alive.... The only pending matter is that of the poet Heberto Padilla. Personally, I haven't succeeded in convincing myself that Padilla's self-criticism was spontaneous and sincere. I don't understand how after so many years of contact with the Cuban experiment, living daily through the drama of the revolution, a man like Heberto Padilla could not have taken before the stand he suddenly took in prison. The tone of his confession is so exaggerated, so abject, that it seems to have been obtained by ignominious means. I don't know whether Heberto Padilla is doing harm to the revolution by his attitude, but his self-criticism certainly is doing a great deal of harm. The proof of this is to be found in the way the text divulged by Prensa Latina was splashed in the hostile Cuban press.... If a germ of Stalinism really exists in Cuba we shall see it very soon, it will be proclaimed by Fidel Castro himself.... In 1961 there was an attempt to impose Stalinist methods, and Fidel Castro denounced it in public and eradicated it in embryo. There is no reason to think that the same wouldn't happen today, because the vitality, the good health of the Cuban Revolution cannot have decreased since that time.... Of course I am not breaking with the Cuban Revolution. Moreover: none of the writers who protested about the Padilla case has broken with the Cuban Revolution so far as I know. Mario Vargas Llosa himself commented on this in a statement subsequent to his famous letter, but the newspapers relegated it to the corner for invisible news. No: the Cuban Revolution is an event of fundamental importance to Latin America and the whole world, and our solidarity with it can't be affected by a blunder in cultural politics, even when the blunder is as large and as serious as the suspect self-criticism of Heberto Padilla....

RG: Are the hopes of intellectuals being accomplished by the Cuban Revolution?

GGM: What I believe to be really grave is that we intellectuals tend to protest and react only when we are personally affected, but do nothing when the same thing happens to a fisherman or a priest. What we ought to do is look at the revolution as an integral phenomenon, and see how the positive aspects infinitely outweigh the negative ones. Of course, manifestations such as the Padilla case are extremely dangerous, but they are obstacles that it shouldn't be hard to surmount. If not it would indeed be grievous, because everything that has been done—making people literate, giving them education and economic independence—is irreversible and will last much longer than Padilla and Fidel. That is my position and I won't budge from it. I'm not prepared to throw a revolution on the rubbish heap every ten years.

RG: Do you agree with the socialism of the Chilean Popular Front?

GGM: My ambition is for all Latin America to become socialist, but nowadays people are seduced by the idea of peaceful and constitutional socialism. This seems to be all very well for electoral purposes, but I believe it to be completely utopian. Chile is heading toward violent and dramatic events. If the Popular Front goes ahead—with intelligence and great tact, with reasonably firm and swift steps—a moment will come when they will encounter a wall of serious opposition. The United States is not interfering at present, but it won't always stand by with folded arms. It won't really accept that Chile is a socialist country. It won't allow that, and don't let's be under any illusions on that point.

RG: Do you see violence as the sole solution?

GGM: It's not that I see it as a solution, but I think that a moment will come when that wall of opposition can only be surmounted by violence. Unfortunately, I believe that to be inevitable. I think what is happening in Chile is very good as reform, but not as revolution.

RG: You said of imperialist cultural penetration—in your interview with Jean-Michel Fossey—that the United States was trying to attract intellectuals by giving them awards and creating organizations where a lot of propaganda went on....

GGM: I have a profound belief in the power of money to corrupt. If a writer, particularly at the start of his career, is given an award or a grant— whether it comes from the United States, the Soviet Union, or from Mars— he is to some extent compromised. Out of gratitude, or even to show that he hasn't been compromised, this help affects his work. This is much more serious in the socialist countries where a writer is supposed to be working for the state. That in itself is the major compromise of his independence. If he writes what he wants, or what he feels, he runs the risk that some official— almost certainly a failed writer—will decide whether it can be published or not. So that I think that as long as a writer can't live by his books he ought to take on some marginal work. In my case it was journalism and advertising, but no one ever paid me to write.

RG: Neither did you accept the office of Colombian consul in Barcelona.

GGM: I always refuse public office, but I rejected that particular post because I don't want to represent any government. I think I said in an interview that one Miguel Angel Asturias was enough for Latin America.

RG: Why did you say that?

GGM: His personal behavior sets a bad example. Winner of the Nobel Prize and the Lenin Prize, he goes to Paris as ambassador representing a government as reactionary as Guatemala's. A government fighting against the guerrillas who stand for everything he says he has stood for all his life. Imperialists don't attack him for accepting the embassy of a reactionary government, because it was prudent, nor does the Soviet Union because he's a Lenin Prize winner. I've been asked recently what I thought of Neruda becoming an ambassador. I didn't say that a writer shouldn't be an ambassador—though I never would myself—but representing the government of Guatemala is not the same thing as representing the Chilean Popular Front.

RG: You must often have been asked how you manage to live in a country with such a dictatorship as Spain's.

GGM: It seems to me that if you give a writer the choice of living in heaven or hell, he chooses hell ... there's much more literary material there.

RG: Hell—and dictators—also exist in Latin America.

GGM: I'd like to clear this matter up. I'm forty-three years old and I've spent three of them in Spain, one in Rome, two or three in Paris, seven or eight in Mexico, and the rest in Colombia. I've not left one city merely in order to live in another. It's worse than that. I don't live anywhere, which causes some anguish. Also I don't agree with an idea that has arisen—and been much discussed lately—that writers live in Europe so as to live it up. It's not like that. One doesn't go in search of that—anyone who wants to can find it anywhere—and often life is very difficult. But I haven't the smallest doubt that it's very important for a Latin American writer to view Latin America from Europe at some given moment. My ideal solution would be to be able to go back and forth, but (1) it's very expensive, and (2) I'm restricted by the fact that I dislike air travel ... although I spend my life in airplanes. The truth is that at the moment I don't care where I live. I always find people who interest me, whether in Barranquilla, Rome, Paris, or Barcelona.

RG: Why not New York?

GGM: New York was responsible for withdrawing my visa. I lived in this city in 1960 as correspondent for Prensa Latina, and although I did nothing except act as correspondent—collecting news and dispatching it— when I left to go to Mexico they took away my resident's card and entered me in their "black book." Every two or three years I've asked for a visa again, but they went on automatically refusing it. I think it was mainly a bureaucratic matter. I've received one now. As a city, New York is the greatest phenomenon of the twentieth century, and therefore it's a serious restriction of one's life not to be able to come here every year, even for a week. But I doubt if I have strong enough nerves to live in New York. I find it so overwhelming. The United States is an extraordinary country; a nation that creates such a city as New York, or the rest of the country—which has nothing to do with the system or the government—could do anything. I believe they will be the ones to create a great socialist revolution, and a good one too.

RG: What have you to say about the solemn title conferred on you by Columbia University?

GGM: I can't believe it.... What I find completely puzzling and disconcerting is not the honor nor the recognition—although such things can be true—but that a university like Columbia should decide to choose me out of twelve men from the whole world. The last thing I ever expected in this world was a doctorate of letters. My path has always been anti-academic; I never graduated as doctor of law from the university because I didn't want to be a "doctor"—and suddenly I find myself in the thick of the academic world. But this is something quite foreign to me, it's off my beat. It's as if they gave the Nobel Prize to a bullfighter. My first impulse was not to accept it, but then I took a plebiscite among my friends and none of them could understand what reason I had for refusing. I could have given political reasons, but they wouldn't have been genuine, because we all know, and we have heard declared in university speeches, that imperialism is not their prevailing system. So that to accept the honor wouldn't involve me politically with the United States, and there was no need to mention the subject. It was rather a moral question. I always react against ceremonies—remember that I come from the most ceremonious country in the world—and I asked myself, "What should I be doing in a literary academy in cap and gown?" At my friends' insistence I accepted the title of doctor honoris causa and now I'm delighted, not only at having accepted it, but also on behalf of my country and Latin America. All this patriotism one pretends not to care about suddenly does become important. In these last days, and more still during the ceremony, I thought about the strange things that were happening to me. There was a moment when I thought that death must be like that ... something that happens when one least expects it, something that has nothing to do with me. Also I have been approached to publish an edition of my complete works, but I emphatically refused this in my lifetime, since I have always thought of it as a posthumous honor. During the ceremony I had the same feeling ... that such things happened to one after death. The type of recognition I have always desired and appreciated is that of people who read me and talk to me about my books, not with admiration or enthusiasm but with affection. What really touched me during the ceremony in the university, and you can't imagine how deeply, was when during the return procession the Latin Americans who had practically taken over the campus came unobtrusively forward saying "Up with Latin America!" "Forward, Latin America!" "Go ahead, Latin America!" At that moment, for the first time, I felt moved and was glad I had accepted.

GENE H. BELL-VILLADA

The Writer's Life

The Story of García Márquez's life is one of steady growth of a number of vocations, all of them interrelated. First, obviously, there is that of writer, both of fiction and journalism (the two of course being narrative crafts), and more broadly his role as lyrical historian of his region and of Hispanic America. Closely linked with his mission as writer are his principles as man of the left. Though he never was a full-time militant, from his twentieth year García Márquez's art and actions were the work of an independent socialist who, in the wake of *One Hundred Years of Solitude*, would use his literary fame and marshal his writing skills publicly to support progressive causes. In addition, being true to his extended family origins, García Márquez would flower most freely as a stable family man and father. Last but not least, he has remained loyally attached to his oldest friends, those who predate his sudden success and wealth. To this day, García Márquez sets aside his afternoon hours as time to be spent with family and friends.

He was born in the sad and unpaved town of Aracataca on 6 March 1927 (not 1928, as generally thought), the eldest child of Luisa Santiaga Márquez and Gabriel Eligio García.[1] His first eight years, however, would be spent with his maternal grandparents, Tranquilina Iguarán and Colonel Nicolás Márquez. The two latter had strongly opposed his parents' marriage, partly because Mr. García was illegitimate and a newcomer to Aracataca but

From *García Márquez: The Man and His Work*. © 1990 by The University of North Carolina Press.

most of all because he belonged to the Conservative camp, against whom Nicolás had fought fiercely in the Thousand Days' War. They tried their best to block the courtship, sending Luisa off to stay with a variety of relatives and even managing to have Gabriel Eligio transferred to Riohacha, on the Guajira. But Gabriel Eligio, very much in love with the colonel's daughter and determined to woo her, would regularly send her loving messages by wire (he was a telegraph operator). And although his perseverance did finally break through the Márquez family barriers, the young couple were then obligated to set up house in distant Riohacha. Later, in a conciliatory gesture, Luisa would be sent to her parents' in order to give birth to baby Gabriel in Aracataca.[2]

The boy's formative experiences were those of the classic extended-family house in which an endless array of cousins, nephews, grandchildren and other distant kin (the colonel's illegitimate children included) are constantly dropping in for a visit. Two sets of memories in particular would stay with him—the adult women, and his grandfather, the soldier. The women ran the household and took good care of little Gabito. Being somewhat superstitious, they were given to saying or doing certain things he would later memorialize. His grandmother Tranquilina, who went blind in old age, used to tell all manner of amazing stories with a straight face, and would talk about people without distinguishing between the quick and the dead. His aunt Francisca wove her own shroud; when he asked why, she replied, "Because I'm going to die, little boy" (OG, 11; FG, 12). Once the job was done she lay down and breathed her last. Besides these actions—now familiar to the novelist's readers—select names were to survive in his books. There was an aunt Petra, and Cotes was the second surname of his mother Luisa. "Iguarán," grandmother Tranquilina's maiden name, was to be retained as that of the materfamilias Úrsula Buendía.

Colonel Márquez was an old-fashioned, small-town gentleman who liked fine lotions, carried a pocket watch with a thick gold chain, and always wore a vest and tie.[3] In his youth, in Riohacha, he had shot a man who had been pestering him, and then left for Aracataca when the counterthreats became impossible. (He often would say, in retrospect, "You can't believe how a dead man weighs you down.") During his combat years he reportedly sired a dozen illegitimate children, but his leadership was also to make Aracataca into a Liberal bulwark, and as an old man he was given to reminiscing about the horrors and glories of war. In 1929, as town treasurer, he provided eyewitness testimony at some celebrated Colombian congressional hearings on the recent banana workers' strike and military massacre. Whenever the circus came to Aracataca the colonel used to take little Gabo along, and at the United Fruit Company stores he would open up the frozen fish boxes and let the boy ponder the miracle of ice. To the end of his days the man would wait fruitlessly for a government pension that was due him, and following his death his widow Tranquilina was to wait even more.[4]

The old colonel died when the boy was only in his eighth year, but he is still remembered by García Márquez as "the person I've gotten along with best and had the best communication ever" (*OG*, 18; *FG*, 18). The memories of the man have clearly served as the inspiration behind many of García Márquez's key personages and narrative events, although, according to the novelist himself, the nameless colonel in *Leaf Storm* is the only one of his characters who actually bears a close resemblance to Colonel Márquez, being all but "a detailed copy of his image" (*OG*, 19; *FG*, 19).

Members of the family used to recall with some disdain the heady days of the "banana fever," the 1910s, when the United Fruit Company (UFCO) expanded into Aracataca, bringing in hordes of migrant workers and a delirious, "gold rush" sort of atmosphere. Though falling world prices and the massive strike had brought UFCO into cyclical decline by 1928, the other-worldliness of the separate Yankee compound would remain vividly imprinted on García Márquez's mind—the wire fences; the ever-neat green lawns; the swimming pools with outdoor tables and umbrellas; the tall, blond, ruddy-faced men in their explorer outfits; their wives decked out in muslin dresses; and their adolescent daughters, playing tennis or going for casual drives in their convertibles around Aracataca (*OG*, 14; *FG*, 14). Such memories of great-power colonialism would mingle with those of family life and eventually become integrated into a mature García Márquez's literary art. Some five miles north of Aracataca there was a banana plantation by the name of "Macondo." The vast farm, now parceled out among local owners, continues to operate today, and in 1988 there still stood a general store bearing a rusted sign saying "Acueducto de Macondo." The living conditions of the workers did not appear to have greatly improved since 1928.

Though García Márquez eventually would bloom as one of the most locally rooted of authors, his biography before the 1960s is characterized by a surprising amount of dislocation and instability. After first attending the Montessori School in Aracataca, in 1936 he was finally sent to live with his parents, whom he had met just recently. They were living in Sucre, a river port whose configuration would later serve as model for the nameless town in *No One Writes to the Colonel* and *Chronicle of a Death Foretold*. Following the death of grandfather Nicolás the boy was dispatched for elementary school as a boarder at the Colegio San José, in Barranquilla. By age ten he was writing humorous verse, a practice that would continue with his transfer to

the Colegio de Jesuitas in that same city. Throughout his school days
"Gabito" would be noted as a slim, taciturn, and introverted boy, averse to
sports, "so serious he was known as 'the Old Man.'"[5]

A scholarship award in 1940 found the boy headed as a boarding
student to the Liceo Nacional de Zipaquirá, a high school for the gifted
located in a small town some thirty miles outside Bogotá. Today a mere
hour's jet flight from the coast, at that time the complicated journey from
Barranquilla required a week's travel—first by steamer up the Magdalena
River (a trajectory the novelist would recount in moving detail more than
four decades hence in *Love in the Time of Cholera*), and then by train further
up into the Andes. Bogotá itself has since evolved into just another bright
cosmopolis with the usual chic brand names and transnational boutiques, but
to the thirteen-year-old from the tropical lowlands it was very much a shock,
with its gray clouds and drizzle, its ever-present chill (temperatures at night
can drop to the forties), its hidebound religiosity (church bells chimed for
rosary at sundown), its emotional reserve, its men in formal black, and its
streets with not a woman in sight (*OG*, 54–56; *FG*, 40–41).

Little Gabito reportedly wept on first seeing this strange *cachaco*
universe. Zipaquirá, in fact, would prove to be even chillier and grayer. The
town's architecture and setting, however, were attractive: the main square,
dominated by its massive early-eighteenth-century cathedral and surrounded
by multistory buildings graced with continuous wooden dark-hued
balconies, looks like a medieval plaza from old Castile transplanted piece-by-
piece onto the Andean savannah. These beauties meant little to the lonely
youth, and twenty-five years later, when writing *One Hundred Years of
Solitude*, García Márquez would make the stuffy Fernanda del Carpio and her
snobbish parents the deluded chief denizens of a sombre, viceregal town
clearly modeled after Zipaquirá. Meanwhile Gabo sought immediate solace
for his adolescent solitude in the bold, vigorous fantasy worlds of Alexandre
Dumas and Jules Verne.

The boy did well in his humanities subjects, less so in the sciences.
There were also some advantages. The Liceo was of good academic quality;
and Gabito's science and mathematics teachers were men of the left who,
during recess, would introduce the bright youngster to Marxist thought and
social and economic history. For their daily entertainment fellow students
would read novels out loud at the barracks-like dormitory; Gabito often
suggested titles. It was in this fashion that he first became acquainted with
The Three Musketeers, *Notre Dame de Paris*, and *The Magic Mountain*, the
latter eliciting lively adolescents' debates as to whether or not Hans Castorp
and Claudia Chauchat bed down together.[6] The first two of these books, it
bears noting, are historical romances that typically combine established fact

and imagined fiction—much as García Márquez would eventually do in his greatest writings.

Meanwhile all these losses and displacements—the death of foster parents, the more problematical relationship to his immediate kin, and the uprootings from places known at a tender age—were giving Gabito an early taste of that adult experience of profound, inexplicable solitude. Aracataca consequently had assumed in his mind the status of a boyhood paradise and lost Eden. A return trip at age sixteen into that very past, however, was to prove crucial to his growth and development. Because grandmother Tranquilina Iguarán de Márquez had recently died, his mother Luisa Santiaga and himself were returning briefly to Aracataca for the prosaic business of selling off the family home. To his surprise, the adolescent boy finds not the idyllic world that has loomed large and mythic in his memory, but an unbearably hot, dusty village, its impoverished wooden shacks as silent and desolate as a ghost town (it is the siesta hour). The strange intensity of the visit is further heightened when his mother happens upon a woman friend from years past, seated quietly in her little shop; the two women embrace and weep speechless in front of the amazed boy for (as he would later recall it) a good half hour[7] (*OG*, 15–16; *FG*, 14–15). Soon thereafter Gabito knows that he has to be a novelist; he starts work on a long narrative entitled *La casa* (*The House*), writing several hundred pages until finally completing and abandoning it in 1953.

Graduating from the Liceo in 1946 and returning to the family fold in Sucre, the young man bowed to parental pressure and in 1947 once again went up to Bogotá, this time to enroll as a law student at the Universidad Nacional. (In Latin America, as in Europe, law is an undergraduate course of study.) One of his professors there was Alfonso López Michelsen, who from 1974 to 1978 would serve as president of Colombia. Among his classmates was Camilo Torres, the future "guerrilla priest," and the two students became close friends. Still, young Gabo felt sadly and thoroughly bored with his law studies, and he performed indifferently. Floating about in a state of chronic personal depression, he led a life confined in the main to the lecture halls, the boarding house, and the nearby cafés, where, book in hand, he would show up unshaven and badly dressed. On weekends he would board a tramway, ride back and forth between terminals, and bury himself in volumes of verse by the Spanish classical authors or by the "Piedra y Cielo" ("Stone and Sky") poets, an important Colombian avant-garde group from the 1930s. Occasionally he and a stranger might strike up a conversation and discuss a poem or two[8] (*OG*, 57; *FG*, 41).

It was during his freshman year in law school that García Márquez wrote and published—almost on a kind of dare—his first still-tentative short story. What happened was that Eduardo Zalamea Borda, then the literary editor and reigning critic at *El Espectador*, had run an essay in which he dismissed the younger generation of Colombian writers as lacking in talent. In spontaneous response to Zalamea's challenge García Márquez produced "The Third Resignation," a somewhat morbid account of a young boy presumed dead in his coffin for eighteen years, yet whose mind remains alive with sensations, memory, and imagination. The nineteen-year-old novice writer submitted the story; to his astonishment it appeared the next Sunday in *El Espectador*'s literary supplement, with an introductory note by señor Zalamea Borda hailing "the new genius of Colombian letters." García Márquez often recalls the serious burden of responsibility he then felt, an almost painful need to be worthy of Zalamea's generous praise and not let the man down.[9] In the next half-decade he wrote and published in *El Espectador* another ten short fictions, most of them equally introspective, no doubt autobiographical in their fantastical close-ups of angst and isolation.

The assassination of Gaitán on 9 April 1948 and the *bogotazo* (see chapter 2) were permanently to alter the aimless, lonely drift of Gabo the late-adolescent and outsider. The hitherto self-absorbed student of law now witnessed an explosion of large-scale collective lawlessness, with who knows how many frenzied thousands caught up in mass rioting and pillaging throughout the city. García Márquez's own circumscribed world suffered the direct effects when the boardinghouse where he'd been staying caught fire, and despite an abortive, tearful rescue attempt on his part, his books and manuscripts were mostly set ablaze. With the Universidad Nacional shut down indefinitely, moreover, Gabo's law studies were now forcibly—perhaps mercifully—interrupted. He sought and obtained transfer to the Universidad de Cartagena, continuing as a so-so student, gradually abandoning the classrooms, and in the end never receiving his bachelor's degree.

The move north was nevertheless the first step in Gabo's return to his Caribbean roots and rediscovery of that culture. His being newly present in the region is also what chanced to lead him to his lifetime occupation as journalist. The appearance of his short story in *El Espectador* had earned him some recognition among coastal literati, and during a casual street encounter with the Afro-Hispanic novelist Manuel Zapata Olivella the latter invited him to do some writing for the recently founded Cartagena newspaper *El Universal*.[10] Soon thereafter the twenty-year-old apprentice had a five-hundred-word daily column of his own, in which his sprightly imagination could range freely over most any topic of his choosing. (Among the subjects he dealt with in his first month as columnist: the accordion, the helicopter, the length of women's skirts, astrology, twins, parrots, Joe Louis, and *Bringing up Father*.) He had gotten off to an auspicious start, for the personal column is a genre of which he would produce thousands of specimens over the years and excel in masterfully throughout his life as a writer.

Around that time García Márquez also befriended the young writers and artists of what eventually came to be known as the "Barranquilla group"—now as much a byword in Colombia as "the Black Mountain Poets" or "the Russian Five" are elsewhere. The spiritual father of the group was Ramón Vinyes, an aged and erudite Catalonian book dealer and prolific writer of unpublished plays and fiction (all in Catalan). Being up on the latest European and U.S. literary trends, he enthusiastically initiated his youthful acolytes—including Gabo, who took the bus trip from Cartagena anytime he could—in many of the leading modernist authors. Later García Márquez would memorialize Vinyes as the wise Catalonian book dealer of Macondo, who passes on Sanskrit primers and other esoteric tomes to the ever-studious Aureliano Babilonia.[11]

Suddenly in early 1949 the Cartagena newspaperman's budding apprenticeship was interrupted when he contracted pneumonia. Bedridden for several months at his parents' place in Sucre, Gabo wrote his Barranquilla friends asking them for some reading matter. They willingly obliged by dispatching three cartons filled with Spanish translations of Faulkner, Hemingway, Joyce, Virginia Woolf, and more.[12]

At the start of 1950 García Márquez moved to Barranquilla, where the largest coastal newspaper, *El Heraldo*, had hired him as a staffer to liven up their pages with a daily column of the sort he had been doing for *El Universal*. The articles began appearing in January 1950, in a narrow-column format under the heading "La Jirafa" ("The Giraffe"), and were morbidly signed "Septimus," after the shell-shocked outsider in Virginia Woolf's *Mrs. Dalloway*. García Márquez used to write his columns during the afternoons, at the offices of *El Heraldo*. After closing time he'd stay behind, working on his novel *Leaf Storm*[13] (*OG*, 62–63; *FG*, 43–44). Later on in the evening there were the all-night book-talk and boozing sessions at the Happy Bar (spelled "Japi Bar") with his friends Alfonso Fuenmayor, Álvaro Cepeda, and Germán Vargas, the young literary Turks of the "Barranquilla group."

El Rascacielos—"The Skyscraper"—was the name of the four-story building located on Calle del Crimen ("Crime Street" [sic]) where García Márquez took lodging in Barranquilla. The bottom floors housed some law offices; the upper ones, a brothel. Gabo had an arrangement to sleep on the top floors after returning from his literary carousals, in whatever boudoir he could find vacant at dawn. On mornings when he was short of money for his bed and shelter, he would leave his manuscript to *Leaf Storm* as security with the gatekeeper. Occasionally, from an adjoining bedroom he might overhear some local politico and one of the "staff" girls engaged in lively talk about the man's many leadership achievements (and otherwise not much action). The whores treated Gabo as a family friend, generously sharing their lunches with him. The grateful novelist would later put much tender and positive feeling into his prostitute characters. One woman in The Skyscraper, an Afro-Hispanic named Eufemia, would reappear in the last chapters of Macondo as the voluptuous Nigromanta, who duly deflowers a bookish and unworldly Aureliano Babilonia. The town bordello also functions as a kind of safe haven in Chronicle of a Death Foretold[14] (OG, 62–63; FG, 43–44).

Young Gabo's professional ties with El Heraldo were to last three full years, through the whole of 1952. From a human and social point of view they constitute the happiest period in García Márquez's life. He had made some intellectually compatible, lifelong friends, and would later pay them the homage of assigning their first names to the only four pals a reclusive Aureliano Babilonia is lucky enough to have. He was brimming with ideas and high spirits and alive with writerly energy, and from ages twenty-two to twenty-five he had his own signed newspaper column in which (within the limits of existing government censorship) he could write pretty much as he pleased. In those years he also was to complete the writing of Leaf Storm, for which during the remainder of his life he would retain a great deal of affection. And, though still financially unsettled, he did not yet find himself faced with the multitudinous pressures and temptations that artistic mastery and worldwide fame would one day bring in their wake.

If 1948–52 are García Márquez's bright happy days of apprenticeship, 1953–67 are the Wanderjähre, the rougher times as journeyman writer and reporter. In December 1952 Gabo left his job (though keeping his friendly ties) with El Heraldo, the day-to-day writing having become too routine for his still-growing talents. The following year, 1953, is a somewhat mysterious period, the documentation and facts being scanty, but Professor Jacques Gilard persuasively argues that it was most probably the year of García Márquez's brief stint (along with Álvaro Cepeda) as an encyclopedia salesman in the Guajira region.[15] The novelist was later to recall that elusive period as one of meager encyclopedia sales but much reading of Virginia Woolf, and the episode itself is gracefully evoked in a distinctive paragraph two-thirds of the way through "Innocent Eréndira," where Cepeda too is mentioned. In the course of that curious little adventure Gabo encountered and conversed with a fellow whose grandfather was the man who long ago had been murdered by Colonel Márquez.[16] Later that year Gabo would temporarily hold a high editorial post at El Nacional, another daily in Barranquilla.[17] There is little sign of major writing activity by García Márquez during those fluid twelve months, evidently a time of transition.

In February 1954 García Márquez moved to Bogotá and began work as a staff reporter for *El Espectador*, the more liberal of the two large national dailies, with almost a century of life to it. The job brought both greater prestige and more restrictions. Much of the writing was on an assignment basis-brief and inconsequential fillers (the editors indicating the allotted space with their thumb and forefinger) or lengthy features on subjects not of great concern to García Márquez, such as a profile series on a famous bicycle racer of the moment.[18] He did produce some memorable reports on, say, the Dead Letter Office and on frontier settlements in the Chocó region near Panama (*OP*, 2:295–323 and 355–60). But, whereas his coastal essays are mostly first-rate, a surprising amount of the Bogotá production is workmanlike and even mediocre.

There were some gains, however. Among García Márquez's multiple tasks was doing movie reviews, and he quickly read up on the existing film bibliography.[19] In the process he would soon become the first-ever regular film critic in Colombia, though not a particularly remarkable or original one. While he did immediately recognize the historic import of Truffaut's *400 Blows*, he also predicted imminent failure for the new wide-screen medium. On the other hand, his independent judgments sometimes aroused the wrath of movie-theater managers, who would put in angry telephone calls in order to register their displeasure over a particular García Márquez review.[20]

García Márquez's almost innocent ability to scandalize certain people became notably manifest in the aftermath of his talks with a sailor named Luis Alejandro Velasco, the sole survivor out of a group of eight castaways from a Colombian navy destroyer that, en route from Mobile, Alabama, had hit unusually rough waters. Velasco was to spend ten days aboard a raft, rowing south, and to García Márquez he now recounted such memorable highlights as the passing airplanes that had ignored him, the captured seagull that he had attempted to devour, the recurrent threats and terror from encircling sharks (one of which actually ate up an oar), the eerie nocturnal sounds of sea fauna, and his own final swim to safety when at last glimpsing the Colombian north shore[21] (*OP*, 3:566–652).

Velasco himself was, García Márquez notes, a "born storyteller," and his tale was intrinsically exciting. Its serialization in *El Espectador* caused something of a sensation, not least because it became evident that the ship's journey had been characterized by shady dealings—overweight contraband, and life rafts unequipped with food or water. Already *El Espectador* had been experiencing various sorts of direct harassment from the Rojas Pinilla dictatorship, and the Velasco stories now elicited threats of real government reprisals. With a view to getting García Márquez temporarily out of trouble, the editors sent him to Geneva to cover the "Big Four" conference, and thence to Rome in case Pope Pius XII were to die from one of his notoriously prolonged hiccup spells.[22] When this latter scoop did not materialize García Márquez enrolled for a few weeks at the Centro Sperimentale di Cinema and also did some traveling in Poland and Hungary. Little did he know that he would be staying in Europe for more than two years, through December 1957.

By mid-1955 García Márquez was arguably the most renowned newspaperman in Colombia, and his time served overseas—it has been said—would mercifully rescue him from the trap of local journalistic fame.[23] As European correspondent for *El Espectador* he would now earn a decent three hundred dollars a month and perform creditably at his new and more difficult set of tasks. Working pretty much alone, and lacking that vast organizational apparatus of the U.S. news agencies, he mostly cribbed from other reports and added his own uniquely personal, humorous, "tropical" touches thereto.[24] His creative side would become especially evident in a lengthy series of articles dealing with two major scandals and trials—one on some French government leaks, another on a sordid and labyrinthine Italian murder case—in which he applied his best techniques of novelistic suspense, suddenly breaking off the series just as the respective solutions were at hand (*OP*, 4:174–236 and 305–98).

García Márquez moved to Paris in January 1956, there finding out to his chagrin that *El Espectador* had been shut down by Rojas Pinilla. A successor daily under the name *El Independiente* was to be launched in February, with Gabo still on the payroll—only to suffer the same fate exactly two months later. At this point García Márquez decided to pocket the money that *El Espectador* had sent him for return fare, and stay on in Paris to write full-time instead. In a hotel garret on Rue de Cujas (a typical Latin Quarter street) he started work on what would be *In Evil Hour*. However, a subplot took on a life of its own to become *No One Writes to the Colonel*, completed after eleven drafts in January 1957.

That bittersweet novella of day-to-day hunger was based in part on the author's experiences of the moment. Waiting in vain for the reopening of *El Espectador*, and having only meager success in rounding up free-lance assignments, García Márquez survived for a protracted spell on returned-bottle deposits and on the good graces of his landlady, who let him accumulate several months' back rent. During these months García Márquez lost so much weight that, commenting on a photo of his which he had sent home, his mother remarked, "Poor Gabito. He looks like a skeleton."[25] It was also the initial stages of the French war in Algeria, and the Parisian police, mistaking the scruffy Colombian for a suspicious Arab, would sometimes harass him on the street[26] (*OG*, 96; *FG*, 65). He also seems to have worked briefly for the Algerian National Liberation Front and even spent an unspecified time in jail. The details, however, remain obscure.

Meanwhile, in August 1956 Plinio Apuleyo Mendoza,[27] an old friend from law school days in Bogotá, had landed an editorial post at *Élite*, a slick picture weekly in Caracas belonging to the Capriles chain (the Hearsts of Venezuela). It was thanks to Mendoza that, through March 1957, Gabo could do some free-lancing for that magazine, though most of the dozen or so hastily written pieces from those months are impersonal and indistinctive, having been targeted for an unfamiliar audience.[28] Later, in the summer of 1957 he and Mendoza (who had just resigned his job at *Élite*) would travel together in East Germany, Czechoslovakia, and the Soviet Union. In the wake of that journey García Márquez wrote some subtly balanced accounts of daily life in the "East-Bloc" countries; it was only as an end result of the Khrushchev "thaw," however, that he was finally able to find a home for them two years hence in *Cromos*, a Bogotá glossy.

November found García Márquez in London hoping to work on his English, but after a month of crafting short stories and shivering in a hotel room he received in the mail a plane ticket to Caracas and a note from Mendoza informing him that *Momento*, yet another slick magazine where he had just been appointed executive editor, was asking García Márquez to join their writing staff. The poverty-stricken novelist actually hesitated before accepting the surprise invitation.[29] Gabo's difficult and uncertain trial years on the old Continent, with their many ups and downs, and the manuscript of one beautifully succinct novella to show for his troubles, were now apparently over.

It was Christmas Eve when he arrived in Caracas, and with Plinio Mendoza's help he soon found a *pensión* room in San Bernardino, a peaceful residential district located near the center of town. García Márquez's Venezuelan phase could not have been better timed. The hated dictatorship of General Marcos Pérez Jiménez was teetering in what would turn out to be its final weeks, and the country was rife with aborted uprisings, clandestine leaflets, and speeches by courageous clerics, as well as frequent night curfews, news blackouts on radio and television, outrages by the security forces, and *pronunciamientos* by General Pérez Jiménez himself. At one point the offices of *Momento* were actually raided by military police who arrested everybody in sight, García Márquez being spared only because he chanced to be out at the time of the lightning sweep.[30]

Following a series of barracks revolts the dictator finally gave up and, on al January, fled for the United States, his suitcases typically stuffed with millions of U.S. dollars. García Márquez now witnessed that mixture of mass jubilation and official caution that characterizes the end of tyrannical regimes, an experience to be captured by him almost twenty years hence in *The Autumn of the Patriarch*. During the subsequent euphoria of the democratic transition he published a few retrospective articles about certain memorable struggles against the dictatorship, such as the thousands of antigovernment leaflets that, at a clash between some women demonstrators and a truncheon-wielding policeman, rained down on them suddenly from the tower of the metropolitan cathedral (*OP*, 3555–64).

In March the Colombian wanderer made an unexpected visit to Barranquilla and married his lifelong sweetheart Mercedes Barcha, a striking beauty of Egyptian origin whom he'd first proposed to when he was age thirteen[31] (*OG*, 27; *FG*, 22). Because of her exotic appearance, his friends used to call her "the sacred crocodile," the nickname by which he would dedicate the volume *Big Mama's Funeral* to her. His well-earned measure of stability, however, was quickly shattered two months later by a crisis within the ranks of *Momento*. On 13 May, in what would become a notorious episode, Venezuelan students stoned and spat upon U.S. Vice-President Richard Nixon; in response the editor-in-chief of the magazine composed an editorial condemning the action, and supporting the United States as "a friendly nation with which we are naturally linked." Taking advantage of a brief absence on the part of their boss, Mendoza and García Márquez affixed the man's initials and ran it as an individual's opinion piece rather than as the magazine's official position. A dispute ensued; the two friends resigned, and García Márquez eventually took a managing-editing job at a gossipy scandal sheet called *Venezuela Gráfica*, a straitjacket that allowed for little free writing time.[32]

Within just months, right-wing dictatorships had tumbled in both Colombia and Venezuela. The ignominious flight of Cuban tyrant Fulgencio Batista on 1 January 1959 and the triumph of Fidel Castro's guerrillas would awaken still greater expectations in a García Márquez caught up in the daily grind and elaborate deceptions of the sensationalist press. Soon thereafter García Márquez was one of several journalists invited by the revolutionary government to witness Castro's "Operation Truth," a media campaign aimed at countering the antileftist bias of the U.S. news agencies. At the trial of Batista henchman Jesús Sosa Blanco, García Márquez heard a catalog of bloody horrors that would further arouse in him the desire to write a novel about Latin dictatorship.

Among the ideas being vaguely entertained by García Márquez at the time was that of returning to Barranquilla and starting a film school there. The Cuban government, however, had decided to launch its own news agency, Prensa Latina, under the direction of an Argentine expatriate named Jorge Massetti. At the behest of Plinio Mendoza, the novelist and his pregnant wife left for Bogotá in May, where the two old friends had the job of mounting a Colombian branch of Prensa Latina. They built from ground zero, organizing shifts, watching teletypes, and sending two daily reports to Havana.[33] Meanwhile, baby Rodrigo was born on 24 August and later baptized by none less than Camilo Torres. In retrospect, 1959 was a very revolutionary year for García Márquez.

Jorge Massetti stopped in Bogotá in 1960 and observed that Prensa Latina needed able writers at other posts. Later that year García Márquez spent six months in Havana, and in early 1961 he started work as one of two staffers at the agency's New York City branch office. Occasional threatening phone calls came from emigré right-wing Cubans who would remind the author of his wife and child; he kept an iron rod by his desk (*OG*, 99; *FG*, 70). On one occasion, during the drive back to his Queens apartment he actually saw a car moving alongside his—with a gun pointed directly at him. Among his major assignments as a U.S. correspondent was to cover President Kennedy's 13 March press conference on the newly founded Alliance for Progress.[34] In mid-year, however, there arose in Cuba the "Sectarianism" crisis whereby the pre-Castro, old Stalinist party types had attempted to maneuver themselves into power, elbowing out Massetti along the way. In a gesture of solidarity with Massetti, García Márquez resigned from his Prensa Latina job.

Finding himself once again unemployed, he, Mercedes, and Rodrigo now embarked on a long Greyhound bus trip that included the American South, García Márquez always having wanted to see from up close the hot, backward, dusty towns only recently immortalized by Faulkner. The family would get a direct taste of Faulkner's world when on several instances, being perceived as Mexicans, they were turned down for hotel rooms. Mexico, ironically, was their destination. With $100 in his pocket and another $120 sent by Plinio Mendoza to the Colombian consulate in New Orleans, Gabo's journey would take him to Mexico City, where he hoped to write film scripts.[35]

Unable at first to secure work in movies, he applied for a job as editor-in-chief of two fluffy periodicals, *Sucesos* (Events) and *La Familia*, recently bought up by Gustavo Alatriste, a well-known media entrepreneur (and producer, among other things, of some of Luis Buñuel's best Mexican films).[36] García Márquez likes to recall how at that time the soles of his own shoes were loose and floppy, and for the job interview, scheduled at a bar, he arrived in advance so as to sit with his legs covered up (*OG*, 100; *FG*, 70). He did get the position, and for two years he handled everything from layout to warmed-over fillers (the periodicals' chief fare).

In the fall of 1963 García Márquez resigned his job at the glossies to begin work at the Mexico City branch of J. Walter Thompson, where he lasted a few months before moving on to the Stanton advertising agency.[37] At about this time he finally began fulfilling his dream of writing film scripts. For the next two years he would write over a dozen of them (some in collaboration with a talented young novelist named Carlos Fuentes), mostly potboiler melodramas filled with duels and shoot-outs and frustrated love.[38] García Márquez would later look back at most of this work in the moving-pictures medium as unsalvageable.

"Landing" after more than a half-decade of uprootedness and floating, García Márquez now began with Mexico City a close relationship almost as constant as that with his native Colombia. Behind him there was some solid if unrecognized literary achievement. During his time with *El Espectador* in Bogotá he had started work on the stories that would make up *Big Mama's Funeral*, crafting them with utmost care over the next five years in Europe and Venezuela, little suspecting that those bittersweet miniatures would one day become anthology and classroom favorites. And in a Paris garret he had conceived and then spent a year giving verbal life to the trim and tragicomical *No One Writes to the Colonel*. First appearing in Colombian newspapers and small journals, neither of these compact narratives would see book form until 1962. Back in Paris he had also begun the troublesome novel that would bear the title *In Evil Hour*. Ironically, it was this flawed work that, still in manuscript, won the 1962 Esso Prize in Colombia, then failing to achieve anything like acceptable print format until 1966. The prize money did help pay the maternity-ward bill for second son Gonzalo, born on 16 April 1962.

Following completion of *In Evil Hour*, García Márquez drifted into a serious case of writer's block. Barring a found manuscript that will prove things otherwise, one can safely state that from 1961 through 1964 García Márquez was unable to come up with a single new, strictly "literary" piece. Future biographers and memoirists may well give us the day-to-day details and the probable causes—financial pressures, demands from his job as well as film work, and personal dissatisfaction with the formal features of his writing thus far—of the author's creative slump. Whatever the reasons, García Márquez must have meant it when around this time he used to say to his friend, the Colombian poet and executive Álvaro Mutis, "I'll never write again."[39]

What finally drew García Márquez out of his slumbers is one of the most dramatic instances ever reported of the sheer power of inspiration. As García Márquez recalls it, he and the family were riding in their Opel along the Mexico City–Acapulco highway, when all of a sudden he found he could imagine every last word of the book he had been trying to get out of him since 1942. "It was so ripe in me that I could have dictated the first chapter, word by word, to a typist."[40] He did a fast U-turn and asked Mercedes to handle the family finances for the next six months while he wrote this novel. And back in his room ("the Cave of the Mafia," as it came to be called) write he did, obsessively, eight hours a day, the book taking on a life of its own as the months rushed by, the author looking glum on the afternoon when he had had to kill off Colonel Buendía, and meanwhile Mercedes secretly pawning the television set, the radio, a wall clock, and an eggbeater, and emergency loans and emotional support coming from various friends, including a Catalan couple next door to whom the book was finally dedicated.

Eighteen months and a ten thousand dollar debt later there were thirteen hundred pages of typescript, plus a variety of working diagrams and sketches which the author promptly destroyed.[41] Earlier in the year Editorial Sudamericana in Argentina had chanced to write García Márquez about the possibility of reprinting his former work, and they agreed to look at his novel-in-progress instead. As he and Mercedes were readying the manuscript for the mails she worried to herself (she would later confess), "And what if, after all this, it's a bad novel?" (OG, 107; FG, 75). Further misadventures took place: as the couple were walking toward the post office the box holding the typescript fell open and some pages started blowing all over the street. And arriving at the stamp window they lacked the money for the full postage, and so mailed out only half the novel, García Márquez rounding up the balance for the second half later in the day.

Having expected good reviews but modest sales—the lot of his previous books—García Márquez was caught off guard by the lightning success. In the initial few months of bestsellerdom and limelight he found himself hotly pursued by reporters seeking interviews, by a publisher offering him a house on Majorca in exchange for his next novel (supposedly to be composed there), by women sending photos of themselves in exchange for his personal mail, and more. Over the next two years the fame would spread worldwide, with major prizes for the book in France and Italy and good sales in the United States.

Soon finding it impossible to work under such conditions, in October 1967 García Márquez and his family packed off to Barcelona with a view to living incognito, putting an end to the phone calls, and writing in peace. A roving García Márquez had once shunned Franco's Spain out of loyalty to exiled Republican friends, but in the late 1960s Barcelona was becoming a center of cultural and political opposition to the regime, and there was also a fair share of expatriate Latin American writers, among them the Peruvian Vargas Llosa, who rapidly became a friend and advocate of the now-celebrated Colombian (until their personal and ideological rift in 1975). In addition, García Márquez wished to observe a right-wing tyranny in its waning days, as part of his research for a novel about Latin dictatorship.

The original plan was to spend maybe a year on the book; it grew into a even-year project. He also found the puritanical austerity of Franco's Spain very much at variance with the flamboyant excess, the amoral eroticism, and tropical informality that had always characterized those Caribbean tyrannies of which he was now creating a historical-geographical composite. Halfway through the long writing process García Márquez and his family took off on a full year's leave, exploring the Caribbean country by country, so that in his mind the novelist might "bring back the fragrance of guava." They returned to Barcelona; his imaginary despot's life crept to its terminal lonesome gasps; and in 1975 (coincidentally the year in which Generalissimo Franco was to die) the long-awaited *The Autumn of the Patriarch* appeared and quickly sold a half-million copies, though its dense and difficult prose would put off many hopeful readers, who had been expecting a return trip to Macondo. With the other book he had always wanted to write now written, García Márquez purchased a house in Pedregal San Angel, a suburb of Mexico City, where, with his wife and visiting sons, he still spends most of his writing year.

In the interim García Márquez had begun using his global fame as an instrument of support for left-wing causes, or for "quiet diplomacy" between warring parties. When in 1972 he received the prestigious Rómulo Gallegos Prize in Venezuela, at the ceremony he publicly donated the entire sum to the parliamentary Movimiento al Socialismo (MAS), and his $10,000 Neustadt Prize (1972) he gave away to the Committee in Solidarity With Political Prisoners. García Márquez was active in the Bertrand Russell Tribunal hearings on South American dictatorships, and he participated in various ways in the campaign of President Omar Torrijos of Panama to have the canal and the adjoining areas placed under Panamanian sovereignty.

With his pen and contacts García Márquez aided the Sandinista guerrillas in the struggle against the forty-year-old Somoza tyranny, and since their victory in 1979 he has made every possible effort to defend them against the vicious U.S. media-cum-military onslaught that followed. On occasion he has used his influence with Fidel Castro to help secure the release of a Cuban political prisoner, and at different moments has served as an intermediary between the Colombian government and certain guerrilla factions. In 1986 he addressed representatives of the "Group of Six" (Sweden, Greece, India, Mexico, Argentina, and Tanzania) on the horrors of nuclear war.

Early in 1981, amid a great deal of international fanfare, the seemingly simple, deceptively brief novel *Chronicle of a Death Foretold* appeared, its two million copies issued in simultaneous editions by Colombian, Spanish,

Argentine, and Mexican publishing houses. At the time García Márquez was in his native land and was considering settling down there once again. On 26 March, however, he returned to Mexico, where he requested political asylum (a fairly traditional Latin American procedure). Back in Bogotá the Liberal government of Julio César Turbay Ayala ridiculed the move and dismissed it as mere publicity-mongering for García Márquez's new book. In the novelist's defense it should be said that Colombia, with its permanent state of siege still in effect, had been rife with rumors of plans for large-scale repression and of lists of a thousand leftist intellectuals marked for arrest, among them García Márquez. In addition, certain M-19 guerrillas had "confessed" that García Márquez was one of their prime sources of funding, and his outspoken views and his Cuban ties would not have been of help should an extreme situation have arisen. Surely the example of the Pinochet coup, which had destroyed Chilean democracy and led to the detention, torture, and death of many left-wing artists—including Pablo Neruda—must not have been far from García Márquez's mind.

Even after world sales of *One Hundred Years of Solitude* had freed him from financial want, García Márquez never was to abandon his journalistic calling. Now, however, he could allow himself the luxury of "advocacy" journalism. Whether reporting on the final struggles of President Allende in Chile, the liberation of Angola from Portuguese rule, the situation in postwar Vietnam, the actions of the Sandinistas, or the literary intellect of French socialist François Mitterrand, García Márquez would bring narrative insight, eloquent prose, and Caribbean wit to matters close to him, and moreover could state his position without fear of being blackballed or sacked. One of the principal venues for these articles was *Alternativa*, a magazine he helped found and fund in Bogotá in 1974. Starting out as a biweekly, it shifted to weekly format within a year, and despite such pressures as a mysterious bomb that damaged its offices in 1975, and constant shortages of cash, it enjoyed more or less continuous publication until it was forced to fold in 1980. An inability to reach sufficiently sizable circulation, combined with a decision not to include advertising, finally rendered the project economically unviable.[42]

In 1980 García Márquez initiated a ritual of repairing to his house in Cuernavaca on Saturdays and composing a weekly column. Syndicated in a couple of dozen Hispanic newspapers and magazines, the pieces dealt with subjects ranging from Bach's cello suites to the "disappearances" of writers under the murderous and stupid Argentine military regime. These little essays were to provide some of the liveliest, wisest, most distinctly personal magazine reading in Spanish for three consecutive years. In addition, by 1982 he had started preliminary work on what he was describing as a love story; an unexpected second windfall, however, was once again radically to change his life and temporarily cut into his creative routines.

In the years following publication of *One Hundred Years of Solitude*, García Márquez had been the recipient of a long fist of international honors, including an honorary doctorate at Columbia University in 1971 (where he refused to wear a necktie) and a medal of the French Legion of Honor from François Mitterrand, whose 1981 presidential inauguration García Márquez attended (along with Carlos Fuentes, Augusto Roa Bastos, and Julio Cortázar). The 1982 Nobel Prize, however, seemed to have come out of the blue. Until then it had been more or less assumed that, for the next round of Latin Americans, the literary Nobel would "naturally" go to Octavio Paz, the avant-garde poet, oracular essayist, and neoconservative elder cultural statesman of Mexico. At age fifty-four, García Márquez now found himself the youngest such laureate since Albert Camus.

He rose to the occasion. When García Márquez and several dozen friends departed Bogotá for Sweden they were bade farewell by President Belisario Betancur himself, who jubilantly declared, "All of Colombia will be keeping Gabo company!" In addition, the entourage included sixty performers from six different Colombian dance and music ensembles who would bring a full week of tropical festivities to the chiaroscuros of Stockholm in the fall.[43] For the ceremonies García Márquez wore not a European coat and tie but the traditional white linen *liqui-liqui* suit of the continental Caribbean.[44] And for the Nobel Lecture he overcame his timidity about public speaking and delivered a stirring evocation of the special beauties and political tragedies of Latin America.[45] There were those who expressed displeasure at the manifestly ideological flavor of the speech, but in all it was the most festive such ceremony in nearly a century. As the coordinator of the events remarked to some friends of García Márquez, "Never in all my years with the Nobel organization have I seen the Swedes in so vibrant a mood."[46]

The originally stated aim of García Márquez was to utilize the prize money to help launch a new newspaper in Colombia, under the name *El Otro* (*The Other One*).[47] However, what with financial difficulties and the obstacles posed merely by the existence of the established press, his worthy project never came to fruition. The will and popularity of a great novelist are not in themselves enough to sustain so ambitious a project as a mass circulation daily.

The aftermath of the Nobel made for months of added obligations, and García Márquez was unable to resume the writing of his novel-in-progress until late in 1983. Taking a sabbatical from his weekly columns from February to September 1984, he rented an apartment in Cartagena—where his parents were now living—and worked on the book eight hours a day, absorbing the old city environment in the afternoons the better to depict it in his narrative. Within a year he returned to his house in Mexico City and there became a convert to the computer, marveling at the speed with which the word processor allowed him to compose the remainder of the novel. In 1985, wearing the three diskettes around his neck, he flew to Barcelona and delivered the "manuscript" to Carmen Balcells, his literary agent. Printers were soon put on rush order—the job was done in two weeks—and the binders were instructed to produce a physical volume that would endure rather than disintegrate on first reading. And on 5 December 1985 a million copies of *Love in the Time of Cholera* were officially issued in the four most populous Spanish-speaking countries.[48] At a formal gathering in Bogotá, former president Alfonso López Michelsen presented the Colombian edition of the novel with an eloquent and learned speech tracing the book's artistic kinships with Proust. Thereafter García Márquez's most significant activities would be his involvement with the executive committee of the Cuban state film school and a new novel entitled *El general en su laberinto* (*The General in His Labyrinth*), based on the life of Simón Bolívar.

His international stature notwithstanding, García Márquez is a man strongly attached to the land of his youth, and indeed his fiction since *The Autumn of the Patriarch* becomes even more local in its preoccupations and focus. Remaining steadfastly loyal to those individuals who gave him emotional and financial sustenance when he most needed them, by the same token he resists the shallow allure and temptations, of media fame and glitter. The only true friends García Márquez actually claims are those predating *One Hundred Tears of Solitude*, and it is they and his closely knit family who shield him from the many solicitors and fortune-seekers that regularly descend upon him at public functions or come knocking at his door. Though a sweet and sociable man who fundamentally takes pleasure in being with other people, were he to attend to even half the requests and invitations that come his way (be they genuine or opportunistic) he would find himself with no time left for his top priorities: writing, family, and friends.

NOTES

1. Though no full-length biography, of García Márquez exists to date, there is ample biographical information scattered about in journalistic pieces, general-interest critical works, and the hundreds of interviews granted by the novelist since 1967. The following narrative of his life pretends to be neither final nor complete, but synoptic, relevant, and useful to the immediate purposes of our study. It has been pieced together from these sources: Oscar Collazos, *García Márquez: La soledad y la gloria*; Gabriel García Márquez, *El olor de la guayaba. Conversaciones con Plinio Apuleio Mendoza*; Stephen Minta, *Gabriel García*

Márquez: Writer of Colombia; Mario Vargas Llosa, *García Márquez: Historia de un deicidio*; and a great many interviews, particularly those compiled in Alfonso Rentería Mantilla, ed., *García Márquez habla de García Márquez*. Last but not least, I must express my scholarly debt to Professor Jacques Gilard for the lengthy biographical "Prólogo" he includes in each of the three main volumes of García Márquez's collected *Obra periodística*, a project that has vastly expanded our knowledge of the life, development, and background of the Colombian author.

2. Vargas Llosa, p. 14.
3. Collazos, p. 12.
4. Vargas Llosa, p. 27.
5. Collazos, p. 16.
6. Interview with Cobo Borda, "Piedra y Cielo me hizo escritor," p. 34
7. Collazos, p. 21.
8. Cobo Borda, p. 34.
9. Vargas Llosa, p. 33.
10. Gilard, "Prólogo" to *OP*, 1:8.
11. Minta, pp. 42–46.
12. Cobo Borda, p. 35.
13. Vargas Llosa, pp. 37–38.
14. Ibid.
15. Gilard, "Prólogo" to *OP*, 1:30–32.
16. "El viaje a la semilla," interview with *El Manifiesto*, in Rentería Mantilla, p. 163.
17. Gilard, "Prólogo" to *OP*, 1:36.
18. Gilard, "Prólogo" to *OP*, 2:8–13.
19. For a detailed examination of García Márquez's work as film critic, see Gilard, "Prólogo" to *OP*, 2:26–60.
20. Ibid., p. 34.
21. Reprinted as a single volume, *Relato de un náufrago* ...; English version, *The Story of a Shipwrecked Sailor*, trans. Randolph Hogan.
22. Gilard, "Prólogo" to *OP*, 2:76–81, and "Prólogo" to *OP*, 3:7–9.
23. Gilard, "Prólogo" to *OP*, 2:83 and 86.
24. Gilard, "Prólogo" to *OP*, 3:25.
25. Plinio Apuleio Mendoza, "18 años atrás," in Rentería Mantilla, p. 91.
26. Collazos, p. 44.
27. Literally "Pliny Apuleius." Classical first names are still fairly common in Latin America, Colombia in particular.
28. Gilard, "Prólogo" to *OP*, 3:33–36.
29. Ibid., p. 50.
30. Ibid., pp. 52–53
31. Ibid., p. 55.
32. Gilard, "Prólogo" to *OP*, 3:60–62. Vargas Llosa, pp. 58–59.
33. Gilard, "Prólogo" to *OP*, 3:62–64.
34. Collazos, p. 71.
35. Vargas Llosa, pp. 65–66.
36. Ibid., p. 66.
37. Ibid., p. 67.
38. For detailed examinations of some of those film scripts, see Vargas Llosa, pp. 67–73, and Collazos, pp. 91–95.
39. Vargas Llosa, p. 75.

40. Ibid., p. 77.

41. González Bermejo, "Ahora doscientos años de soledad," p. 55.

42. This phase of García Márquez's journalistic activity is itemized and commented on in Benson, "García Márquez en *Alternativa* (1974–1979)" and "García Márquez en *Alternativa* (1978–1980)."

43. Mera, untitled preface to *Aracataca Estocolmo*, p. 60.

44. Collazos, p. 233.

45. The address, "The Solitude of Latin America," is included in McGuirk and Cardwell, *Gabriel García Márquez*, pp. 207–11.

46. Nereo López, "Testimonio del fotógrafo," in *Aracataca Estocolmo*, p. 95.

47. Collazos, pp. 245–46.

48. Caballero, "El amor en los tiempos del Nobel," p. 32.

HARLEY D. OBERHELMAN

Hemingway's Presence in
the Early Short Fiction (1950–55)

O ne of the most complete studies of the presence of Hemingway in García Márquez's short fiction was done by his sometime friend and fellow novelist Mario Vargas Llosa in his 1971 signal study, *García Márquez: Historia de un deicidio* (*García Márquez: History of a Decade*; 150–56). Hemingway, among others, is correctly identified as one of García Márquez's principal "cultural demons," especially in his early fiction. *Into the Mainstream*, Luis Harss and Barbara Dohmann's collection of conversations with ten contemporary Latin-American writers, describes García Márquez's relationship with Hemingway as "platonic; a matter of general stylistic tendency," but, the authors continue, the difference between García Márquez's Faulknerian first short novel, *La hojarasca* (1955; *"Leaf Storm" and Other Stories*, 1972) and his second, *El coronel no tiene quien le escriba* (1958/1961; *"No One Writes to the Colonel" and Other Stories*, 1968) is the same difference as "between profligacy and absolute economy" (324).

LEAF STORM

The "profligacy" of *Leaf Storm* clearly marks it as García Márquez's most Faulknerian work. Written during the years that he spent on the coast in Cartagena and Barranquilla, it shows the plot pattern and style of the author

From *The Presence of Hemingway in the Short Fiction of Gabriel García Márquez*. © 1994 by York Press, Ltd.

of *As I Lay Dying*. In its creation of Macondo, a fictional town based on the realities of the author's native Aracataca and the Caribbean coastal region, one can see the presence of Faulkner's Jefferson and Yoknapatawpha County, likewise based on his native Oxford and Lafayette County, Mississippi. *Leaf Storm*'s three long, intercalated monologues recall the multiple narrators of Faulkner's *The Sound and the Fury*, and the moral and economic pillage of Macondo by the North American banana company is reminiscent of the carpetbaggers who invaded Jefferson and Yoknapatawpha County following the Civil War.

The axis around which the memories of the past swirl in *Leaf Storm* is the dead body of a mysterious French doctor whose strange and defiant actions caused great hostility in Macondo. The vicissitudes of burying the remains of a prominent or controversial figure were to appear frequently in García Márquez's later fiction, but the exemplary burial sequence in Faulkner is the struggle to overcome the forces of fire and flood in *As I Lay Dying* so that Addie Bundren's family can transport her remains to Jefferson for interment according to her wishes and the promise made by her husband on her deathbed. Both novelists, of course, are ultimately indebted to the archetypal burial scene in Sophocles's *Antigone*. In both novels there is a pervasive feeling of solitude and the suggestion of decadence and decay. Both works are derived from a social conflict between one's ethical sense of responsibility to give proper burial to an unpopular or controversial figure and societal pressures to allow the emotional reactions of the community to intervene.

In the early 1950s, when García Márquez was still at work on *Leaf Storm*, he began to read Hemingway in an effort to neutralize the overpowering effect and the "aftertaste" of Faulkner's prose. In "Gabriel García Márquez Meets Ernest Hemingway" he states that Faulkner "doesn't seem to have an organic system of writing, but instead walks blindly through his biblical universe, like a herd of goats loosed in a shop full of crystal" (16). To dismantle a page of Faulkner's prose leaves the distinct impression that one is left with extra springs and screws that do not fit when the page is reassembled. Hemingway, by contrast, leaves the screws and springs of his "literary carpentry" fully exposed. For this reason, García Márquez concludes that "Faulkner is a writer who has had much to do with my soul, but Hemingway is the one who had the most to do with my craft" (16). This transfer of stylistic allegiance to Hemingway resulted in an effaced narrative style, not unlike Henry James's rhetoric, and "a more deliberate and explicit treatment of the social and political questions that had formed part of the milieu of *Leaf Storm*, but were not in themselves objects of attention" (Janes 29).

Both Hemingway and García Márquez had yet another factor in common, their early training in journalism. This led to their use of objective reality as the source of all of their writings. Their approach, however, is in sharp contrast. For García Márquez reality includes the world of magic, superstition, and fantasy—all part of everyday life in Spanish America, he affirms. Hemingway, on the other hand, always sought "the real thing;" i.e., stark, bare realism that searches out the fraction of the iceberg protruding from the waters. Stated another way, "the real thing" is the search for a sensory detail that sparks an emotional response in Hemingway's prose. In 1960 Hemingway told Luis Guevara that "the journalist is a minor novelist. He has to narrate putting aside literature in order to be understood; we novelists who previously have been journalists know better than anyone" (24; my translation). García Márquez developed his style slowly from his reading of Hemingway among others and gradually abandoned first-person narration in favor of a Hemingwayesque, unobtrusive third-person recorder. Hemingway, on the other hand, was limited early in his career to the inflexible style book of the *Kansas City Star* that instructed its writers to "Use short sentences. Use short first paragraphs. Use vigorous English, not forgetting to strive for smoothness. Be positive, not negative" (Miscellaneous Publications, Hemingway Collection, JFK Library). García Márquez gradually abandoned first-person narration in favor of a behind-the-scenes third-person narrator.

"THE WOMAN WHO CAME AT SIX O'CLOCK"

García Márquez had used such a narrator in an early short story, "La mujer que llegaba a las seis" ("The Woman Who Came at Six O'Clock"), first published in *Crónica* on June 24, 1950, and reprinted two years later in *El Espectador*. The story's initial publication in *Crónica* establishes García Márquez's first contacts with Hemingway around 1950 after he had just arrived in Barranquilla. By his admission the tale is more an imitation of Hemingway than one of his own typical short stories. Two years later he sent the story to *El Espectador* together with a letter to Gonzalo González, a journalist from the coast who worked for years in Bogotá. In the letter he details the story's genesis: it was the result of a bet with Alfonso Fuenmayor that he could not write police fiction. García Márquez dashed off what he called "the worst love story I could write" and won the bet with Fuenmayor (*OP* 1: 724; my translation). In the same letter he mentioned that the Losada publishers had rejected *Leaf Storm*, the novella he finally was able to publish in 1955. He related as well that he had just returned from dusty, sleepy Aracataca, the town where he was born and where he spent the first eight years of his life, and Valledupar, where singing seemed to be the major pastime. He planned to use these experiences in his 700-page novel, "La casa" (The House), which some fifteen years later evolved into the highly praised *One Hundred Years of Solitude*. Both the short story and the letter, titled "Auto-crítica" (Self-Criticism), were published in the March 30, 1952, issue of *El Espectador* (*OP* 1: 724–26).

The model for "The Woman Who Came at Six O'Clock" is the much anthologized Hemingway short story, "The Killers." It was one of three stories Hemingway penned in a Madrid boardinghouse the snowy afternoon of May 16, 1926, when the bullfight program was canceled due to inclement weather. It was first published in the March 1927 edition of *Scribner's Magazine*. Later that year it appeared in the collection *Men Without Women*. Alfonso Fuenmayor published the first Spanish translation of "The Killers" in the October 1945 issue of *Revista de America*. It was reprinted twice, once in *Estampa* in 1949, and in *Crónica* a year later. *Crónica* was the same review where García Márquez was first to publish "The Woman Who Came at Six O'Clock," also in 1950. There is little doubt that "The Killers" was one of the first translations of Hemingway available to García Márquez, and its mark on "The Woman Who Came at Six O'Clock" is undeniable.

"The Killers" is set in a small-town restaurant in Summit, Illinois. Two professional assassins, both Chicago hit men, have come to annihilate a Swedish boxer named Ole Andreson, a frequent diner at the restaurant. The action begins around five o'clock in the afternoon, and Andreson usually arrives about six. After eating, the hit men tie up Nick Adams, a reappearing character throughout the course of Hemingway's fiction, and Sam, the black cook. They threaten George, the owner of the establishment, and make him dispatch other would-be diners. Shortly after seven it is apparent that Andreson will not appear; the hit men leave, and George goes back to the kitchen to untie Nick and Sam.

In the second half of the story Nick rushes to the rooming house where Andreson lives in order to warn him of the danger to his life. Andreson is passive and refuses to appeal to the police for protection or to leave town. The idealistic Nick is unable to comprehend Andreson's decision and later tells George that he himself has decided to get out of Summit. George agrees that leaving town is a good idea and recommends that Nick not think more about the disagreeable incident. While the reasons for the assassination plot are never totally revealed, it is clear that Nick Adams slowly begins to imagine the horror of the "awful thing" that precipitated the attempted homicide. This open-ended conclusion was to provide García Márquez with a pattern for much of his later short fiction as well as for "The Woman Who Came at Six O'Clock."

The García Márquez short story is likewise set in a restaurant, and, as the title suggests, maintains a limited time frame into which the action fits. The six characters of "The Killers" are reduced to two: a prostitute simply called "Reina" (Queen), and the lovelorn restaurant owner, José, sometimes referred to by his nickname, Pepillo. Reina is a punctual patron (like Ole Andreson), and she always arrives precisely at six. The use of the Spanish verb llegaba in the imperfect tense in the story's title suggests "used to arrive" as a more accurate translation (Bell-Villada 141). Reina embodies both the hit men of "The Killers" as well as their would-be victim, Andreson. The rectitude of a youthful Nick Adams can be seen in José whose nickname connotes innocence. It is doubtful, however, that José even begins to comprehend Reina's basic request, that he tell anyone who asks that on that particular day she arrived a quarter of an hour earlier.

This story is atypical of García Márquez's early fiction in that it uses an omniscient narrator and an extraordinary amount of dialogue. Reina is the talkative protagonist; José limits his part of the conversation to brief reactions and commentaries. Reina's plan is readily apparent to the reader: she always comes to the restaurant at six o'clock, and indeed she did come at the usual time on the day the story takes place. "Today is different," she fabricates; "I didn't come at six today, that's why it's different" (*CS*). José, checking his ever accurate clock on the restaurant wall, immediately disputes her affirmation.

Reina's remarks a few minutes later reveal that her purpose is to cajole José in order to use him as an alibi to cover the fact that she has just murdered one of her clients. She successfully extracts from him a declaration of his eternal love along with a promise that he will defend her even if she is accused of the murder of a depraved client. The naive José finally agrees to her request, at which point she confesses to him that, like Nick Adams in the Hemingway story, she is going to leave town and prostitution as well. Up to this point she has only asked him to say that she arrived at a quarter of six. Now at the end, in exchange for her promise to find José a little windup bear on a string, Reina asks for fifteen more minutes. José is to declare that she came at five-thirty.

Both "The Killers" and "The Woman Who Came at Six O'Clock" describe the dichotomy between good and evil. The basic innocence of Nick Adams and José is set in contrast to the abject world of the hit men, Ole Andreson, and Reina. These latter characters represent the underworld of crime and prostitution. Nick Adams, on the other hand, is an idealistic youth who discovers a corrupt world on a fall day in a small Illinois town. José, his counterpart, is a credulous restaurant owner who is easily deceived. At a point shortly before the action begins, both Andreson and Reina have undergone a basic transformation in their lives; Andreson has decided to stop running from his pursuers, and Reina has decided to leave prostitution and to go "where there aren't any men who want to sleep with [women]" (*CS* 65). While Andreson seems to have resigned himself to death, Reina seeks a better world where she can escape the role of victim.

Structurally, the two short stories have a great deal in common. Both take place within about an hour's time. The two separate scenes of "The Killers" (the incident in the restaurant and Nick Adams's attempt to warn Andreson) become a single setting in García Márquez's tale. The two stories contain large amounts of dialogue, and this sets "The Woman Who Came at Six O'Clock" apart from later García Márquez fiction. Writing in "Auto-crítica," García Márquez believes that the dialogue is the story's principal defect (*OP* 1: 724). The original *Crónica* version published in 1950 contained "sewer dialogue;" appalling but more authentic, García Márquez thinks. This was especially true of the lines spoken by Reina. The 1952 version published by *El Espectador* and reissued in subsequent collections of short stories is an expurgated, "disinfected" version that the author deems less authentic. Both of these stories have an open ending. The ultimate fate of Andreson as well as the fate of Reina are unknown. While the two restaurant owners and Andreson stay behind, the announced departures of Nick Adams and Reina provide a sense of ending to both narratives in that these protagonists have finished one phase of their lives and now seek a better future. Nick Adams is to reappear in later Hemingway fiction, but Reina and José have not yet been resurrected by García Márquez.

THE STORY OF A SHIPWRECKED SAILOR

Early in 1954 García Márquez's close friend, the poet and critic Álvaro Mutis, invited him to return to Bogotá to do film reviews and editorials for *El Espectador*. At the time García Márquez had already published some ten short stories, twenty-nine "Punto y aparte" articles in *El Universal*, some 400 "La jirafa" columns in *El Heraldo*, and various fragments of short fiction. *Leaf Storm* was written, once rejected, and not to appear until May 31, 1955. The six years spent in Cartagena and Barranquilla had been artistically productive. In Bogotá he worked from February 1954 until July 1955, at which time *El Espectador* sent him to Europe as a foreign correspondent.

The most memorable series García Márquez wrote after returning to Bogotá was fourteen installments in *El Espectador* that recounted the story of a Colombian sailor, Luis Alejandro Velasco, one of eight crewmen on the destroyer Caldas who had fallen overboard and disappeared during a putative storm in the Caribbean in February of 1955. The fourteen articles appeared during the period April 5–22 and represented an intense period of writing in order for García Márquez to satisfy his avid reading public. The newspaper's circulation almost doubled during April, and readers scrambled to buy back issues. The series was so popular that *El Espectador* reissued all the installments in a special edition that printed more copies than any other previous Colombian newspaper. This edition was illustrated with photographs the survivors had taken on the high seas; one could easily see some boxes of contraband merchandise with their factory labels on the top deck.

Velasco's story contained a political and moral time bomb that enraged both the navy and the government of the dictator, Gustavo Rojas Pinilla. Velasco related that the Caldas was returning to Cartagena from Mobile, Alabama, where it had been for eight months while its electronic equipment and gunnery were being repaired. The alleged storm caused the eight crewmen to be washed overboard about two hours before the Caldas arrived in Cartagena. But ten days later Velasco washed up half dead on the coast after having drifted on a raft without food or water for more than a week. He was later given a hero's welcome in the capital, but after twenty six-hour interviews with García Márquez it came out that the cause of the accident was not a storm at all, but rather the shifting of the boxes of luxury contraband articles on the ship's deck during rough seas. This revelation caused the wrath of the navy as well as the government of Rojas Pinilla. Disclaimers were printed on the first page of the April 27 edition of *El Espectador*, but the newspaper nevertheless published the special edition the next day together with the telltale photographs. In 1970 García Márquez reprinted the series as a book called *Relato de un náufrago* (*The Story of a Shipwrecked Sailor*, 1982). It included a prologue that left no doubt about the author's polemical intent. "The account, like the destroyer, was loaded with ill-secured moral and political cargo," García Márquez added (*Sailor* viii).

The dictatorship countered with a series of drastic reprisals that months later resulted in the closure of the newspaper. Despite pressure and threats, Velasco refused to recant a single word of his story. He was forced to leave the navy, and some months later a reporter found him working in a Bogotá bus station. Life had passed him by, but the aura of a hero who had told the truth persisted. When Rojas Pinilla caused the eventual shutdown of *El Espectador*, García Márquez, working as a correspondent in France at the time, was forced to begin a nomadic exile, drifting like Velasco on the raft of financial insecurity without the salary he once received from the newspaper. Two years later the dictatorship collapsed and the nation "fell to the mercy of other regimes that were better dressed but not much more just" (*Sailor* ix).

If William Faulkner's *As I Lay Dying* informed the pages of *Leaf Storm*, then *The Old Man and the Sea*, Hemingway's 1952 masterpiece, most certainly was; the inspiration for *The Story of a Shipwrecked Sailor*. Jacques Gilard believes that García Márquez wrote *Sailor* as if he had accepted a challenge to compete with Hemingway. Gilard establishes the fact that García Márquez's reading of *Old Man* in translation as published by *Life en español* caused him to reevaluate Hemingway's contribution to literature in a more favorable light (*OP* 2: 64n76). This early reading of Hemingway occurred between 1952 and 1953 when García Márquez was selling encyclopedias in the heat of Riohacha on the Guajira Peninsula. He no doubt recognized *Old Man* as a major work—one that was to restore Hemingway's flagging reputation and facilitate his nomination for the Nobel prize two years later. Gerry Brenner sees it as a masterwork that "speaks across historical periods to a broad range of readers ... [and] deals freshly or complexly with recurrent human issues" (28). *Old Man* engages readers emotionally and intellectually, Brenner believes, while at the same time they measure its treatment of such issues against the yardstick of daily existence. It is generally granted that García Márquez was inspired by the theme and style of *Old Man*, a work fresh in his memory when he was suddenly called on to interview Velasco and interpret his odyssey.

In *Old Man*, Santiago, who has fished the Gulf Stream for decades, is in his eighty-fourth day without landing a fish. For the first forty days he was accompanied by a young friend, Manolin, but the rest of the time he has fished alone. On the eighty-fifth day he ventures out farther than usual and successfully hooks a giant marlin. An epic struggle ensues that is to last three days. Santiago is called upon to use all of his strength and experience to capture the prize. It is not until the afternoon of the second day that he finally sees the mighty fish break above the water with a gigantic leap. Santiago and the enormous marlin two feet longer than his skiff— momentarily confront each other. Finally on the third day Santiago works him close enough to the skiff to harpoon him and secure him to the boat for the journey home.

The third day brings another confrontation, this time with a great shark and a school of scavenger sharks that rip off huge chunks of the marlin's flesh. Santiago clubs them desperately until he loses his last weapon. "Now it is over, he thought. They will probably hit me again. But what can a man do against them in the dark without a weapon?" (*Old Man* 130). Santiago sails into the harbor late on the third day with the skeleton of the great fish lashed to the side of his vessel. He stumbles back to his shack and is asleep when Manolin looks in on him the next morning. He brings Santiago some hot coffee, and they make plans to go out fishing again.

There is a presumed basic difference between *Old Man* and *Sailor*: the former is a product of Hemingway's invention while the latter is a written account of Velasco's retrospection. Neither of these hypotheses is entirely correct. In a letter to *Esquire* dated April 1936, Hemingway recounts an episode that was to provide him with the basic plot of *Old Man*:

> Another time an old man fishing alone in a skiff out of Cabanas hooked a great marlin that, on the heavy sashcord handline, pulled the skiff far out to sea. Two days later the old man was picked up by fishermen sixty miles to the eastward, the head and forward part of the marlin lashed alongside. What was left of the fish, less than half, weighed eight hundred pounds. The old man had stayed with him a day, a night, a day and another night while the fish swam deep and pulled the boat. When he had come up the old man had pulled the boat up on him and harpooned him. Lashed alongside the sharks had hit him and the old man had fought them out alone in the Gulf Stream in a skiff, clubbing them, stabbing at them, lunging at them with an oar until he was exhausted and the sharks had eaten all that they could hold. He was crying in the boat when the fishermen picked him up, half crazy from his loss, and the sharks were circling the boat. (Brenner 28–29)

While the fisherman in this anecdote is not Santiago, his ordeal sketches a story line to which Hemingway adds such qualities as endurance, self-sufficiency, love, and respect for the noble creature represented by the giant marlin. Santiago is an idealized, archetypical hero, even a saint if one considers that his name translates as "Saint James," the patron saint of Spain, an apostle, and also a fisherman. Hemingway's Santiago was born in the Canary Islands off the coast of Africa. (It is worth noting that Santiago on several occasions dreams about the lions he saw as a young man on visits to the nearby African mainland.) Santiago left his native islands to bring his heroic values to Cuba, much like thousands of others who emigrated from Spain and settled there before him. It is generally believed that Hemingway based the character of Santiago on Carlos Gutiérrez and Gregorio Fuentes, his mates on the yacht Pilar, both born in the Canary Islands (Capellán 109–10). García Márquez reports in his 1981 *New York Times Book Review* article that Hemingway spent a great deal of time in the rugged fishing village of Cojímar, just east of Havana, where he could observe the daily life of the men he was to immortalize in the person of Santiago (17). A few days after Hemingway's death the fishermen of Cojímar erected a bust of their friend in the plaza, now called Plaza Hemingway. It faces one of the docks where Hemingway moored the Pilar.

Earl Rovit believes that "the saga of Santiago is an attempt, among other things, to represent the whole of man's experience through a system of symbolic correspondences" (69). Hemingway once told a reporter, "I tried to make a real old man, a real boy [Manolin], a real sea and a real fish and real sharks. But if I made them good and true enough they would mean many things" (Rovit 70–71). He followed the traditional pattern of the quest or the journey that ultimately produces a higher level of reality, the "real thing," i.e., a transcendent level of being. His original premise, however, is based on what he observed in Cojímar and while fishing in the Gulf Stream. *Old Man*, therefore, is based on "real" events and people in much the same manner utilized by García Márquez in *Sailor*. Both share a common thesis: the winner must take nothing. Santiago "wins" the giant marlin, in the end stripped of its flesh by scavenger sharks; Velasco "saves" his life only to suffer repudiation by the dictatorship when he discloses the "real" course of events aboard the Caldas. In the epigraph to his 1933 collection of fourteen bitter stories, *Winner Take Nothing*, Hemingway writes: "Unlike all other forms of lutte or combat the conditions are that the winner shall take nothing; nor... shall there be any reward within himself." This concept is closely related to Hemingway's use of the term *nada* (nothingness), the ominous, terrifying absence of meaning to which all human beings must respond. Velasco in *Sailor*, Santiago in *Old Man*, and humanity in general face the bleak chaos of the tabula rasa. The nothingness of Velasco's life after the government repudiates him is a clear case of life imitating art; Santiago faces the nothingness of a marlin's skeleton, but he responds by planning another fishing expedition with Manolin.

When the fourteen installments that were to make up *Sailor* first appeared in 1955, it was apparent that the principal intention was to entertain the reading public. Rojas Pinilla's government had a severe censorship code in place, and the opposition press could attack the state only in an indirect fashion. The inclusion of photographs of the contraband in the April 28 special edition further exacerbated the tenuous relationship between the government and *El Espectador*. Another consideration is the fact that the series was first published under the general title *La verdad sobre mi aventura* (The Truth about My Adventure), and Velasco was clearly named as author. First Velasco and later García Márquez, as well as the entire staff of *El Espectador*, were to encounter the vengeance of the Rojas Pinilla dictatorship that closed down the newspaper from 1956 to 1958. However by 1970, when the series was published as a book, García Márquez assumed the full responsibility of authorship for *Relato de un náufrago* ... and included a prologue, "La historia de esta historia" (The History of This Chronicle). He asserts that it would have been politically dishonest to halt publication of the series in 1955 simply because it offended the government; the dictatorship was therefore forced to satisfy itself by patching up the truth with rhetoric and misrepresentation (*Sailor* viii).

The 1970 edition of *Sailor* and its 1986 English translation include a long subtitle: [*The Story of a Shipwrecked Sailor*] *Who Drifted on a Life Raft for Ten Days Without Food or Water, Was Proclaimed a National Hero, Kissed by Beauty Queens, Made Rich through Publicity, and Then Spurned by the Government and Forgotten for All Time*. Its mock-epic subtitle recalls the cry of a huckster at a rural fair or a town crier centuries ago. It pokes fun at Colombia's penchant for worshiping beauty queens while at the same time it sketches an outline of the story's contents. It moves the journalistic series into the realm of creative writing with both a serious and a festive intent and confirms the thesis that the story is Velasco's, but the style and method are in every respect García Márquez's design.

Sailor clearly falls into the category of the nonfiction novel, a genre popular both in the United States and Spanish America in recent years. George McMurray places it within the boundaries of "the so-called New Journalism" and describes it as topical journalism, tied to particular events and combining "detailed, factual observation with stylistic techniques, structures and, on occasion, authorial imagination typical of fiction" (1992, 111). It is an attempt to convert the amorphous material of real experience into art. Within the categories of the nonfiction novel, *Sailor* is a clear example of the testimonial novel in which the author or the individual interviewed by the author (Velasco, in this instance) is the first-person narrator of the work. Readers of the García Márquez novel are likely to see Velasco as the true hero, whose survival against all odds demonstrates an unusually high degree of courage, determination, and physical strength often associated with the prototypical hero of the testimonial novel. In this respect Hemingway's Santiago bears comparison with Velasco, especially in view of García Márquez's well-known admiration for Hemingway at the time he interviewed the Colombian seaman.

Sailor makes use of a classic genre, the narrative of shipwreck, in which the castaway experiences a broad range of feelings: hunger, solitude, thirst, and survival anxiety. It continues this traditional shipwreck genre as cultivated by Melville, Stevenson, Núñez Cabeza de Vaca, Garcilaso de la Vega el Inca, and Cervantes. While Hemingway's *Old Man* is not technically a shipwreck tale, without a doubt it does provide García Márquez with short, exemplary sentences as a model for his prose, a gripping story line, images and similes in accord with the barren waters that encircle both protagonists, and an exploration of the twilight zone between reality and fantasy.

VERA M. KUTZINSKI

The Logic of Wings:
Gabriel García Márquez and
Afro-American Literature

Night is an African juju man
weaving a wish and a weariness together
to make two wings.

> (Robert Hayden, 'O Daedalus,
> Fly Away Home')

One of the main differences between the work of those writers who comprise the so-called literary 'mainstream' in the United States and that of major Latin American authors from the Caribbean is the way in which the latter group accepts Afro-American culture as a vital part of its cultural identity.[1] Nicolás Guillén once wrote that the African element brings the definitive mark to the cultural profile of (Latin) America,[2] and we only have to look at the writings of Alejo Carpentier, Guillermo Cabrera Infante, Miguel Barnet, Antonio Benítez Rojo, Lydia Cabrera (who may well deserve to be called Cuba's Zora Neale Hurston), and even Adalberto Ortiz to recognize the validity of such a claim. The following citation from Lydia Cabrera's introduction to her famous *El monte* further corroborates this. 'There is no doubt,' she writes, 'that "Cuba is the whitest island of the Caribbean." But the impact of the African influence on that population, which regards itself as white, is nonetheless immeasurable, although a superficial glance may not discern this. You will not be able to understand

From *García Márquez*, Robin Fiddian, ed. © 1995 by Longman Group Limited.

our people without knowing the blacks. That influence is even more evident today than it was in colonial times. We cannot penetrate much of Cuban life without considering that African presence, which does not manifest itself in skin color alone.'[3] The validity of Cabrera's comments extends far beyond Cuba, and I intend to substantiate that proposition by examining the uses of Afro-American myth and history in the writings of Gabriel García Márquez. One may well ask what the work of García Márquez has to do with Afro-American culture and literature, and justly so, since there appears to be very little evidence in his novels and stories of such a connection. Unlike Carpentier, for instance, García Márquez never wrote *about* blacks. He belongs to a generation of Latin American writers who arrived on the scene well after the heyday of the Afro-Antillean movement in the twenties and thirties, but for whom questions about Latin America's cultural identity and about an authentic Latin American literature nevertheless remain issues of no less importance now than fifty or sixty years ago. Afro-American culture continues to occupy a fairly prominent position when it comes to those questions, and this is nowhere more evident than in the Caribbean, of which García Márquez is undoubtedly a part.

Although his work is strongly indebted to the modern offsprings of the *novela de la tierra*, as is revealed by the similarities between Rómulo Gallegos's *Doña Barbara* (1929) and 'Big Mama's Funeral' (1962),[4] there is also another, more distinctly Caribbean, aspect to García Márquez's writings. This already becomes apparent when we consider 'Big Mama's Funeral' in connection with Cabrera Infante's *Three Trapped Tigers* (1967) and his 'Meta-final', which although initially conceived as the end of *Three Trapped Tigers*, was published separately in 1970.[5] What is important here is not only the remarkable resemblance between the voluminous black singer Estrella, 'the Queen, the Absolute Monarch of Cuban music', and Big Mama, 'absolute sovereign of the Kingdom of Macondo',[6] but the way in which this resemblance renders accessible the source from which both of these female figures spring: the legendary black Dominican Má Teodora Ginés. The famous 'Son de la Má Teodora' is, as Roberto González Echevarría has pointed out in his excellent discussion of the subject, 'a synthesis of the Spanish, African and *taíno* (Arawak) cultures that composed the Caribbean'.[7] As such, the 'Son' is perhaps the earliest cultural ritual (it dates back to the second half of the sixteenth century) which celebrates the breakdown of ethnocentrism in the Caribbean by establishing a kind of contrapuntal coherence that later writers, notably Carpentier in his *Explosion in a Cathedral* (1962), will attempt to develop into a fully fledged theology.[8]

Gabriel García Márquez very consciously places himself within the historico-cultural framework represented by the 'Son de la Má Teodora'. His following remarks, taken from a recent interview, leave no doubt about this.

My grandparents were descendants of Spanish immigrants, and many of the supernatural things they told me about came from Galicia. But I believe that this taste for the supernatural, which is typical of the Galicians, is also an African inheritance. The coast of the Caribbean, where I was born, is, like Brazil, the region of Latin America where one most feels the African influence. In this sense, the trip I made to Angola in 1978 was one of the most fascinating experiences I have ever had. I believe that it divided my life into two halves. I expected to encounter a strange world, completely foreign, and from the moment I set my feet down there, from the moment I smelled the air, I found myself immediately in the world of my childhood. Yes, I found myself face to face with my entire childhood, customs and things which I had forgotten. This also included the nightmares I used to have as a child.

In Latin America we have been trained to believe that we are Spaniards. This is true in part, because the Spanish element forms part of our peculiar cultural make-up and cannot be denied. But I discovered during that trip to Angola that we are also Africans. Or better, that we are *mestizos*. That our culture is *mestizo*, that it is enriched by diverse contributions. Never before had I been conscious of this.... In the Caribbean, to which I belong, the boundless imagination of the black African slaves mixed with that of the native pre-Columbians and then with the fantasy of the Andalucians and the supernatural cult of the Galicians. This ability to view reality in a certain magic way is characteristic of the Caribbean and also of Brazil. From there has evolved a literature, a music and a kind of painting like that of Wifredo Lam, all of which are aesthetic expressions of this part of the world.... I believe that the Caribbean has taught me to see reality in a different way, to accept supernatural elements as something that is part of our daily life. The Caribbean is a distinctive world whose first magic piece of literature is *The Diary of Christopher Columbus*, a book which speaks of fabulous plants and mythical worlds. Yes, the history of the Caribbean is full of magic....[9]

What García Márquez is proposing here as the founding principle of his writings is a kind of magic realism that is strongly suggestive of the Carpenterian concept of a 'marvelous American reality' in that it presupposes a certain faith, an acceptance of the supernatural as part of ones daily life. There are faint allusions to this in an earlier interview, but they are by far not as revealing, or even as serious, as the above pronouncements.[10] What is indeed most striking about the above passage is that García Márquez describes his experiences in Angola in terms which suggest a kind of homecoming, a return to the forgotten, but yet very familiar, world of his childhood in the Caribbean. His image of Africa is that of a native land, and the symbolic value of such a statement should not be underestimated. Shall we then dismiss this as a case of fanciful nostalgia simply because it comes from a writer with no black ancestry in the strict genealogical sense?

I have said earlier that there appears to be little evidence in the work of García Márquez of a connection with and possible indebtedness to Afro-American culture. It is true that such a link is difficult, if not impossible, to discern as long as we keep searching for the kinds of explicit references and allusions we encounter for instance in Carpentier's *The Kingdom of This World*, Barnet's *Autobiography of a Runaway Slave*, César Leante's *Capitán de Cimarrones*, or Adalberto Ortiz's *Juyungo*. With very few minor exceptions, there are no black characters in García Márquez's texts, but that fact alone, as I have already suggested in my brief remarks about 'Big Mama's Funeral', is misleading given the sources from which figures such as Big Mama spring. What I would now like to examine in some detail are two stories, which more than likely were among those childhood memories rekindled by García Márquez's visit to the African continent: his own 'A Very Old Man with Enormous Wings' (1968), which, in the translation, is subtitled 'A Tale for Children', and Juan Rodriguez Freyle's story of Juana García, which appears in *El carnero* (1636) and has been widely anthologized under the titles of 'Las brujerías de Juana García' or 'Un negocio con Juana García.'"[11]

There appears to be no immediate connection between those two texts outside of the obvious fact that both their authors are Colombian. On closer look, however, we find that both stories share not only the same geocultural space (that of the Caribbean coast of Colombia), but also, even more importantly, cluster around the same fundamental trope: that of flying. Interestingly enough, this key metaphor is almost completely obscured in the English translation of the story of Juana García, who is introduced as a freed Negress who 'was something of a witch', whereas the original reads, 'Esta negra era un poco *voladora*' (my italics, p. 137), which literally means, she 'could fly a little bit'. On the one hand, Juana García is, as Enrique Pupo-Walker has pointed out, undeniably a variation on Fernando de Rojas's

Celestina.[12] But on the other hand, the association of sorcery with flying, brought about by the use of 'voladorá' and 'volatería' (p. 140) instead of 'bruja' and 'brujería', which are the more common terms for witch and witchcraft, adds to Rodriguez Freyle's character a dimension which is even more distinctly Afro-American than the fact that Juana García is black. To be sure, Pupo-Walker's point that the story of Juana García is 'a precursor text of the Afro-Hispanic narrative'[13] is well-taken, but for even more profound reasons than he himself may suspect.

The metaphoric link between flying and sorcery (or magic) is of vital importance to the entire Afro-American literary canon. There are numerous tales about and allusions to flight in Afro-American folklore, all of which are, in one way or another, versions of what is commonly known as the myth of the flying Africans. 'Once all Africans could fly like birds; but owing to their many transgressions, their wings were taken away. There remained, here and there, in the sea-lands and out-of-the-way places in the low country, some who had been overlooked, and had retained the power of flight, though they looked like other men.'[14] In this sense, those who have retained the gift of flight are the guardians of Afro-America's cultural tradition. These keepers of traditional values and beliefs are the sorcerers and conjure-(wo)men, almost archetypal figures of notable prominence in Afro-American literature.[15] One of those figures is that of the old man, who appears in the following version of the folktale 'All God's Chillun Had Wings'.

> The overseer and the driver ran at the old man with lashes ready; and the master ran too, with a picket pulled from the fence, to beat the life out of the old man who had made those Negroes fly. But the old man laughed in their faces, and said something loudly to all the Negroes in the field, the new Negroes and the old Negroes. And as he spoke to them they all remembered what they had forgotten, and recalled the power which had once been theirs. Then all Negroes, old and new, stood up together; the old man raised his hands; and they all leaped up into the air with a great shout; and in a moment were gone, flying, like a flock of crows, over the field, over the fence, and over the top of the wood; and behind them flew the old man. The men went clapping their hands, and the women went singing; and those who had children gave them their breasts; and the children laughed and sucked as their mothers flew, and were not afraid.[16]

The function of the old man in this traditional Afro-American tale corroborates Lydia Cabrera's observation that the practices and rites of the

black sorcerers are directed toward the well-being of their community.[17]
That this community, specifically in the Caribbean, also includes a large
number of white members, who are not necessarily converts to *santería*,
voodoo, or any of the other Afro-American religions in that region, but
nonetheless avail themselves of the special knowledge and services of the
'brujos' or 'brujas', is quite evident from the story of Juana García. We are
told that the Negress's confession to the Archbishop, who is also the Chief
Inquisitor, 'implicated various other women ... and rumor had it that many
had been caught in the net, among them ladies of importance' (p. 142).
Enrique Pupo-Walker has aptly pointed out that this tale 'confirms—on the
most intimate planes of the cultural process—the presence of blacks as a
basic factor of the new social context'.[18] Similarly, the kind of socio-cultural
interpenetration or synchretism here is substantiated by the fact that Juana
García, also admitting as part of her confession that she had 'flown' to
Bermuda at the time of the sinking of the *Capitana* and the subsequent
drowning of the two *oidores* which is mentioned at the beginning of the story,
'had taken wing [echo a volar] from the hill behind the Church of Nuestra
Señora de las Nieves, where one of the crosses stood' (p. 143). The hill, ever
since known as 'the hill of Juana García', is a symbolic space that
accommodates both the official religious emblem and popular magic. But it
is not without a certain irony that Juana García should choose, as point of
departure for her flight, that is, for the practice of powers which literally
surpass those of the officially recognized religion, the very same place where
the Catholic Church had erected the symbol of its imperial authority. The
Negress's powers defy, if not outrightly mock, such institutional authority, in
much the same way as her punishment for such open defiance recreates an
image which perpetuates and significantly solidifies that mockery: '[The
Archbishop] imposed on her as a penance that she be placed on a raised
platform in Santo Domingo at the hour of high mass, with a halter around
the neck and a burning candle in her hand' (p. 143). Even Juana García's
lament that she alone was made to pay while all the others had been absolved
to save the face of the vice royalty, cannot distract from what is also suggested
by her standing on that platform with a halter around her neck (doubtlessly
to keep her from flying away!) and a lighted candle in her hand. What is
intended as punishment ultimately yields an image that surreptitiously
asserts the very powers whose existence it is supposed to crush: not only does
the halter around Juana García's neck indirectly verify her power of flight by
attempting to restrain it. In addition, the burning candle in her hand recalls
a phenomenon associated, according to Lydia Cabrera, especially with the
black sorcerers from Haiti and Jamaica, whose victims are said to carry a
lighted candle in their hands as a warning to other mortals.[19] This is quite

appropriate given that the sorceress had been carried off to Santo Domingo, where the punishment is administered.

It is not entirely coincidental that this particular scene should evoke a famous historical incident which also occurred in Santo Domingo about a hundred years later: the burning of Macandal in 1758, which is one of the key events in Carpentier's *The Kingdom of This World*. The analogy between these two punishment scenes as described by Rodriguez Freyle and Carpentier respectively is obvious enough and need not be discussed in any great detail. What is most relevant to our topic is the striking recurrence in the scene of Macandal's execution of the flight metaphor: 'The bonds fell off and the body of the Negro rose in the air, flying overhead, until it plunged into the black wave of the sea of slaves.'[20] Although Macandal's body was indeed consumed by the fire, the black slaves were undeterred in their belief that he had saved himself through his 'volatería': 'That afternoon the slaves returned to their plantations laughing all the way. Macandal had kept his word, remaining in the Kingdom of This World. Once more the whites had been outwitted by the Mighty Powers of the Other Shores.'[21] Macandal's flight, like Juana García's, constitutes an undisguised mockery of institutionalized authority and its feeble attempts to impose shackles on something that has no *body* to bind. In the story of Juana García, this corrosive mockery is subtly reinforced by the fact that the notice she admits to having posted on the walls of the *cabildo* in Bogotá imitates an official document: it is complete with the exact date, only lacking the 'proper' signature.[22] It may be argued that one of the functions of the story of Juana García within that particular chapter of *El carnero* is to explain the origin of that mysterious notice, which, although seemingly peripheral, serves as a kind of supplement to the actual plot, the 'deal' with the pregnant woman.

Supplements also play an important role in García Márquez's tale about 'A Very Old Man with Enormous Wings', which is, as we shall see, part of the literary canon generated by the trope of flying. This story differs from Rodriguez Freyle's and Carpentier's versions in that its curious protagonist, if he can be called that at all, is not black. In fact, there is a great deal of confusion about who or what this strange winged creature actually is:

> The light was so weak at noon that when Pelayo was coming back to the house after throwing away the crabs, it was hard for him to see what it was that was moving and groaning in the rear of the courtyard. He had to get very close to see that it was an old man, a very old man, lying face down in the mud, who, in spite of his tremendous efforts, couldn't get up, impeded by his enormous wings. (p. 105)

While the huge buzzard wings of this 'drenched great-grandfather' now 'forever entangled in the mud', substantially impede his own physical movements, they seem to have exactly the opposite effect on the inhabitants of this unidentified town, which is another version of Macondo—but with a difference. Macondo, as we know from *One Hundred Years of Solitude*, is located in the interior of Colombia, whereas the town we encounter in this story is clearly situated on the Caribbean coast. This is not only evident from the very beginning of the text, where we hear about Pelayo throwing the dead crabs into the sea; García Márquez is careful throughout the story to remind his readers of that specific location. Unfortunately, these more or less subtle reminders—references to Martinique, the Caribbean, and Jamaica— have been, for some reason, either changed or completely removed from the text of the translation.[23] Furthermore, it should not be overlooked that the old man speaks 'an incomprehensible dialect with a strong *sailor's* voice' (my italics, p. 106). At first glance, all these details may appear relatively insignificant to the actual narrative. On closer look, however, they indicate the importance García Márquez attributes to the Caribbean as a cultural context within which to cast the winged old man.

The 'inconvenience' of the wings gives rise to all kinds of speculation about the stranger's identity: some regard him as the victim of a shipwreck; others claim that he is an angel knocked down by the three-day rain; and Father Gonzaga almost predictably suspects that he is one of the devil's carnival tricks.

> The parish priest had his first suspicion of an impostor when he saw that he [the old man] did not understand the language of God or know how to greet his ministers. Then he noticed that seen close up he was much too human: he had an unbearable smell of the outdoors, the backside of his wings was strewn with parasites, and his main feathers had been mistreated by terrestrial winds, and nothing about him measured up to the proud dignity of angels. Then he came out of the chicken coop and in a brief sermon warned the curious against the risks of being ingenuous [sic: simple-minded].... He argued that if wings were not the essential element in determining the difference between a hawk and an airplane, they were even less so in the recognition of angels. (p. 107)

Yet these wings, parasite-infested as they may be, are of crucial importance, not so much for determining the actual identity of the fallen freak, but for comprehending how and why García Márquez employs the trope of flying as a foundation for his own particular version of a more or less 'marvelous' American reality.

Described and examined in quite some detail in this story, the wings are the visible metaphoric extensions of the Afro-American myth of flying. They almost literally grow out of that myth, which itself is an appendage, a *supplement* in the Derridean sense, to the body of Hispanic culture in the Caribbean. It is quite telling in this regard that the doctor, who could not resist the temptation of examining the 'angel', should be struck by 'the logic of his wings'—'They seemed so natural in that completely human organism that he couldn't understand why other men didn't have them too' (p. 111). The logic of the wings, as it were, is the logic of the supplement, which is at once complementary and additional; it is both a part of as well as apart from the cultural and textual context in which it appears. This ambiguity is precisely what characterizes the position of the bird/man within that community into which he has been accidentally thrown. He is a stranger, yet he is familiar; he appears to be human, yet he is more than that; he is, in short, a being which cannot easily be contained within non-contradictory definitions. In this sense, the old man's ambiguous anatomy is already sufficient to place him, much like Juana García and also Macandal, in direct opposition to the kind of authority to which Father Gonzaga appeals for 'a final judgment on the nature of the captive' (p. 109). The priest 'promised to write a letter to his bishop so that the latter would write to his primate so that the latter would write to the Supreme Pontiff in order to get the final verdict from the highest courts' (p. 107). Clearly, Rodriguez Freyle's Juana García, Carpentier's Macandal, and García Márquez's old man with enormous wings are all mythical figures which exist outside and in defiance of the authority of the law, which in all three cases attempts, rather unsuccessfully, to confine them within the limits of a fixed definition or identity, to make them adhere to the conceptual categories officially employed to define reality and truth.

It is important to note that intimate connection between the law, which assures permanence and identity, and the kind of writing which may be called 'legal' in the sense that it does not tolerate contradictions and ambiguities.[24] This writing is used as a means of social control in that it seeks to impose indelible marks of the official authority vested in it by the bureaucratic apparatus of either Church or State. In García Márquez's story, this link is most evident in a passage which emphasizes the inherently violent nature of such inscriptions of authority. The particular act of violence we witness significantly assumes another, very specific, cultural dimension once we consider that it was a common practice among slaveholders in all parts of the New World to brand their slaves as punishment for certain offenses. This form of punishment was most frequently administered to recaptured runaways, so that they could easily be identified by their mark of possession.

> The only time they [the curious gathered in front of the chicken coop] succeeded in arousing him [the old man] was when they burned his side with an iron for branding steers, for he had been motionless for so many hours that they thought he was dead. He awoke with a start, ranting in his hermetic language and with tears in his eyes, and he flapped his wings a couple of times, which brought on a whirlwind of chicken dung and lunar dust and a gale of panic that did not seem to be of this world. Although many thought that his reaction had been one not of rage but of pain, from then on they were careful not to annoy him, because the majority understood that his passivity was not that of a hero taking his ease but that of a cataclysm in repose. (p. 109)

Again, this scene is somewhat reminiscent of Macandal's execution in *The Kingdom of This World*, which I have mentioned earlier in connection with the end of the story of Juana García. There is a remarkable figurative analogy here between Macandal's moving the stump of his arm in a 'threatening gesture which was none the less terrible for being partial'[25] at the very moment that the flames were beginning to lick his legs and the old man's flapping his wings when touched by the hot branding iron. Both gestures cause a panic among the crowd of spectators, who are instantly reminded of the destructive powers latent in the kind of magic ascribed in similar ways to these two characters as well as to Juana García. This invites us to consider in more detail an important quality shared by these three figures: they are all believed to be sorcerers and as such invested with special curative powers. It is not an exaggeration, then, to describe each as what Derrida has called a *pharmakos* (healer, wizard, magician, sorcerer).[26] The term is particularly appropriate because of its ambiguity, which results from the continuous vacillation of its meanings between all kinds of positive and negative connotations.

The characteristic ambiguity of the *pharmakos* is perhaps most apparent in the case of Macandal, whose acquired knowledge of plants and herbs enables him to orchestrate a large-scale poisoning of the white slaveholders and their families, thus 'curing' the blacks from the pains of their bondage. In contrast, Juana García's poison is much more subtle. By offering the promiscuous young wife of a Spanish merchant concrete evidence of his husband's own infidelity in the form of a sleeve from his mistress's dress, she enables the woman to conceal, and even legitimize by way of blackmail, the accidental result of her adultery (the child who is born and disowned during her husband's long absence). Juana García's services implicitly sanction such marital transgressions and thus pose a threat to the moral order as well as to the public image of the colony. Her magic poisons not the bodies, but the minds of the residents of Bogotá. The ambiguous powers of García Márquez's mysterious old man are suggested in a variety of ways. Both the fact that the sick infant of Pelayo and Elisenda recovers almost immediately after the 'angel's' appearance in their courtyard as well as the arrival of pilgrims from all over the Caribbean in hope of miraculous relief from their illnesses and deformities indicate that he might possess the positive qualities of a healer.

> The most unfortunate invalids on earth [sic: of the Caribbean] came in search of health: a poor woman who since childhood had been counting her heartbeats and had run out of numbers; a Portuguese man [sic: a Jamaican] who couldn't sleep because the noise of the stars disturbed him; a sleepwalker who got up at night to undo the things he had done while awake; and many others with less serious ailments. (p. 108)

But all the winged sage offers those invalids, whose unusual, if not absurd, afflictions cannot but strike us as somewhat Borgesian,[27] are 'consolation miracles, which were more like mocking fun' than serious remedies: 'the few miracles attributed to the angel showed a certain *mental disorder*, like the blind man who didn't recover his sight but grew three new teeth; or the paralytic who didn't get to walk but almost won the lottery, and the leper whose sores sprouted sunflowers' (my italics, p. 110).

Those extraordinary 'consolation miracles' are, of course, further manifestations of the same kind of supplementarity which, as we have seen, determines the logic of the old man's wings. This logic in its characteristic ambiguity is akin to the inherently contradictory nature of the *pharmakos*; in fact, the wings are a synecdochial representation of the *pharmakon*, which is the magic power of transformation earlier described as 'volatería'. What we are dealing with, in short, is not a condition of mental disorder, but a method capable of both enriching and at the same time endangering the stability of the accepted, official version of an historical reality and an historical process which, in each of the three texts, is represented by a figure of public authority: the Governor of Santo Domingo in *The Kingdom of This World*; the Chief Inquisitor in *El carnero*; and Father Gonzaga in 'A Very Old Man with Enormous Wings'. This conceptual method, which avails itself of the paradoxical logic of the supplement or *pharmakon* in order to disrupt and destabilize conventional Western ideas of order as well as the formulaic language in which these ideas are cast, significantly links Macandal's poison, Juana García's sleeve, the wings of the old man and his consolation miracles.

Although it might be argued that the Platonic/Derridean concepts of the *pharmakos* and the *pharmakon* as applied to these texts lift them out of their specific cultural and literary context by reducing their figurative properties to universals, it ought to be noted that the inseparable bond between *pharmakos/pharmakon* and flight already preempts such a reading. The *pharmakos* as 'volatería' is endowed with irreducible culture-specific meanings, and as such verifies the continued existence of distinct Afro-Americanisms in twentieth-century Latin American literature. These Afro-Americanisms are pronounced enough to generate a separate canon, but at the same time it has to be emphasized that this canon, unlike its North American counterpart, does not simply consist of texts produced by a clearly defined 'minority'. Rather, it is composed of texts which add Afro-American myth and history to Latin America's repertoire of founding fables. Afro-America thus becomes an integral part of the literature of the Hispanic Caribbean, but it is integrated into this larger cultural and literary context without losing its distinctiveness or authenticity. Viewed from this perspective, it is not all that surprising that even a writer like García Márquez should, among other things, lay claim to the same cultural heritage as a black writer from the United States, and it is certainly no coincidence that the relationship between those groups which comprise the cultural/literary establishment in the United States and particularly the Hispanic Caribbean is quite similar to that between so-called white America and its black community. This has been historically true approximately since the turn of the century.

Such generalizations of course require at least some evidence. Without leaving the immediate realm of our discussion, which has been predominantly but not exclusively literary so far, I would thus like to call attention to a poem by the late Robert Hayden entitled 'For A Young Artist', which, as indicated by the author himself, is a tribute to García Márquez's 'A Very Old Man with Enormous Wings'.[28] That an Afro-American poet like Hayden should single out this particular short story as the basis for one of his best-known poems at a time when literary critics and historians were for the most part very much preoccupied with cutting the American literary canon into thin ethnic slices, is a statement of some importance which, if nothing else, indicates the existence of a substantial lag between American literature and its criticism. Without overstating the importance of Hayden's symbolic gesture, it is safe to say that the relationship between his poem and García Márquez's story is, in many ways, representative of a larger pattern of cross-cultural interpenetration in modern American literature. Hayden is by no means an exception in this regard, and it is worth noting that the work of other contemporary black writers from the United States—among them the poets Jay Wright and Michael Harper as well as the novelist Gayl Jones—reflects a similar interest in Latin America.

But let us look more closely at the textual relationship between 'For a Young Artist' and 'A Very Old Man with Enormous Wings'. Obviously, what attracted Hayden most to this story was García Márquez's peculiar practice of the traditional Afro-American flight metaphor. For Hayden, as for García Márquez, the gift of flying is intimately associated with the poetic power to unsettle and transform language by making it referentially and representationally ambiguous, by freeing it from the constraints of singular, fixed meanings. Like the old man in both the poem and the story, this language '*twists* away/from the cattle-prod' (my italics, p. 8), and, in doing so, assumes a semantic multiplicity or plurivalence that is as elusive as the 'angel', who, after finally dragging himself out of the chicken coop, 'seemed to be in so many places at the same time that they grew to think that he'd been duplicated, that he was reproducing himself all through the house' (p. 111). This elusiveness, which is significantly figured as a process of multiplication, of endless supplementation, already anticipates the ultimate achievement of flight at the end of both texts.

> He strains, an awk-
> ward patsy, sweating strains
> leaping falling. Then—
>
> silken rustling in the air
> the angle of ascent
> achieved.
>
> (p. 10)

The preparatory intensity of movement created by the verbal cluster 'sweating strains/leaping falling' builds up toward a similar kind of elusiveness, which is prefigured by the hyphen ('Then—') and culminates in the complete disappearance of the persona in the poem's final stanza. It is interesting that in neither one of the two texts do we actually witness the moment of flying. We only hear the 'silken rustling' of the wings and Elisenda's 'sigh of relief, for herself and for him, when she saw him [the old man] pass over the last houses' (p. 112). The moment of flight is clearly a moment of depersonalization: The winged old man ceases to be a presence, in Elisenda's life as well as in the texts themselves, and becomes an 'imaginary dot on the horizon of the sea'. What remains in the text, *as* text, is the 'angle of ascent' which, as a metaphor for the textual representation of flight, significantly replaces what we may call the 'ascent of the angel'. Hayden's seemingly playful pun, the turning of 'angel' into 'angle', is the key event in the poem. It signals the transformation of character into trope, and thus comments on García Márquez's text—and by extension on the execution of Macandal and the story of Juana García—in a most profound way. The trope is what supplements mere representation by adding to it an allegorical dimension, so that representation can become a vehicle for allegory. This, in and by itself, is nothing new or unusual. But Hayden's realization that certain texts in Latin American literature are vehicles for specific Afro-American myths and allegories is an insight that opens many new possibilities for studying processes of canon-formation in American literature(s).

NOTES

1. One notable exception to this fairly general rule is, of course, the work of William Faulkner, whose novels, as is known, had a tremendous impact on the modern Latin American narrative.

2. See NICOLÁS GUILLÉN'S Prologue to *Sóngoro consongo* (1931) and his poem 'Llegada' [Arrival] in *Obra Poética 1920–1972* (La Habana: Instituto Cubano del Libro, 1974), Vol. I, pp. 114–116.

3. LYDIA CABRERA, *El monte. Igbo finda ewe orisha, vititi nfinda. Notas sobre las religiones, la magia, las supersticiones y el folklore de los negros criollos y del pueblo de Cuba* (La Habana: Ediciones C.R., 1954), p. 9. My translation.

4. This is discussed in ROBERTO GONZÁLEZ ECHEVARRÍA's 'The Concept of Culture and the Idea of Literature in modern Latin America: *Doña Bárbara* Writes the Plain' in his *The Voice of the Masters: Writing and Authority in Modern Latin American Literature* (Austin: The University of Texas Press, 1985).

5. An annotated translation of 'Meta-final' [Meta-End] by ROBERTO GONZÁLEZ ECHEVARRÍA appears in the *Latin American Literary Review* Special Issue on Hispanic Caribbean literature, VIII, 16 (Spring–Summer, 1980) 88–95.

6. 'Meta-End', p. 89; 'Big Mama's Funeral', in *No One Writes to the Colonel and Other Stories*, trans J.S. Bernstein (1968; New York: Harper and Row, 1979), p. 153.

7. 'Literature of the Hispanic Caribbean', *Latin American Literary Review*, VIII, 16 (Spring–Summer, 1980): 7.

8. See GONZÁLEZ ECHEVARRÍA, *Alejo Carpentier: The Pilgrim at Home* (Ithaca: Cornell University Press, 1977), esp. Chapters 2 and 5.

9. *El olor de la guayaba: Conversaciones con Plinio Apuleyo Mendoza* (Bogotá: Editorial de la Oveja Negra, 1982), pp. 54–55. My translation.

10. See ARMANDO DURÁN, 'Conversaciones con Gabriel García Márquez', *Revista Nacional de Cultura*, 39 (1968): 31; also *The Pilgrim*, p. 112.

11. In the following those two texts will be referred to by page number only. The editions I am using are: (1) *Leaf Storm and Other Stories*, trans. by Gregory Rabassa (1972; New York: Harper and Row, 1979); for the corrections I made in this translation the reader should consult *La increíble y triste historia de la cándida Eréndira y de su abuela desalmada*

(Barcelona-Caracas: Monte Avila, 1972), pp. 11–20; (2) *El carnero*. Con notas explicativas de Miguel Aguilera (Bogotá: Editorial Bedout, 1976). The translations from *El carnero* are mine.

12. ENRIQUE PUPO-WALKER, '*El carnero* y una forma seminal del relato afro-hispanico', *Homenaje a Lydia Cabrera*, ed. Reinaldo Sánchez and José A. Madrigal (Barcelona: Ediciones Universal, 1977), p. 255. For a more detailed discussion see also his *La vocación literaria del pensamiento histórico en América: Desarrollo de la prosa de ficción: Siglos XVI, XVII, XVIII y XIX* (Madrid: Gredos, 1982), pp. 123–55.

13. '*El carnero* y una forma seminal del relato afro-hispánico', p. 256.

14. 'All God's Chillun Had Wings', in Langston Hughes and Arna Bontemps (eds), *The Book of Negro Folklore* (New York: Dodd, Mead and Co., 1958), p. 62. See also: 'Flying People', in J. Mason Brewer (ed.), *American Negro Folklore* (Chicago: Quadrangle Books, 1968), pp. 308–9; 'How Spider Read the Sky God's Thoughts' (Ashanti), in *African Myths and Tales*, ed. with an introduction by Susan Feldman (New York: Bell Publishing Co., 1975); PUPO-WALKER, *La vocación*, p. 141; and LYDIA CABRERA, *El monte*, pp. 23–4.

15. One of the best-known examples of this is *The Conjure Woman* stories by CHARLES W. CHESNUTT (1899; Ann Arbor: The University of Michigan Press, 1969).

16. *The Book of Negro Folklore*, p. 64.

17. *El monte*, p. 16.

18. PUPO-WALKER, *La vocación*, p. 115.

19. *El monte*, p. 24.

20. *The Kingdom of This World*, trans. by Harriet de Onis (1957; New York: Collier Books, 1970), pp. 51–2.

21. *The Kingdom*, p. 52.

22. See *El carnero*, p. 129.

23. Compare the second paragraph on p. 108 of the translation to the last paragraph on p. 14 of the original.

24. See JACQUES DERRIDA, *Dissemination*, trans. with an introduction and additional notes by Barbara Johnson (1972; Chicago: The University of Chicago Press, 1981), p. 113.

25. *The Kingdom*, p. 51.

26. *Dissemination*, p. 130.

27. See, for instance, 'Funes, the Memorious'.

28. 'For a Young Artist' appears in *Angle of Ascent: New and Selected Poems by Robert Hayden* (New York: Liveright, 1975). All further textual references are to this edition.

STEPHEN M. HART

Magical Realism in the Americas:
Politicised Ghosts in One Hundred Years of Solitude, The House of the Spirits, and Beloved

A quota system is to be introduced on fiction set in South America. The intention is to curb the spread of package-tour baroque and heavy irony. Ah, the propinquity of cheap life and expensive principles, of religion and banditry, or surprising honour and random cruelty. Ah, the daiquiri bird which incubates its eggs on the wing: ah, the fredonna tree whose roots grow at the tips of its branches, and whose fibres assist the hunchback to impregnate by telepathy the haughty wife of the hacienda owner; ah, the opera house now overgrown by jungle. (Barnes 1984: 104)

Julian Barnes's witty reduction of magic realism to a formula—in effect it is an ironic pastiche—shows how far we have come since the heady days of the 1940s and '50s when magic realism was spluttering into being in Latin America. And yet, since magic realism is nowadays something of a genre in its own right, this has led to some problems with definition, precisely because of the way it has crossed national, linguistic, and genre boundaries. Quite apart from its Spanish-American variety there have been studies of magical realism in West African Fiction (Cooper 1998), in German-speaking countries, in Italian, Flemish, Spanish, French, Polish, and Hungarian literatures (Weisgerber 1987a). There have been studies of magic realism in the visual arts, in painting and cinema (Jameson 1986, Delvaux 1987, Gerard

From *Journal of Iberian and Latin American Studies* Vol. 9, No. 2 (December 2003). © 2003 by Taylor & Francis, Ltd.

1987, Hadermann 1987). Indeed, quite a strong case can be made for seeing magic realism's favoured genre as the visual arts; it had its indisputable roots in the German art movement, Neue Sachlichkeit in the 1920s (Weisgerber 1987b).

There is an enormous bibliography on the subject of magical realism and, rather than review even part of it, I shall propose a working definition (the secret of magical realism lies in its ability to depict reality objectively but with a magical dimension) and test the following hypothesis: the phantom in magical realist fiction is the projection within an ideologically riven nation of a subaltern forced to "disappear" as a result of lying (in both senses of the term) on the wrong side of the political, gender, or race line. I want to apply this hypothesis to three novels, Gabriel García Márquez's *One Hundred Years of Solitude* (1978/1967), Isabel Allende's *The House of the Spirits* (1988/1982), and Toni Morrison's *Beloved* (1997/1987).

One Hundred Years of Solitude is now universally seen as a classic, "the Latin American Don Quixote" as the *New Yorker* hailed it (see front cover of the Picador translation by Gregory Rabassa). The novel focuses on the five generations of the Buendía family who live in the mythical town of Macondo over a period of 100 years, beginning with the patriarchal figure José Arcadio Buendía and ending with the child Aureliano who, since he is the product of incest, is born with a pig's tail, a fact which seals the fate of the Buendías. A leitmotif of the novel is the sense in which occurrences seen as supernatural in the First World (such as ghostly apparitions, human beings with the ability to fly, levitate, disappear or increase their weight at will) are presented as natural from a Third World perspective, while occurrences seen as normal in the First World (magnets, science, ice, railway trains, the movies, phonographs) are presented as supernatural from the point of view of an inhabitant of the Caribbean.

García Márquez has said that he learned the tricks of his trade from his grandmother: "The tone that I eventually used in *One Hundred Years of Solitude* was based on the way my grandmother used to tell stories. She told things that sounded supernatural and fantastic, but she told them with complete naturalness" (see http://www.themodernword.com/gabo/gabo-mr.html). One of the best examples of this technique occurs in the famous scene when Remedios the Beauty is carried up to heaven while hanging out the sheets to dry. The magic nature of the event is muted by the various realistic details which surround its portrayal. First of all García Márquez introduces the detail of a sheet billowing in the wind as a preamble to Remedios's levitation. The realist detail about the wind allows us to visualise this extraordinary event. Furthermore, Márquez introduces a number of other touches—Amaranta's lace petticoats, Remedios's waving goodbye to her sisters on the ground, the insects and flowers in the garden, and the time it occurred (4 o'clock)—which imbue the scene with an empirical air. Finally, there is the crowning detail—her sister's reaction: "Fernanda, burning with envy, finally accepted the miracle, and for a long time she kept on praying to God to send her back her sheets" (García Márquez 1978: 195). Both details—her jealousy, and the desire to get her sheets back—provide empirical legitimacy to a miraculous event.

But García Márquez has not only referred to his grandmother as a source. In fact, she could be more readily described as the vehicle, since the real source is those beliefs buried in popular culture, what Florencia Mallon calls the "buried treasures of popular imaginings" (1995: 329). García Márquez has said that the Caribbean gave him the ability to see the magical side of life: "In the Caribbean, to which I belong, the unbridled imagination of the black African slaves got mixed up with the beliefs of the pre-Colombian natives and then with the fantasy of the Andalusian" (quoted in Hart 1994: 12). A cursory reading of the autobiography of a runaway slave, *Biografía de un cimarrón* (1966) by Esteban Montejo, and edited by Miguel Barnet, would tend to confirm García Márquez's view. Esteban Montejo was interviewed in 1963 at the age of 103, and had lived as a runaway slave in the second half of the nineteenth century in Cuba. Esteban Montejo regales his reader with tales of headless horsemen, witchcraft, zombies, mischievous ghosts, unexplained lights over cemeteries, witches who can take their skin off at will, leaving them hanging up behind the door, and wizards who can fly back in a few minutes from Cuba to the Canary Islands, and yet his account does not present any of these events as if they are anything unusual. Here is a brief example:

> The witches were another one of those weird things. In Ariosa I saw them catch one. They caught her with sesame seeds (*ajonjolí*) and mustard, and she was trapped to the spot. As long as there's a little grain of sesame on the floor, they can't move.

> So they could fly off the witches used to leave their skins behind. They would hang them up behind the door and then they would fly off, just wearing their bare flesh. [...] All of them were from the [Canary] Islands. I've never seen any Cuban witches. They would fly here every night from the Canary Islands to Havana in a few seconds.

> Even nowadays when people aren't so scared, they still leave a light on in the house where there are small children sleeping just

so the witches don't come along interfering with them. If they did
that would be the end of them, because witches are very partial to
little children. (Barnet 1998: 125–26; my translation)

Certainly some of these popular imaginings have found their way into
Márquez's inkwell and, with this idea in mind, I want to turn to one of his
most famous ghosts who appears in chapter 15 of *One Hundred Years of
Solitude*. In that chapter—you will recall—we hear about how three thousand
banana plantation workers on strike are gunned down by the army, an event
which is modelled on a real event, the massacre of banana plantation workers
which occurred at 1:30 am on 6 December 1928 in Ciénaga, Colombia, on
the orders of General Carlos Cortés Vargas (Posada Carbó 1998). In real life,
as García Márquez found out to his amazement, 10 years after the actual
event, when he visited the scene, nobody could remember exactly what
happened. In the novel, reactions vary as to what happened:

> The woman measured him with a pitying look. "There haven't
> been any dead here", she said. "Since the time of your uncle, the
> colonel, nothing has happened in Macondo." In the three
> kitchens where José Arcadio Segundo stopped before reaching
> home they told him the same thing: "There weren't any dead."
> (García Márquez 1978: 251)

The comment made by the authorities to the accusation of mass murder of
political undesirables is priceless: "'You must have been dreaming', the
officers insisted. 'Nothing happens in Macondo, nothing has ever happened
in Macondo, and nothing ever will happen in Macondo. This is a happy
town'" (García Márquez 1978: 252). This sense of two conflicting versions
as to what happened, this bifocalism, coalesces around the testimony of the
main witness to this slaughter, José Arcadio Segundo, who, as we soon
discover, is in all likelihood what we normally understand by the term
"ghost".

  At one point in chapter 15, we find out about how José Arcadio
Segundo has been hiding in Melquíades's room, and we assume that he is
about to be captured when the military officer arrives to search the Buendía
household. The officer orders the door to Melquíades's room be opened, and
although the members of the household can see him sitting on the side of the
bed, the officer apparently does not see him. We read: "He [the officer]
paused with his glance on the space where Aureliano Segundo and Santa
Sofía de la Piedad were still seeing José Arcadio Segundo and the latter also
realised that the soldier was looking at him without seeing him" (García

Márquez 1978: 254). This moment of antimony in García Márquez's novel is similar to that juncture in Carpentier's *The Kingdom of this World* (1990/1948) in which we have two versions of an event (did Macandal's soul fly out of his body, or did it not?; for further discussion, see Hart 2001). In both cases the subaltern seems to see the ghost whereas the figure of authority does not. Whereas the standard definition of a ghost is a "soul or spectre of a dead person usually believed to inhabit the netherworld and to be capable of returning in some form to the world of the living" (*EB* 1995: 242), ghosts often operate in magic-realist fiction as disembodied memorialisations of a trauma experienced by the subaltern, normally in the past. Given that the non-subaltern, or controlling, agencies of society are actively involved in suppressing knowledge of trauma of this kind, it is not surprising that, from an empiricist-official point of view, ghosts do not exist. Ghosts, thus, rupture the socio-spatio-temporal membrane of society and, in magic-realist fiction, operate as traces of subaltern trauma. This is why I believe that we can talk in magic realist fiction about politicised ghosts.

Given that I have mentioned the idea of politicised ghosts this appears to be an appropriate moment to turn to Isabel Allende's *The House of Spirits*, in which we find what I will call the "subalternised supernatural". John Beverley has argued that "what Subaltern Studies makes visible is precisely the fissured character of the national narrative itself, the way it is intersected by other histories, other modes of production, other values and identities" (1995: 16), and the other history which Allende's texts forces us to glimpse or confront is herstory rather than history. One idea which is often expressed by Isabel Allende in her interviews is her fervent hope that, one day, there will be "a more feminine world, a world where feminine values will be validated" (see www.motherjones.com/mother_jones/SO94/allende.html). This idea, understandably enough, is carried over into her fiction. It is undeniable that the principal aim of *The House of the Spirits* is to tell the recent history of Chile from a feminine, some would say feminist, point of view.

There are clearly points in this novel when García Márquez's formula is grist to Allende's mill. Like her Colombian forebear, Allende portrays a world in which the everyday and the supernatural coexist. Rosa the Beautiful, for example, is described in such terms as to make us wonder if she is really of this world. She has green hair, seems to float when she walks, and, because of her beauty, is able to mesmerise men (Allende 1988: 22). As a child Clara the Clairvoyant was known to have spirits hovering around her, to be telepathic (as when she knows the identity of the murderer of the schoolchildren before the police do [1988: 77]), and able to interpret dreams (1988: 74–5). Clara is also skilled at premonition. She predicted the death of her godfather (1988: 75), her own marriage (1988: 82–3), even her father's hernia (1988: 76). Perhaps most remarkable, she is able to move objects without touching them (1988: 77). And as the novel shows, this gift is passed onto female children and grandchildren. Clara's world, as her grandchild, Alba, notes when reading the former's notebooks, is one "where the prosaic truth of material objects mingled with the tumultuous reality of dreams and the laws of physics and logic did not always apply" (1988: 82).

But it is important to remember that Allende consciously gives the world of magic realism a feminine touch, since it is the women who have a sixth sense and not the men. Indeed, Esteban Trueba seems to spend much of his time attempting to stop the neighbours finding out about Clara's and Blanca's powers of divination because of the public scandal this may produce. Likewise the novel specifically refers to the spiritual powers that the women possess as allowing them to construct a new solidarity between women, in effect, a passport to survival in a man's world. The three Mora sisters, for example, who befriend Clara, "discovered a way to transmit mental energy [...] which enabled them to give each moral support in difficult moments of their daily lives" (1988: 125). This knowledge becomes crucial later on for Alba when she is held in a prison camp and suffering daily torture. She is sustained by the apparition of her grandmother, Clara, from beyond the grave (1988: 414), and by her prison companion, Ana Díaz (1988: 425–7). That Ana Díaz's support is the mirror image of Clara's tends to make Clara's magical apparition more believable, confirming once more one of the central techniques of magic realism. Clara's ghost, we might say, is another example of the politicised ghost which inhabits magic realism's pantheon. The ghost returns to Alba and encourages her to create a monument to those who lost their lives in Pinochet's brutal dictatorship, which turns into *The House of the Spirits*. In this way the novel reasserts the primacy of the feminine, and shows how female "intuition" is underpinned not only by a sixth sense (clairvoyance, premonition, and telepathy), but also by a sense of political justice. For Allende, clearly, ghosts are, first of all, female and, second, left wing, that is, not only *desaparecidos* but *desaparecidas*.

I now want to turn my attention to my final text—Toni Morrison's novel *Beloved*, first published in 1987—and explore some of the similarities it has to Latin America's brand of magic realism. *Beloved* seems at first glance to be a strange bedfellow for García Márquez's *One Hundred Years of Solitude* and Allende's *The House of the Spirits*. As Deborah L. Madsen points out, though, Morrison's work is not easy to pigeonhole, and few critics have registered any specific similarities between Morrison's work and that of the Latin American magic realists (Madsen 1998). Stelamaris Coser, however, proposes seeing a number of US authors as well as Latin-American authors in terms of what she calls the "extended Caribbean", and she identifies a number of similarities between them, including what she calls allusion to "the African roots of the Americas" (1994: ix). I want to take up the idea enunciated here by Coser when she says that Morrison grafts "onto Latin American novels the gaze of black women in the United States" (1994: 2), and look specifically at cross-linkings between *Beloved*, *The House of the Spirits* and *One Hundred Years of Solitude*. (I ought to mention that Coser has pointed to an intertextual link between Morrison's *Song of Solomon* and *One Hundred Years of Solitude* [1994: 1–2], but not between the latter novel and *Beloved*.)

Beloved is based on the true story of a female runaway slave in Kentucky called Margaret Garner. At about 10 o'clock on Sunday 27 January 1856, eight slaves escaped from the estate of Archibald K. Gaines situated in Richmond Station, Boone County, 16 miles to the south of Covington in northern Kentucky. When their escape was discovered Mr Gaines made chase, crossed the Ohio River into Cincinnati, and discovered that they were hiding in a house of a black slave called Kite, near the Mill Creek bridge. The house was surrounded by the posse but before they could capture the slaves Margaret Garner slit the throat of her two-year-old daughter, and tried unsuccessfully to do the same with her two sons (whom she simply wounded). As she said when captured, she would rather kill all her children than have them returned to slavery in Kentucky. The incident shook the United States and fuelled the already high feelings among abolitionists (for more discussion of the legal ramifications after the murder, see May 1999). Morrison decided to tell the story, not only because it was part of her local folklore—she is from Ohio—but because the story touches a nerve in the American psyche.

Slavery is a period of history that the United States would sooner forget. As Morrison once said of *Beloved* (incorrectly as it happens): "this has got to be the least read of all the books I've written because it is about something that the characters don't want to remember, I don't want to remember, black people don't want to remember, white people don't want to remember. I mean, it's national amnesia" (quoted in Heinze 1993: 180). The reference to Margaret Garner's story is what might be called the realism of the novel, its roots in specific historic circumstances. The most extraordinary part of the novel occurs, however, when Morrison blends that realism with a magical event, the resurrection of the murdered child. To do this she relied on her own experience. In her childhood, as she has pointed out in an interview, "we were saturated with the supernatural" (quoted in Foreman 1995: 300). Her books are the same. *The Song of Solomon*, I quote, "is about Black people who could fly. That was always part of the folklore in my life; flying was one of our gifts" (quoted in Foreman 1995: 300). Proof that this was not simply a childhood belief is the fact that Morrison has stated she maintains a relationship with her dead father (quoted in Heinze 1993: 159–60).

The fantastic is not incorporated into her literary text, though, in a straightforward way, for *Beloved* is very much a liminal, almost chiaroscuro fiction. It is set in the mid-1800s, in a liminal zone somewhere between the Sweet Home of Kentucky and the abolitionist haven of the North, in the liminal zone between life and death: Beloved, murdered as a small baby by her mother, Sethe, comes to live with her mother in house no. 124. Beloved is also liminal, somewhere in between a baby (she is totally dependent on her mother, Sethe's love), and an adult (she has sexual relations with Paul D). A *Sunday Times* review of the novel spoke of how Morrison "melds horror and beauty in a story that will disturb the mind forever" (quoted in Heinze 1993: 178), and, while it is a beautifully written novel with an uncannily accurate and believable sense of slave talk and slave thought in the times of the Civil War in Kentucky, I want to focus on the horror of the novel, and the horror of the novel resides inside Sethe's unhinged mind. This horror, indeed, has cultural roots. Heinze has argued that Beloved represents "not only the spirit of Sethe's daughter; she is also the projection of the repressed collective memory of a violated people" (Heinze 1993: 179), and I want to explore this idea in greater depth.

There are a number of points at which the imaginative ideology of *Beloved* intersects with that of *One Hundred Years of Solitude*: (i) the portrayal of ghosts in a mundane context, (ii) the use of ghosts to allude to a subalternised supernatural, (iii) the use of the supernatural as a means of drawing attention to the ideological rifts within a given society, that is, highlighting the fact that what exists for one group does not exist for another. This rivenness is, as we have seen, central to the notion of magic realism. The supernatural is presented in Morrison's novel in a gradual sense (unlike in the film version of the novel in which too many of the loose ends are tied up). Our first indication that something is wrong with House no. 124 occurs when Paul D attempts to go in the front room:

> Paul D tied his shoes together, hung them over his shoulder and followed her through the door into a pool of red and undulating light that locked him where he stood.
> "You got company?" he whispered, frowning.
> "Off and on," said Sethe.
> "Good God." He backed out the door onto the porch. "What kind of evil you got in there?"
> "It's not evil, just sad. Come on. Just step through." (1997: 8)

Similar in this to the rhetoric of magic realism prevalent in Latin America, the supernatural is something which is taken for granted by the "inner circle" of people in the novel. Paul D can feel its presence. The two brothers felt it, and it was such an undeniable presence that they ran away from home, never to return. Baby Suggs accepts it as natural, and even argues that it's not as bad as it could be: "Not a house in the country ain't packed to its rafters with some dead Negro's grief. We lucky this ghost is a baby" (1997: 5). Stamp Paid, the companion of Baby Suggs, can hear the eerie noises emanating from the house: "he heard its voices from the road" (1997: 171). People are so scared of House no. 124 that nobody will go in there (1997: 171). And finally, at the end of the novel, the community of women go to the house to find out whether the baby has really returned from the dead, and to see if it has been whipping Sethe. At which point Beloved disappears, and all that we have is the sighting by a boy down at the river who sees "cutting through the woods, a naked woman with fish for hair" (1997: 267), presumably running back down to the river.

What is important about the supernatural as presented in *Beloved* is that it is a subalternised reality, that is, it is directly expressive of societal oppression, and is related to the repression of the African-American in nineteenth-century US society: "White people believed that whatever the manners, under every dark skin was a jungle. Swift unnavigable waters, swinging screaming baboons, sleeping snakes, red gums ready for sweet white blood. In a way, he thought, they were right" (Morrison 1997: 198). Related to his unspoken, unexpressed reality bubbling just beneath the level of skin are the unfathomable thoughts of the women who live in no. 124: "Mixed in with the voices surrounding the house, recognisable but undecipherable to Stamp Paid, were the thoughts of the women of 124, unspeakable thoughts, unspoken" (Morrison 1997: 199). The novel, as we can see, is constructing a web of associations between the unconscious, the socially repressed, women within a patriarchal society, and, last but not least, the ghost of what Baby Suggs calls "some dead Negro's grief". The supernatural expressed in *Beloved* is, thus, an ethnicised, subalternised world which points to the enormous chasm between white and black worlds. The white people cannot see or hear the ghosts not because—as a scientist might argue—they cannot exist in scientific terms, but because they themselves are the very agents of repression in the first place. To admit that they exist would be tantamount to admitting that social oppression exists. Racism is predicated on the desire to keep Negro ghosts in the no-man's land of death. The novel is careful to note that the tragedy of Beloved's murder is the direct result of the inhumane treatment that Sethe received when she was living at Home Sweet Home in Kentucky, something she did not want her children to experience, preferring to kill them than allow them to be captured by the slave-catcher and taken back. As the schoolteacher puts it, soon after discovering the carnage in the shed: "you just can't mishandle creatures and expect success" (Morrison 1997: 150).

What is most remarkable about *Beloved* is its use of language. It is perhaps indicative of Morrison's temperament that the central focus of her Nobel acceptance speech should have been language. She spoke of the oppression that exists within language which "limits knowledge", "hiding its racist plunder in its literary cheek", within that "arrogant pseudo-empirical language crafted to lock creative people into cages of inferiority and hopelessness" (Morrison 1994: 18). Rather than being a "device for grappling with meaning, providing guidance, or expressing love", language had been turned into something she calls "tongue-suicide" (Morrison 1994: 15). Morrison rejects the use of language as an ordering machine; as she eloquently puts it: "How dare you talk to us of duty when we stand waist deep in the toxin of your past?" (Morrison 1994: 27).

It is this "toxin of the past" which Morrison, via her novel, is attempting to exorcise. And, though many critics see *Beloved* as a bleak novel, since it is the story of how a ghost returns—like a zombie from a horror story—in order to pull her mother's hair out, and whip her every day—it is important to recall that it is as a result of female solidarity that the ghost of America's past is banished. And here I might mention that there is a similarity between *Beloved* and *The House of the Spirits*. Ella and her 30 or so female friends surround house no. 124 and sing in order to blow the devil away; Beloved is subsequently forced to flee, and—again an important detail—Sethe does not commit a second murder (as she would have done if this were an Aeschylan tragedy). She (no doubt at Beloved's instigation) attempts to murder Edward Bodwin, the man who—ironically enough—stopped her going to the gallows in the first place, but Ella punches Sethe on the chin, and stops her dead. So we could say that the cycle of revenge has been broken. And it is surely significant that the novel should end with a reconciliation scene between Sethe and Paul D. His last words to her, "me and you, we got more yesterday than anybody. We need some kind of tomorrow" (1997: 273), express a degree of hope for the future, even if, we feel, Sethe is on her last legs. And the epilogue which is punctured by the refrain "It was not a story to pass on" (1997: 275)—an idea echoed by the author herself when she said the slavery of the past was something everyone wanted to forget—needs to be put into perspective, for it is surely truer to say that the story has indeed been passed on. The political ghosts of America's past have finally been laid to rest. And yet....

REFERENCES

Allende, I. (1988) *The House of the Spirits*, pans. Magda Bogin, New York: Bantham [Spanish original 1982].

Barnes, J. (1984) *Flaubert's Parrot*, New York: McGraw Hill.

Barnet, M. (1998) *Biografía de un cimarrón*, Barcelona: Siruela [Spanish original 1966].

Beverley, J. (1995) *Subalternity and Representation*, Durham: Duke University Press.

Carpentier, A. (1990) *The Kingdom of the World*, pans. Harriet de Onus, London: Andre Deutsch [Spanish original 1948].

Cooper, B. (1998) *Magical Realism in West African Fiction: Seeing with a Third Eye*, London: Routledge.

Coser, S. (1994) *Bridging the Americas: The Literature of Paula Marshall, Toni Morrison, and Gayl Jones*, Philadelphia: Temple University Press.

Delvaux, A. (1987) "Du roman à l'écran: L'Homme au crâne rasé", in Weisgerber 1987a, pp. 262–9.

Encyclopedia Britannica (1995) Chicago: Encyclopedia Britannica, vol. 5.

Foreman, P.G. (1995) "Post-on Stories: History and the Magically Real, Morrison and Allende on Call", in L. Parkinson Zamora and W.B. Faris (eds), *Magical Realism: Theory, History, Community*, Durham: Duke University Press.

García Márquez, G. (1978) *One Hundred Years of Solitude*, trans. Gregory Rabassa, London, Picador [Spanish original 1967].

Gerard, F.S. (1987) "Delvaux et Bertolucci: Deux visions du no man's land à l'écran", in Weisgerber 1987a, pp. 270–90.

Hadermann, P. (1987) "Le réalisme magique en peinture", in Weisgerber 1987a, pp. 245–60.

Hart, S.M. (1994) *Crónica de una muerte anunciada: Critical Guide*, London: Grant and Cutler.

———. (2001) *Reading Magic Realism from Latin America*, Bloomsbury Publishing: ISBN 0747556202, Internet course.

Heinze, D., (1993) *The Dilemma of "Double Consciousness": Toni Morrison's Novels*, Athens, GA: University of Georgia Press.

Jameson, F. (1986) "On Magic Realism in Film", *Critical Enquiry*, 12: 301–25.

Madsen, D.L. (1998) "Toni Morrison", in P. Schellinger (ed.), *Encyclopedia of the Novel*, Chicago: Fitzroy Dearborn, vol. II, pp. 870–1.

Mallon, F. (1995) *Peasant and Nation: The Making of Postcolonial Mexico and Peru*, Berkeley: University of California Press.

May, S.J. (1999) "Margaret Garner and Seven Others", in W.L. Andrews and N.Y. McKay (eds), *Toni Morrison's Beloved: A Casebook*, Oxford: Oxford University Press, pp. 25–36.

Morrison, T. (1994) *Lecture and Speech of Acceptance, upon the Award of the Nobel Prize for Literature*, New York: Alfred A. Knopf.

Morrison, T. (1997) *Beloved*, London: Vintage [1987].

Posada Carbó, E. (1998) "La novela como historia; *Cien años de soledad* y las bananeras", *Boletín Cultural y Bibliográfico*, 35: 3–19.

Weisgerber, J. (ed.) (1987a) *Le Réalisme magique: Roman, peinture et cinéma*, Paris: Éditions l'Âge d'Homme.

———. (1987b) "La locution et le concept", in Weisgerber 1987a, pp. 11–32.

STEVEN BOLDY

One Hundred Years of Solitude
by Gabriel García Márquez

According to many testimonies, like García Márquez's exact contemporary the Mexican Carlos Fuentes or the Colombian critic many years younger than both, Michael Palencia-Roth, *Cien años de soledad* (*One Hundred Years of Solitude*, 1967) is the one novel where Latin Americans recognize themselves instantly: their own social, cultural reality, their families, and the history of their countries.[1] It is also the mirror in which a generation of Europeans and North Americans, by the millions, since its publication have discovered the magical reality of an exotic continent, and a taste for its hallucinatory literature.[2] Are they reading the same novel?

One dimension of the "magical realism" which has been seen to characterize the novel is the simultaneous invocation of different mentalities, genres, sorts of truth and experience. The homely and the banal, the content of the hagiographical and the style of the chronicle come together when the priest can levitate only after imbibing drinking chocolate. A similar combination gives Remedios ascending to heaven and Fernanda's annoyance at losing her sheets in the ascension. The conjunction of genres generates synesthesia, the mixing of different senses: "un delicado viento de luz" ("a delicate wind of light").[3] The metaphor and the literal come together when Remedios, as femme fatale, has her suitors die from falls into latrines, kicks to the head from stallions, gun shots. The economic power of the United

From *The Cambridge Companion to the Latin American Novel*, Efraín Kristal, ed. © 2005 by Cambridge University Press.

Fruit Company is translated into meteorological omnipotence when it causes a rainstorm of four years eleven months and two days. One dimension does not cancel or neutralize the other or fuse with it: the prose moves with apparent effortlessness from one to the other, as a Moebius strip.

Cien años de soledad generously invites reading, offers great textual pleasure, but merely tolerates interpretation. One has the impression that weighty motifs which in contemporary modernist texts by Fuentes or Cortázar would cry for analysis and commentary, such as solitude, incest, nostalgia, apocalyptic wind, are here *trompe l'oeil*, simulacra, honey pots for incautious exegetical flies. The uneven fortune of the many interpreters within the novel counsels caution. Aureliano José, who had been destined to live many happy years, is murdered because of an incorrect reading of the cards: "la bala [...] estaba dirigida por una mala interpretación de las barajas" (136; "the bullet was directed by a mistaken reading of the cards"). Aureliano Babilonia finally deciphers the manuscript only to read about himself deciphering the manuscript. Like Lonröt in Borges's "La muerte y la brújula," whose investigation shows that the final victim is to be himself, the interpretation is simply a mirror "un espejo hablado" (350; "a spoken mirror"), an image of the same.

Two very disparate models for his prose which García Márquez often mentions in just about the same breath reflect the novel's tight interweaving of different dimensions: the national and the cosmopolitan, the local and the universal, the historical and the mythical. These are the conversational style of his grandmother, Tranquilina Iguarán Cotes, and the text of Franz Kafka's *The Metamorphosis*. When at the age of seventeen he discovered that it was possible to write straightforwardly that one morning Gregory Samsa woke up to find he had been turned into an insect, he knew then that he would become a writer. Kafka used the same method in German as Márquez's grandmother in Spanish: "She would tell me the most atrocious things without batting an eyelid, as if it was something she had just seen."[4] In the established mythology around the genesis of the novel, Tranquilina has another lieutenant in his aunt, known locally to have an answer to every question. When a villager took her a strangely misshapen egg, she calmly judged that it belonged to a basilisk and should be burned; which it was.[5] The novel is the story of a town, Macondo, and six generations of a Colombian family, the Buendías, with a stubborn tendency to incest, to being ravaged by solitude, haunted by the fear of engendering the child with a pig's tail which is born to Aureliano Babilonia and his aunt Amaranta Úrsula in the final pages.[6] It is the story of real Colombian history, not so different from that of other Latin American republics: the struggle between Liberals and Conservatives and the Civil War of 1899–1902, the treaty of Neerlandia, the banana boom of the first decades of the century, the transfer of power from the *criollos* to multinational companies, the strike and massacre of workers in 1928, and the economic ruin of the area by the Caribbean coast. It is also a mythical narration of the original foundation involving murder and incest, exodus (before genesis), the prophetic dream of Macondo, the "ciudad ruidosa con casas de paredes de espejo" (28; "noisy city of mirror-walled houses"), various biblical-style plagues ranging from insomnia to love, and a final apocalyptic hurricane. The focus of the novel slips constantly and deftly between these three planes.

A key apparent dichotomy which the novel handles memorably is that between the referential and the metatextual. The novel has two patriarchs, José Arcadio Buendía, who founded and built the city with his wife and cousin Úrsula Iguarán, and the gypsy Melquíades, master of the occult, who wrote the manuscript in which the whole history of Macondo was predicted: city and text, action and thought. The manuscript is a classic *mise en abyme*, the novel within the novel which is deciphered at the end, and which is similar but probably not identical to the text of *Cien años de soledad*, though some critics follow Vargas Llosa in having Melquíades as the narrator of the whole novel. When the text ends, so does Macondo; it does not exist outside its representation (in this and other novels). Crucially, no opposition is clear-cut in the novel: Buendía moves from action and politics to an obsession with alchemy and science; Melquíades brings practical artifacts such as magnets and false teeth and cures the plague of insomnia. Roberto González Echevarría has persuasively identified Melquíades as an avatar of the Argentine arch-anti-realist writer Jorge Luis Borges. His room contains two works associated with Borges: the encyclopedia and *The Arabian Nights*. It is an image of the novel as an archive of the textual mediations, the authorizing paradigms of Latin American literature such as the chronicles, the *relación*, scientific travel literature, anthropology.[7]

The task of deciphering the manuscript is passed through the generations of Buendía males, but the two most obsessively involved, Aureliano Babilonia and his great uncle José Arcadio Segundo, are also the two figures most linked to censured political and historical knowledge: the massacre of the banana workers by the authorities in connivance with the United Fruit Company. Moreover, Aureliano is the son of the only proletarian to join the family: Mauricio Babilonia. The actual massacre took place at Ciénaga railway station in 1928, and knowledge of it was virtually erased from public knowledge and memory. Márquez reproduces real names of soldiers and words of the official decree. José Arcadio Segundo was involved in organizing a strike and witnessed the killings. He was taken as dead with hundreds of corpses to be dumped into the sea but escaped to discover that the inhabitants of Macondo had mysteriously forgotten about the massacre overnight: magical realism brilliantly used as political satire. He passes on the forbidden knowledge to Aureliano Babilonia. In the final days of dusty and forlorn decadence in Macondo, Aureliano finds a companion who shares his knowledge: the descendent of the liberal general Gerineldo Márquez, called Gabriel. This final pair in a way mirrors the founding patriarchs. While Aureliano is caught up by his destiny in the apocalyptic wind and will never leave the room of Melquíades, Gabriel Márquez exercises his free will and leaves Macondo for the wider world, for Paris to live in a hotel room later occupied by the characters of Cortázar's *Rayuela*, presumably to initiate the literary career which would culminate in the writing of *Cien años de soledad*.[8]

The presence of Borges, whose most influential short stories and essays such as *Ficciones* and *Otras inquisiciones* were written in the forties and fifties, is emblematic of his importance for the generation of the sixties novelists often known as the Boom. Though Márquez, a figure of the left and a strong supporter of the Cuban Revolution, disliked the conservative politics of Borges, he read him constantly. The textual and intellectual sophistication of the Argentine, his whimsical games with literary originality and tradition, the linguistic and the real, provide the tools and consciousness which allow the new novelists to go beyond the old realisms which preceded them, and beyond the Manichaeism of committed versus elitist literature, between the postmodern and historical fiction. In Hutcheon's terms *Cien años* is a "historiographical metafiction."[9] In Borges's "Tema del traidor y del héroe" we already see the history of the IRA being rewritten using plots from Shakespeare.

Another myth about the genesis of Márquez's novel, described by Márquez as "the decisive episode in my life as a writer"[10] introduces us to the central theme of return, recovery of the past, nostalgia. Michael Bell provides a usefully schematic comparison. Just as Cervantes's *Don Quixote* offers a satirical critique of the chivalric romance, yet is also an affectionate recreation of its long-lost values, so García Márquez's characters are destroyed by a negative nostalgia, yet his novel is a wistful celebration of his grandparents' house and world.[11] Another parallel would be the return of Juan Rulfo and his character Juan Preciado in *Pedro Páramo* (1955) to a Comala which at once "huele a miel derramada" ("smells of spilt honey")[12] and is the desolate site of the ghosts of the tormented dead. García Márquez had been brought up in the house of his grandparents at Aracataca, and the house is in many ways the living, and dying, protagonist of the novel. His grandfather Nicolas was the model for José Arcadio Buendía and, together with the liberal General Uribe Uribe, of Coronel Aureliano Buendía. The banana boom, with the exciting influx of strangers and migrant workers, the *hojarasca*, was still a vibrant memory in the town and his family; the house was filled by its ghosts. Aracataca was a rich, peculiar world of folk wisdom, local and family myths. When García Márquez was fifteen, after having lived what he experienced as exile from his luminous Caribbean roots, that is in the boarding school near the cold and inhospitable Bogotá, he accompanied his mother back to Aracataca to sell the family house. He found there his past ruined by the passage of time. "And it was a dusty and stifling place; it was a terrible midday, you breathed the dust."[13] His mother meets an old friend and they silently cry in each other's arms for half an hour.

García Márquez's novel is a literary battle to recover the Aracataca of his childhood from the ravages of time, a battle fought on many fronts, a gloriously undecided war. In the first nine chapters, presided over by the patriarch José Arcadio and the rival matriarchs Úrsula and Pilar Ternera, life is good; the final eleven, presided over by the parallel triad of José Aureliano, Fernanda del Carpio, and Petra Cotes, mirror them darkly as the tide turns in favor of decay. Two sites register the change most memorably. One is the Spanish galleon found in the jungle by the founding patriarch, and revisited many years later by his son the Colonel during one of the thirty-two rebellions he staged and lost. The first experience paradoxically fixes the wreck in a state of pristine and seductive atemporality: "Frente a ellos, rodeado de helechos y palmeras, blanco y polvoriento en la silenciosa luz de la mañana, estaba un enorme galeón español. [...] Toda la estructura parecía ocupar un ámbito propio, vedado a los vicios del tiempo y a las costumbres de los pajaros." (18; "Before them, surrounded by ferns and palms, white and dusty in the silent morning light, was an enormous Spanish galleon. [...] Its whole structure seemed to occupy a space of its own, immune from the vices of time and the customs of birds.") Viewed by the Colonel with a tired cynicism born of a long fight over power, "lo único que encontró fue el costillar carbonizado en medio de un campo de amapolas" (18; "the only thing he found was the charred rib-cage in the middle of a field of poppies"). The other is the room of Melquíades, perceived by some, in spite of being closed for many years, as luminous and immaculate, while others such as the soldier who comes to capture José Arcadio Segundo see only filth and spiders' webs.

In terms of the biblical book of Revelation Macondo is both Babylon and New Jerusalem, with a typical inversion: New Jerusalem is founded before Babylon is destroyed. The prophesied "city of mirror-walled houses," the "river of diaphanous waters which dashed over a bed of polished stones" (9), evoke the holy city whose light was "like unto a stone most precious, even like a jasper stone, clear and crystal" (Rev. 21:11), the "pure river of water of life, clear as crystal" (Rev. 22:1). It is this New Jerusalem which becomes the final unreal Babylon destroyed by the hurricane. Just as "with violence shall that great city Babylon be thrown down, and shall be found no more at all" (Rev. 18, 21), so in the final lines of the novel, "las estirpes condenadas a cien años de soledad no tendrán una segunda oportunidad sobre la tierra" ("family lines condemned to a hundred years of solitude will not have another chance on earth"). Other similar inversions suggest the perversity of destiny in Macondo. In Revelation the fifth angel and the inhabitants of the bottomless pit torment those who "do not have the seal of God in their forehead" (Rev. 9:4). The seventeen sons of the Colonel who have the indelible crosses on their foreheads after an Ash Wednesday ceremony are hunted and shot one by one by the Conservative troops. Throughout *Cien años de soledad* time is a protean force. From an original time of creation and energy, for the founding José Arcadio it simply stagnates and stops, and he sinks into madness as every day for him becomes Monday: "La máquina del tiempo se ha descompuesto" (73; "The mechanism of time has gone wrong"), he confusedly laments. For others, especially after returning from a journey or a war, the passing of time becomes intolerably painful. As repetitions of phrases and situations take over from flow, time becomes a meaningless circle: "Es como si el mundo estuviera dando vueltas" (253; "It's as if the world were turning round and round,") exclaims Úrsula. In the second part of the novel, the word nostalgia becomes almost as frequent as solitude throughout. Its power is fatal. The Colonel, for example, hears the noise of a circus and "por primera vez desde su juventud pisó conscientemente una trampa de la nostalgia" (229; "for the first time since his youth he knowingly stepped onto a trap of nostalgia") as he recalls again the founding moment when his father takes him to see the ice. He leans on the chestnut tree and dies with his head between his shoulders like a little chicken.

Two key characters return to their roots and their death drawn by nostalgia: the vivacious and ultramodern Amaranta Úrsula returns to the terminally decaying Macondo only to bleed to death after giving birth to the pig-tailed baby as the first such baby born to the family had died over one hundred years previously at the beginning of the whole cycle. The *sabio catalán* is a bookseller and the intellectual mentor of the group of friends of Aureliano Babilonia, who share the names of García Márquez's friends when he lived in Barranquilla. He is a double of Melquíades, with his own set of manuscripts. After many years in Macondo he returns to the Mediterranean village of his birth, "derrotado por la nostalgia de una primavera tenaz" (336; "defeated by the nostalgia for a tenacious spring"). Once there, he feels the same nostalgia for Macondo and is caught between two facing mirrors:

"aturdido por dos nostalgias enfrentadas como dos espejos" (339). This leads him to urge them to leave Macondo and declare that the past is a mirage, that the springs of one's youth are irrecuperable: "en cualquier sitio que estuvieran recordaran siempre que el pasado era mentira, que la memoria no tenía caminos de regreso, que toda primavera antigua era irrecuperable." With this he leads them out of captivity in the spell of Macondo, with the exception of course of Aureliano Babilonia.

The image of the mirrors is a significant and recurring one. For the Catalan it is negative. The twins Aureliano Segundo and his brother use their synchronized movements as a party trick with mirrors, "un artificio de espejos" (151). They can also be seen to comment, however, on the attraction of the same in the Buendía family. From a literary point if view, it is also a key image of the way in which the novel attempts to capture time and produce a sense of simultaneity. Melquíades seems to achieve this magically in his manuscript: "no había ordenando los hechos en el tiempo convencional de los hombres, sino que concentró un siglo de episodios cotidianos, de modo que todos coexistieran en un instante" (350; "he had not ordered events in conventional human time, but concentrated a century of everyday episodes so that they all came together in one instant"). Gabriel García Márquez has to content himself with sentence and narrative structure.

Many critics have analyzed techniques such as narrative loops, enumeration, hyperbaton, coexistence of the past and the present in key sentences.[14] At the beginning of the sixth chapter, just as the Colonel Aureliano Buendía is embarking on his long military career, one breathtaking, cleverly modulated paragraph lists the most dramatic moments of that career. When we come to read the episodes at length over the next few chapters, it is as if they had already happened, or were destined to happen; being anticipated and later chronicled the events belong to two times, past and future. Other enumerations follow events, as when Úrsula wonders whether José Aureliano Segundo is falling into the Buendía family habit of doing just to undo ("hacer para deshacer" 267). His own actions would belong not so much to the chronology of his own life as to a timeless pattern. Retrospectively, moreover, Amaranta with her shroud, the colonel with his gold fish, José Arcadio Segundo with the parchments, are also inserted into the pattern. Often a single event is briefly mentioned at the beginning of a chapter or section after which the narrative loops back into the past and progresses until the event is reached and fully explained. The chapter closes in on itself as does the Buendía family, or the universal time scale of genesis and apocalypse.

According to Mario Vargas Llosa, the technique used in the memorable first sentence of the novel provides the narrator with a watchtower from which to survey and link all the events of the novel. "Muchos años después, frente al pelotón de fusilamiento, el coronel Aureliano Buendía había de recordar aquella tarde remota en que su padre lo llevó a conocer el hielo." ("Many years later, facing the firing squad, Colonel Aureliano Buendía was to remember that remote afternoon when his father took him to discover ice.") From an undefined present the narrator evokes the future of a past moment, expressed with the ubiquitous "había de" with its hint of inevitability, from which this same past is recalled. We have again the facing mirrors that will reflect and forge the labyrinthine time of the novel. Only in the seventh chapter does the Colonel face the firing squad. Most first-time readers of the novel surely assume that he will die at that point, but he is saved. The predictive function of narrative is subtly evoked and questioned.

The inseparability and complex mirroring of past and the future, of prediction and narration of the past, ultimately, of freedom and destiny make the reading of *Cien años de soledad* a rich and nuanced experience. The warring temporal dimensions are sometimes associated with characters. Úrsula Iguarán is the mother of the legitimate first generation of children born in Macondo; Pilar Ternera bears the following generation, illegitimately, to Úrsula's sons. These rival matriarchs live through almost all the novel, but while Úrsula is the seat of memory for the family, Pilar tells the future by reading cards. Like all oppositions in the novel, this one is gradually undone, inverted, endowed with paradox and complexity. On one occasion Pilar's prediction that Aureliano would face a serious danger connected with his mouth actually changes the future and ensures that she is wrong. Aureliano shoots himself in the chest rather than in the mouth in order to frustrate Pilar's prediction, and in the process fails to die. Úrsula too is wrong on this occasion: when she sees her milk pan full of maggots, she announces that Aureliano has been killed. During the insomnia plague, when the link between sign and thing slips from the people and amnesia sets in, prediction replaces memory when Pilar Ternera must read the cards to discover the past.[15] In her great old age, Pilar realizes that experience is more powerful than telling cards; while in hers, Úrsula lives so exclusively in her memories, that these become "un futuro perfectamente revelado y establecido" (333; "a perfectly revealed and established future").

The narration in the past tense of *Cien años*, which speaks of free will and a creative engagement with history, coexists with various types of prediction which speak rather of determinism, predestination—the prophecies of characters, recurring family traits, and the well-known outcomes of the myths evoked: Oedipus will come to grief, Genesis predicts Apocalypse. The tension is structurally built into the novel, which has in a sense two texts, even if one is more or less virtual: the chronicle of the Buendía family which we read and the text of Melquíades, composed during the action of the novel and finally deciphered, as in Revelation and Daniel, at the end of time. The characters make heroic intellectual efforts to read the parchments, but then it was fated that they should do so.[16]

García Márquez has repeatedly stated that his favorite book is Sophocles's *Oedipus the King*. The unburied corpse from Sophocles's *Antigone*, burial in general, where one is buried, in Colonus or Thebes, Riohacha or Macondo, haunts the Colombian's texts from *La hojarasca*, to *El otoño del patriarca*. In *Cien años* just a couple of examples are the sack with the bones of the parents of Rebeca and the arrival from Bogotá of the coffin with the putrefying remains of Fernanda's father. It can be argued that incest in *Oedipus the King* (Faulkner's *Absalom, Absalom!* and *Pedro Páramo* have a similar role) seems to attract García Márquez as a force of destiny, a curse, rather than as a theme in itself. Whereas the themes of solitude and power permeate most of his texts, incest figures as a major concern only in *Cien años*. Predictions structure many works: that Santiago would be murdered in *Crónica de una muerte anunciada*, that the Patriarch's body would be found in such and such a way. Melquíades's parchment seems to function in a similar way to the Delphic oracles in Oedipus's case: Oedipus busily goes about trying to work for the polls, discover the murderer of Laius and lift the plague, and discovers that his own predicted destiny, which he had fought so hard to avoid, had *already* been fulfilled.[17] His investigation is his own free-willed action yet reveals his fate fulfilled. Aureliano's deciphering of the manuscript reveals that he was already destined to suffer the curse brought on by his destiny of incest and produce the pig-tailed child so persistently evaded by his family. Destiny and freedom are often two sides of the same coin; when any life has ended or when a book is completed, what happens within it becomes destiny. Melquíades's parchment graphically reminds us of this truism.

When the first Aureliano uses the gold he had been given to go to the brothel to gild the door keys, his mother laments that children inherit the idiosyncrasies of their parents and adds that this is as horrendous as a pig's tail. It is clear that the incest associated with the tail is mostly a metonym for deterministic inheritance in general. The traits which reappear from generation to generation echo those of Faulkner's Southern families. Some have positive results, the enterprising streak which builds an ice factory or brings the train to Macondo; others such as loneliness or the inability to love do not. Much has been made of the characteristics of the Arcadios' and the Aurelianos in the novel; physical and social, cerebral and withdrawn, but of course what distinguishes them at birth is not so much parentage, genes, but an arbitrary name, which takes on ironically magical powers. Josefina Ludmer works to dissolve such determinism by name, by demonstrating just how extraordinarily complex the mechanism of inherited traits is. She observes that such are the labyrinthine echoes between disparate situations, characters and periods that rather than any sort of chronological line, one has a multidirectional movement, a baroque space, infused with "a sort of cosmic narcissism."[18] Her description echoes Melquíades's notion of simultaneity.

Cien años de soledad was constantly in García Márquez's mind for some fifteen years, since the time when he had tried unsuccessfully to write it and the mythical moment on the road to Acapulco when he had the revelation that he should write it like his grandmother spoke, and he closed himself into his Mexico City flat for a year and a half to write it. It is a novel written with "all the tricks of life and all the tricks of the trade."[19] It compresses or expands all the anecdotic richness of his previous work, giving the impression to the reader of being the tip of a vast iceberg. The reader's experience that in it he can see both sides of the moon at the same time[20] is translated by at least two critics into the aphorism of Gramsci: "pessimism of the intellect, optimism of the will."[21] When one thinks of sex in the novel, the first image is celebratory: Aureliano Babilonia carrying a bottle of beer on his erect "inconceivable masculinity" (328), women clamoring to buy a raffle ticket to win a time in bed with José Arcadio, the riotous "chillidos de gata" (325; "cat-like squeals") of Amaranta Úrsula. Then one remembers the misery: the torment by incestuous desire of Amaranta, her fearful rejection of the loves of her life, Pietro Crespi and Gerineldo Márquez. When Aureliano Buendía loses his virginity, he feels "el ansia atolondrada de huir y al mismo tiempo de quedarse para siempre en aquel silencio exasperado y aquella soledad espantosa" (31; "the bewildered urge to flee and at the same time to remain forever in that exasperated silence and that awful solitude"). When asked what critics had most blatantly missed about his novel, García Márquez answered: "its main quality: the author's immense compassion for all his poor creatures."[22]

NOTES

1. See Carlos Fuentes, "Gabriel García Márquez and the Invention of America," in his Myself with Others: Selected Essays (London: André Deutsch, 1988), p. 190, and Michael Palencia-Roth, Gabriel García Márquez: la línea, el círculo y las metamorfosis del mito (Madrid: Gredos, 1983), p. 10.

2. See Gerald Martin's excellent study "On 'Magical' and Social Realism in García Márquez," in Bernard McGuirk and Richard Cardwell (eds.), Gabriel García Márquez: New Readings (Cambridge University Press, 1987), p. 103.

3. Gabriel García Márquez, *Cien años de soledad* (Buenos Aires: Sudamericana, 1970), p. 205. Page numbers in the text refer to this edition. All translations are my own.

4. Gabriel García Márquez, *El olor de la guayaba: conversaciones con Plinio Apuleyo Mendoza* (Barcelona: Bruguera, 1982,), p. 41.

5. See, for example, Mario Vargas Llosa, *García Márquez: historia de un deicidio* (Barcelona and Caracas: Monte Avila, 1971), p. 24.

6. Similar in many ways to Faulkner's Yoknapatawpha County and Juan Carlos Onetti's Santa María.

7. See Roberto González Echevarría, *"One Hundred Years of Solitude*: The Novel as Myth and Archive," in Robin Fiddian (ed.), *García Márquez* (London and New York: Longman, 1995), pp. 79–99.

8. Characters from other contemporary Latin American novels also stray into the pages of *Cien años de soledad*, such as Carlos Fuentes's Artemio Cruz (2–54) and Victor Hugues from Alejo Carpentier's *El siglo de las luces* (84).

9. See Linda Hutcheon, *A Poetics of Postmodernism: History, Theory, Fiction* (New York and London: Routledge, 1991), p. 129.

10. Vargas Llosa, *García Márquez*, p. 90.

11. Michael Bell, *Gabriel García Márquez* (London: Macmillan Press, 1993), p. 67.

12. Juan Rulfo, *Pedro Páramo* (Mexico City: Fondo de Cultura Económica, 1971), pp. 22.

13. Vargas Llosa, *García Márquez*, p. 90.

14. The most thorough analysis of the structure of the novel is that of Josefina Ludmer in her *Cien años de soledad: una interpretación* (Buenos Aires: Tiempo Contemporáneo, 1974).

15. In Borges's story "Funes el memorioso" total recall, not amnesia, is the consequence of insomnia.

16. Palencia-Roth has good sections on the apocalyptic dimension of the novel, and the relationship with Sophocles. See also the chapter on Márquez in Lois Parkinson Zamora's *Writing the Apocalypse: Historical Vision in Contemporary US and Latin American Fiction* (Cambridge University Press, 1989).

17. See Bernard Knox's introduction to *Oedipus the King*, in Sophocles, *The Three Theban Plays* (Harmondsworth: Penguin, 1982), esp. p. 1150.

18. Ludmer, *Cien años*, p. 145.

19. García Márquez, *Guayaba*, p. 90.

20. See Ernst Völkening, cit. by Gerald Martin, p. 100.

21. Michael Wood, *Gabriel García Márquez: One Hundred Years of Solitude* (Cambridge University Press, 1990), pp. 6–7.

22. García Márquez, *Guayaba*, p. 111.

FURTHER READING

Bell, Michael, *Gabriel García Márquez*, London: Macmillan Press, 1993.

Fuentes, Carlos, "Gabriel García Márquez and the Invention of America," in Carlos Fuentes, *Myself with Others: Selected Essays*, London: André Deutsch, 1988.

García Márquez, Gabriel, *El olor de la guayaba: conversaciones con Plinio Apuleyo Mendoza*, Barcelona: Bruguera, 1982.

González Echevarría, Roberto, *"One Hundred Years of Solitude*: The Novel as Myth and Archive," in Robin Fiddian (ed.), *García Márquez*. London and New York: Longman, 1995.

Ludmer, Josefina, *Cien años de soledad: una interpretación*, Buenos Aires: Tiempo Contemporáneo, 1974.

Martin, Gerald, "On 'Magical' and Social Realism in García Márquez," in Bernard McGuirk and Richard Cardwell (eds.), *Gabriel García Márquez: New Readings*, Cambridge University Press, 11987.

Palencia-Roth, Michael, *Gabriel García Márquez: la linea, el círculo y las metamorfosis del mito*, Madrid: Gredos, 1983.

Parkinson Zamora, Lois, *Writing the Apocalypse: Historical Vision in Contemporary U.S. and Latin American Fiction*, Cambridge University Press, 1989.

Vargas Llosa, Mario, *García Márquez: historia de un deicidio*, Barcelona and Caracas: Monte Ávila, 1971.

Wood, Michael, *Gabriel García Márquez: One Hundred Years of Solitude*, Cambridge University Press, 1990.

DIANE E. MARTING

The End of Eréndira's Prostitution

Ends are ends only when they are not negative but frankly transfigure
the events in which they are immanent.

(Frank Kermode 175)

The criticism of Gabriel García Márquez' works usually accomplishes the
difficult task of considering both his formal innovations and his criticisms of
Latin American society and politics, but in the secondary literature on "La
increíble y triste historia de la candida Eréndira y de su abuela desalmada"
(1972), the magical, fairy-tale elements have been analyzed much more
thoroughly than its main theme of oppressive child prostitution. For
example, Joel Hancock discusses "Eréndira and the Brothers Grimm"
(1978); Barbara B. Aponte examines "el rito de iniciación" (1983); Marta
Morello-Frosch analyzes the "función de lo fantastico" (1984–85); Efrén
Ortiz gives the story "una lectura mítica" (1980); Antonio Benitez Rojo calls
Eréndira "la Bella Durmiente de García Márquez" (1987); Roberto Reis
writes that the "estructura de Poder" is questioned through the use of the
fantastic (1980); Jasbir Jain calls it "The Reversal of a Fairy Tale" (1987) and
Mario Vargas Llosa places his comments on Eréndira within a chapter titled
the "Hegemonía de lo imaginario" in his 1971 biography of García Márquez,
Historia de un deicidio.

From *Hispanic Review* Vol. 69, No. 2 (Spring 2001). © 2001 Hispanic Review.

The social problem that "La increíble historia" addresses deserves a more frontal treatment. (I will use this short form of the story title to distinguish it from the film, for which I will use the character's name within quotation marks: "Eréndira"). Overlooked in comparison to genre and myth, the story's social themes and realist strategies reveal García Márquez' early interest in criticizing aspects of women's oppression. In this article I first remind readers of the Colombian author's insistence on the autobiographical origins of the Eréndira–Abuela pair, and then discuss prostitution in several other texts by him. Finally I seek to explain the controversial ending of "La increíble historia" by highlighting its faithfulness to its genesis and analyzing where the fiction diverges both from those origins and from literary norms. My contention is that Eréndira's prostitution is comparable to the massacre of the banana workers in *Cien años de soledad* in that they are narrathemes based on real events which are treated by the fictions as unreal. In *Cien años*, the historical massacre is represented, but then the sole survivor cannot find anyone to believe his testimony. All deny his tale and declare him mad. Hyperbole and improbability weight the evidence in the fiction in favor of the massive coverup, the Big Lie in which a massacre on such a scale never could have happened. Yet history has witnessed such an event. Similarly, the nature of Eréndira's slavery is couched in the language of fable and fairy tale, giving the appearance of fictionality, of its impossibility or untruth in any literal sense. Hyperbole and improbability have led to reader incredulity. Yet Eréndira's barbaric treatment by her grandmother and the huge number of men who have paid-sex with her in fact could happen and does happen in reality.

According to published interviews with the author, "La increíble historia" is based on an experience when, as a sixteen-year-old, García Márquez saw an eleven-year-old girl working as a prostitute. She was accompanied by a woman whom he presumed to be a relative. At a decisive moment in the fictional Eréndira story, the text similarly anchors itself in the reporter's look, in personal testimony, rather than the omniscient authority of a storyteller. The episode with the bordello prostitutes is witnessed by a first-person, participant narrator who enters the text on the page before (126), interrupting the third-person omniscient narration. Like García Márquez' newspaper account of seeing the young prostitute abused by a relative, this unnamed participant narrator is a young man. In this segment, a group of sex workers from the local brothel are angry because Eréndira has attracted all their customers to wait in lines at her tent. They attack Eréndira and carry her out into the street naked, leaving her trapped there and the dogchain by which she is locked to the bed is made visible for all to see (127–28). Within the plot, the writer-witness' brief eye-witness testimony marks the spot where Eréndira begins to take steps toward her definitive liberation by planning her grandmother's murder.

The new narrator, a writer, tells of the time in his past when as a traveling encyclopedia salesman he saw Eréndira's encampment near the country's border:

> Las conocí por esa época, que fue la de más grande esplendor, aunque no había de escrudiñar los pormenores de su vida sino muchos años después, cuando Rafael Escalona reveló en una canción el desenlace terrible del drama y me pareció que era bueno para contarlo. (126)

He writes that although he saw them years before, he could not tell her story before he knew how the story ended. Unlike the actual author who repeats Eréndira's story in a series of his works, the narrator-writer was prevented from writing about her until he knew from Escalona that the grandmother had been killed. And unlike García Márquez who saw the young prostitute in excruciating poverty, the narrator sees her living in wealth.

Lodged at a crucial juncture in the story, the temporary disturbance in the omniscient narrative surface appears just after Eréndira is separated from her grandmother a second time (The first time was when she was kidnapped and taken to the convent). This brief first-person account interrupting the third-person narration occurs after Eréndira's frustrated escape with Ulises, when her "instinto de libertad prevaleció contra el hechizo de la abuela" (123), an escape which could have served to end the story, but did not. The bubble of first-person narration contains descriptions of the carnival town in which she is forced back to work with the dogchain added to prevent similar escapades. The ending was false, and merely leads to more of the same work, with greater humiliation and less personal freedom.

The writer Gabriel García Márquez first wrote about seeing the young prostitute in *Cien años de soledad* (1967; One Hundred Years of Solitude, 1979) in which the adolescent boy who would become Colonel Aureliano Buendía feels pity for a young prostitute in similar circumstances (52–54). A screenplay followed because, the Colombian wrote, he could not imagine their story as a novel—only as a drama in images ("Chronicle" 12). This first screenplay was never filmed although fragments have been published. After waiting four years for it to be filmed, García Márquez rewrote his memory of the two women as fiction. This 1972 novella which I am discussing here became in its turn the source for a second screenplay, "Eréndira," the basis for the film directed by Mozambique-born, Brazilian Ruy Guerra in 1982. The Guerra film combines "Muerte más allá del amor," another short story from the same collection, with "La increíble historia" as per García Márquez' second film script. The 1972 novella is the first complete written version to survive, and it varies significantly from the first and second scripts, as well as from the Guerra film.

While several of García Márquez' works feature women characters who are "matriarchs," powerful women whose concerns nevertheless revolve around children, church, and kitchen (Úrsula Buendía, Fermina Daza, La Mamá Grande), few of his works of any length have neglected to mention prostitutes, and early criticism often remarked that his portrayal was partial, negative, conservative or realistic (Hazera, Sayers Peden, Siemens, Álvarez Gardeazábal). A brief list of important prostitutes in his works would include: Pilar Ternera and Petra Cotes in *Cien años de soledad*; the Patriarch's mother Bendición Alvarado in *El otoño del patriarca* (1975); and Florentino Ariza's friends in the hotel in *Amor en los tiempos del colera* (1985). In the case of widow of Nazaret from this novel, sexual liberation is positively associated with prostitution when she tells Florentino, "Te adoro porque me volviste puta" (209). The narrator of *Crónica de una muerte anunciada* spends the hours before Santiago Nasar's murder in bed with a prostitute, María Alejandrina Cervantes. The short stories "Muerte más allá del amor" and "El mar del tiempo perdido" in the Eréndira collection feature prostitutes and at the same time are the stories most closely related to "La increíble historia."

In a 1983 *Playboy* interview, Claudia Dreifus asks García Márquez why he writes "with great warmth about prostitutes." He answered that his reasons are sentimental:

> Prostitutes were friends to me when I was a young man. Real friends. The environment I grew up in was very repressive. It wasn't easy to have a relationship with a woman who wasn't a prostitute. When I went to see prostitutes, it wasn't really to make love but more to be with someone, not to be alone. The prostitutes in my books are always very human and they are very good company. They are solitary women who hate their work. (Dreifus 177–78)

If his fiction is any indication, García Márquez also hates "their work." He laments the exploitation prostitutes suffer, but he does not disapprove of the workers themselves. Indeed, an odd idealization of the brothel and the prostitute can be seen. Here is an example from Amor en los tiempos del colera:

> Cuando Florentino Ariza llegaba del empleo se encontraba con
> un palacio poblado de ninfas en cueros, que comentaban a gritos

los secretos de la ciudad, conocidos por las infidencias de los propios protagonistas. Muchas exhibían en sus desnudeces las huellas del pasado: cicatrices de puñaladas en el vientre, estrellas de balazos, surcos de cuchilladas de amor, costuras de cesáreas de carniceros. Algunas se hacían llevar durante el dia a sus hijos menores, frutos infortunados de despechos o descuidos juveniles, y les quitaban las ropas tan pronto como entraban para que no se sintieran distintos en el paraíso de la desnudez. (108)

An idealization of the brothel and the prostitute occur together with a protest against the serious risks they incur and against other negative consequences of the conditions under which they labor. Their profession is dangerous due to the exposure to disease, to the prostitutes' vulnerability to physical attack, especially among the streetwalking population, to repression from authorities, and also due to their general marginality. But they are not to blame for the conditions in which they work.

In the *Playboy* and other interviews, García Márquez also does not condemn the male customers of whores, unless the men use coercion or violence. Many sympathetic male characters in his works are either clients or friends of female sex workers. Since there is no blame placed on the people buying or selling sex in his fiction, the usual gender division between those who pay (men) and those who charge (women) appears as if a simple, neutral, sociological fact, unproblematized in the fiction.

In *Cien años de soledad, Crónica de una muerte anunciada, Amor en los tiempos del colera, El general en su laberinto* (1989), and "La increíble historia," hypocritical attitudes toward those who receive money for sex cause the loneliness—the solitude—of the prostitute. The existence of the profession is attributed to greed and its violence to the abuse of power. In *El otoño del patriarca* especially, written during the same years as the 1972 version of "La increíble historia," prostitution is a specific manifestation of more generalized economic and political oppression. For example, the Patriarch uses food in his sexual games with the unnamed school girl who falls in love with him (222–23). With an irony typical of García Márquez, the real whore from the port complains about the Patriarch's waste of good food when she is going hungry (226). With the exception of the Patriarch, however, the prostitutes' economic problems in García Márquez rarely come from the customers who pay them, but frequently from public officials and pimps who take the money the women earn.

In *La prostitución en Colombia, una quiebra de las estructuras sociales* (1970, 1976), Saturnino Sepúlveda Niño describes in non-statistical format for the lay reader some of the salient characteristics of prostitution in Colombia during the 1960s and 70s. In his conclusions, he comments:

> En las ciudades sobre el rio Magdalena, sobre todo, hay relación directa entre la prostitución y los ingresos fiascas municipales. La solidez económica municipal depende de la foración de cantinas, cabarets, y casas de lenocinio, a través de los impuestos y multas por su funcionamiento. (169)

In Mexico, a similar abuse on the part of the authorities appears in Irma Gutiérrez' testimonial account, "Un problema laboral y sanitario, Irma Gutiérrez: Basta de prejuicios y discriminación para las prostitutas" (1977), an interview of Gutiérrez by García Flores. One of the first women doctors to treat prostitutes in Pachuca, Hidalgo, Gutiérrez speaks of her prostitute patients as if all the different groups who attack the sex workers had a cumulative effect on the women's personalities:

> Son personas agresivas, ¿cómo no van a serlo si sufren agresión tras agresión? Les pagan para que se dejen manejar como objetos; se les niega diariamente su condición de persona. Si a eso agregamos que los dueños de los locales y los cantineros donde trabajan, y los hombres que les dan prótección las explotan, que las autoridades las extorsionan, que son agredidas fisicamente, bueno ¿no seria anormal que no fueran agresivas? A mí nunca me agredieron; hicieron una manifestación cuando tuve que irme, porque las traté como personas. (375–76)

Additionally, according to Sepúlveda Niño's surveys, most Colombian prostitutes begin to work between the ages of 15 and 18; they usually leave the profession around age 25. García Flores writes of the Mexican parallel that "la investigación de trabajadores del Departamento Federal, [decía que de] 1,753 prostitutas [la] edad promedio era de 22 años" (374). Prostitutes in Latin America come most frequently from the countryside, are unmarried, in good health, and, according to the Colombian study, have an average of 1.6 children each. Sepúlveda Niño's figures number Colombia's prostitutes at more than 150,000 and growing.

García Márquez said he saw the eleven-year-old prostitute and her relative who inspired the story when he was 16. Born in 1928, the author would have seen the pair of women around 1944. What were the laws regarding prostitution like in Colombia at this time? Before a 1962 law suppressing all registration of prostitutes and decriminalizing prostitution in

Colombia, laws from the 1940s prohibited prostitution in Bogotá and regulated it in "zonas de tolerancia" in Antioquia, according to Sepúlveda Niño: "La reglamentación, donde existe, incluye ubicación de zonas de tolerancia, prohibición para menores, expedición de carnets, control venereo, horas y días de salida de las prostitutas a los centros de la ciudad, etc." (164). Prostitution was regulated by a city or department (county), and not coordinated federally (his studies were of Puerto Berrio and Bogotá). When the registration of prostitutes was abolished in 1962, García Márquez would have been 34 and an experienced journalist. During the time when registration existed, a prostitute did not have the right to take a walk when and where she wanted, even to look for other type of work, and instead was strictly limited. Through his work, the author probably was aware of the change. Only forcing someone into prostitution, or working as a minor remained a crime in 1972, when García Márquez rewrote his memories as a short story. It is possible García Márquez stresses Eréndira's very young age because prostitution itself was legal in Colombia at this time, whereas forcing a minor into prostitution was doubly illegal, although very young age is also an added attraction in itself in this brutal business.

In the newspaper article about his inspiration for "La increíble historia," García Márquez states that the girl-prostitute he had seen as a boy had been "seduced at ten by a lustful shopkeeper who traded a ripe banana for her virginity" ("Chronicle" 12), yet his fictional character Eréndira is forced physically to submit to her first customer. She enters the profession by the second most common means mentioned in Kathleen Barry's study, *Female Sexual Slavery* (1979): she was purchased and beaten into submission (91).[1] The most common way in which women begin to work as prostitutes is "through seduction by being promised friendship and love" (5) by a man, who himself or with the help of another, brings her to the brothel or to the streets. This initial willingness complicates the woman's and society's attitude toward her subsequent victimization because it gives the appearance of choice to all that occurs. As with date rape, agreeing to be with a man or even agreeing to work for him initially does not give him license to do violence or to force her later. But Eréndira does not "choose" prostitution: for a man, for economic survival, to feed her children, or for gain. She is unequivocally forced by the shopkeeper and the *Abuela*. The circumstances of Eréndira's becoming a prostitute emphasize the two adults' abuse of their legal, moral, physical and magical power over a child. In this way, the Colombian's protest against injustice becomes the salient feature, avoiding the more ambiguous questions surrounding prostitution when an adult woman is involved.

For many readers, the description of the long lines of men waiting to pay for a few minutes with Eréndira are unrealistic and part of a grotesque and unreal imaginary. Vargas Llosa wrote: "La anécdota muda de objetiva en imaginaria por exageración: lo extraordinario no es que Eréndira ejerza la prostitución sino el numero 'imposible' de sus clientes" (634). I disagree: her grandmother's calculations of her debt repayment schedule allow us to estimate that Eréndira services around a hundred men a night once her tour has gotten into full swing. However exaggerated the number may appear, and however frequently hyperbole may be a technique in this and other García Márquez' works, this number of tricks is not out of the range of possibility for certain kinds of sex workers in documented studies.

I base my calculations on the following (admittedly sketchy) figures. At the beginning the *Abuela* tells the shopkeeper who buys Eréndira's virginity that her granddaughter owes her over a million pesos (90). In the early episode of the *carguero de camión* who wants to buy Eréndira, after she had worked a short while, the Grandmother quotes a price of 871,895 pesos (94). After about six months, she calculates that Eréndira will have to work for over eight years (97), that is, she must work for at least 8 1/2 years in all:

> Habian transcurrido seis meses desde el incendio cuando la abuela pudo tener una visión entera del negocio.
>
> —Si las cosas siguen asi—le dijo a Eréndira—me habras pagado la deuda dentro de ocho años, siete meses y once días.
> Volvio a repasar sus cálculos con los ojos cerrados, rumiando los granos que sacaba de una faltriquera de jareta donde tenia tambien el dinero, y precisó:
>
> —Claro que todo eso es sin contar el sueldo y la comida de los indios y otros gastos menores. (97)

Of course, the *Abuela* has no intention of letting Eréndira repay the debt and continually finds ways to pocket the fruit of her labor. In this sense, a comparison with the foreign debt of third world countries has been sustained. But let us do the rest of the math anyway, to determine a baseline for her work conditions.

If the first six months is like every other six months, and she needs 8 1/2 years to repay the million pesos, then every six months she repays one/seventeenth of the debt, or approximately 58,826 pesos. In general the *Abuela* seems to charge 50 pesos per man (95,127), with a few exceptions.[2] At this rate, Eréndira must be paid for 1,176 men per six months period. If she worked every day, six months would be 182.5 nights. The average number of men per night then is 6.27. Since Eréndira travels and has days when she does other work, she probably has double or triple that many men, at least twenty to thirty, per working night over the years. This number is much lower than the number of those who wait on line, but there must be many who do not manage to enter her tent before business is closed for the evening.

For reasons that are obvious, the number of tricks earned by prostitutes each night is not usually the object of research, whereas their health and the reasons they begin this work frequently are. Nevertheless, the lines of men awaiting Eréndira are not unlike some of the worst cases which Kathleen Barry found during her research:

> There are small prostitution hotels in one part of the North African *quartier* of Paris known as *maisons d'abattage*.... In each of the *maisons d'abattage* (literal translation: houses of slaughter), six or seven girls each serve 80 to 120 customers a night. On holidays their quota might go up to 150. After each man pays his 30 francs (approximately $6.00) at the door, he is given a towel and ushered into a room. A buzzer sounds after six minutes, and he must leave immediately as another man comes in. The girl never even gets out of bed. (3–4)

The number of Eréndira's tricks is not as impossible as one would like to think, sadly, but neither is it a worst case scenario. Nor is her hard work *fantastic*, in the sense of mysterious or unexplainable, in the same way that the Grandmother can survive huge doses of poison, or that the trees belonging to Ulises' father grow oranges with diamonds inside. Her sexual slavery is not ontologically comparable to the magical qualities love imparts to Ulises or to the long-distance telepathy the lovers share. The number of men who enter Eréndira's tent, and the lines of waiting men outside, unlike the Grandmother's green blood, represent scenes which can and do occur in reality. In other words, not only are the characters in the story based on a real event seen by the author, but the sociological characteristics of the prostitution described in the fiction have existed.

If the mystery of the fantastic elements had been primary, then social concerns would have to take a back seat to metaphysical or intellectual concerns, whereas the horror of Eréndira's life in fact drives the story. The desire to set Eréndira free from her victimization is a major fictional objective. Once the horrific conditions are recognized as realistic elements, the narrator's sympathy for Eréndira as a child sex slave can be rightly seen as one more of many foreshadowings of her future emancipation from everything and everyone from her world of prostitution, and not her future with Ulises. For that same reason, García Márquez needs to discount Ulises as her savior. The author does this first of all by downplaying any love for Ulises on her part, at the same time he shows Eréndira's increasing dependence on him. When Ulises returns and suggests to Eréndira that they flee together across the border, she does not think it is possible, and is so uninterested that she answers him: "Nadie puede irse para ninguna parte sin permiso de su abuela" (119), as if she were a very young child explaining the facts to another. But Ulises shows her a revolver, opens an orange to show her the diamond inside, and Eréndira lets herself be convinced. At this moment of the story, the diamond, the truck, and the revolver interest Eréndira more than a romantic escapade or even Ulises' promises of rescue. Reasonably enough, she wants to be sure of the success of the attempt before undertaking anything. She shows herself practical—even shrewd and calculating.

Another related alternative ending, in addition to a happy wedding for the two lovers, another ending which is never explored textually, would have been for Ulises to purchase her freedom from the Grandmother with diamonds stolen from his father's magic oranges. Earlier, the *Abuela* seems perfectly willing to sell her to the *carguero* for the amount still owed. According to Ulises, each of his father's diamond-bearing oranges is worth 50,000 pesos (104), so he would need only 18 oranges, assuming Eréndira had not been able to reduce the debt at all. The Grandmother's calculations always err and always err in her own favor, but still two dozen oranges may have been enough for Ulises to buy Eréndira from her monstrous slaver. Perhaps Ulises' parents would have been opposed to his buying her, but that hardly seems an obstacle. Ulises' most frequent activity in the novella is stealing: he steals the money to pay for his first visit to Eréndira's tent from his father's wallet, then he steals his father's truck, revolver, and oranges for his attempt to run away with her. After he leaves home for the last time, he steals to live: Ulises "atraveso el desierto escondido en camiónes de paso, robando para comer y para dormir, y robando muchas veces por el puro placer del riesgo, hasta que encontro la carpa en otro pueblo de mar" (132). The uselessness of his revolver attests to his ineffectual nature, ironically named for a wily and intelligent hero whose loyal wife is under siege from many suitors.

The reason this possibility of his purchasing her is silenced in the text is that the ending must be one of Eréndira's absolute freedom from her past—not merely her transfer as property from Grandmother to Ulises, and not merely her manumission from the Grandmother. To escape, Eréndira wishes for the death of her cruel taskmistress and only sees Ulises as a means to this end. Her alternatives are limited, since escape from her servitude while the *Abuela* is alive thus far has proven impossible. The religious authorities did not succeed in separating her from her whale-like relative and the civil authorities did not want to; they conspire to keep her working. But the first-person narrator interrupts the tale to say that it is precisely the way the story ends that allows him to write about it: once he learned of "el desenlace terrible del drama me pareció bueno para contarlo" (126).

Indeed, what could be this terrible ending which Rafael Escalona revealed in his song? The documentary literature on the subject of how women leave prostitution is quite sparse, but Sepúlveda's research indicates that, in Colombia in the 1960s, prostitution was a temporary job, and frequently a part-time one as well. Gutiérrez also said of the Mexican prostitutes:

> Había muchas que llevaban una doble vida. Adentro tenían un nombre diferente al de afuera. Llevaban doble vida y hacían hasta lo imposible porque sus familias y sus amigas no se enteraran de su vida nocturna. Había mujeres casadas, con hijos, esposas de policias que vivían una situación desesperada y se prostituian para ganar un poco de dinero. (375)

Another Colombian study, this time of prostitutes in Bogotá in 1990, found that the average time women work as prostitutes is 5.1 years, with many (21.5%) quitting within the first year. But leaving prostitution alive and well is rarely treated in fiction; the classics of the genre in world literature lead one to believe that all prostitutes die young, victims of violence or disease, while still in the business. These are cautionary tales, warning of the dangers of entering the profession. In literature, García Márquez' story is unusual, therefore, not because a violent death is required for Eréndira to escape prostitution, but because the death is not hers, but her evil grandmother's.[3] Eréndira's safe and voluntary exit from sex work is again homologous to social science discourse which studies the realities of prostitution, like the numbers of men she serviced, and the conditions of sex slaves internationally. She escapes and takes the money *she* earned. García Márquez' literature is still a cautionary tale which warns that the life is horrible, but it also encourages; if you are forced into it or are forced to continue it, then his narrative writes you as one who has options and who will succeed. In compensation for straying from the norms of literature, "La increíble historia" thus gains not only a homology to reality, but also poetic justice as well. The Abuela's death may occur with slapstick humor, as Ulises unsuccessfully attempts to poison her and to blow her up; it is the Grandmother's resistance to all these attempts that earns the novella its adjective "increíble," not the conditions of Eréndira's prostitution or her escape from it.

There are those who will question the idea of poetic justice and reply that Eréndira's lack of gratitude toward Ulises for his murder of the Grandmother, when she abandons her lover and does not look back, prevents the closure which poetic justice requires, because Ulises does not receive his just rewards for killing the Grandmother. I submit that Eréndira's disappearance without him was the only way to end her slavery completely. To close her story, she must start over and not be held in the world of prostitution, even by her gratitude to a past customer. It is an unwincing realist strategy for the text to narrate Eréndira's careful removal from the grandmother's cadaver of the burning gold bars which she will need in the future, together with her unhesitating abandonment of the suitor she does not love to deal with the consequences of the murder he has committed. He killed the Grandmother for love of Eréndira; she accepted his help because she needed to escape.

In the epigraph with which I opened this paper, Frank Kermode writes that the ends of stories must "transfigure the events in which they are immanent." When Eréndira recovers her earnings and leaves Ulises, "La increíble historia" is transfigured. Its romantic tendencies become ironic, its love story vestigial. Its muckraking protest against the Grandmother and her ilk, in contrast, moves into the foreground. The narrator's and the reader's desire to see Eréndira unbound from her "cadena de perro" (128) is satisfied, and that must be enough for Ulises and for our sense of poetic justice.

NOTES

1. The feminist movement's relation to prostitution during the 1970s and 1980s, although neither monolithic nor uniform, was one of discovery. The almost universal assumption in this literature is that much passing for knowledge about sex work is actual patriarchal, paternalistic, or moralistic misinformation, and the best source for the truth is the women who know the life firsthand. Anonymous accounts are common, and fiction, when based on experience, not unheard of. A Venezuelan volume, while less explicitly related to the feminist movement, certainly has a similar goal to the English-language works under consideration, that is, to make the prostitutes' life stories better known (Bourgonje).

2. When they leave the first town, Eréndira "pago el viaje y el transporte de los muebles haciendo amores de veinte pesos con el carguero de camión" (92). Later the amounts become approximate. "Al principio había sido tan severa que hasta llegó a rechazar un buen cliente porque le hicieron falta cinco pesos. Pero con el paso de los meses fue asimilando las lecciónes de la realidad, y termino por admitir que completaran el pago con medallas de santos, reliquias de familia, anillos matrimoniales, y todo cuanto fuera capaz de demostrar, mordiendolo, que era oro de buena ley aunque no brillara" (97).

3. Another Spanish-American exception occurs in Rosario Ferré's story, "Cuando las mujeres quieren a los hombres," in which Isabel la Negra stops working as a prostitute when her rich client leaves her half his wealth.

WORKS CITED

Álvarez Gardeazábal, Gustavo. "Las formas de hacer el amor en *Cien años de soledad.*" *Explicación de Textos Literarios* 4 Suppl. (1976): 39–63.

Aponte, Barbara B. "El rito de la iniciación en el cuento hispanoamericano." *Hispanic Review* 51.2 (Spring 1983): 129–46.

Barry, Kathleen. *Female Sexual Slavery.* New York: New York UP, 1979.

Bell, Laurie, ed. *Good Girls/Bad Girls: Feminists and Sex Trade Workers Face to Face.* Seattle, WA: Seal P, 1987.

Benítez Rojo, Antonio. "'Eréndira,' o la Bella Durmiente de García Márquez." *Cuadernos Hispanoamericanos* 448 (Oct. 1987): 31–48.

——— and Hilda O. Benítez. "Eréndira liberada: la subversión del mito del macho occidental." *Revista Iberoamericana* 128–29 (1984): 1057–75.

Bourgonje, Flor. *La luna se desangra por el otro costado: testimonios sobre la prostitución en Caracas.* Caracas: Ateneo de Caracas, 1980.

Burgos, Fernando. "Hacía el centro de la imaginación: 'La increíble y triste historia de la candida Eréndira y de su abuela desalmada.'" *Inti* (1982–1983): 71–81.

Cámara de Comercio de Bogotá. *La prostitución en el centro de Bogotá: censo de establecimientos y personas. Análisis socioeconómico.* Bogotá: Cámara de Comercio de Bogotá, 1991.

Cancino Moreno, Antonio. *El derecho penal en la obra de Gabriel García Márquez.* Bogotá: Iibería del Profesional, 1983.

Delacoste, Frederique and Priscilla Alexander. *Sex Work: Writings by Women in the Sex Industry.* Pittsburgh: Cleis P, 1987.

Dreifus, Claudia. "*Playboy* Interview: Gabriel García Márquez, A Candid Conversation with the Nobel Prize Winner about His Novels, His Friend Fidel Castro, and Life, Love, and Revolution in Latin America." *Playboy* 30.2 (Feb. 1983): 65–77; 172–78.

Ferré, Rosario. "Cuando las mujeres quieren a los hombres." *Papeles de Pandora.* Mexico: Joaquín Mortiz, 1976.

García Flores, Margarita. *Cartas marcadas.* México, D.F.: Difusión Cultural, Departamento de Humanidades, 1979.

García Márquez, Gabriel. *Amor en los tiempos del cólera.* Buenos Aires: Suderamericana, 1985.

———. *The Autumn of the Patriarch.* Tr. Gregory Rabassa. New York: Harper & Row, 1976.

———. "Chronicle of a Film Foretold: How I Found the Seed for Eréndira in a Chance Encounter in the Tropics." Tr. Lisa Wyant. *American Film* (72 Sept. 1984): 12–13; *El Espectador* [Bogotá] 3 November 1982.

———. *Cien años de soledad.* Buenos Aires: Sudamericana, 1967, 1989.

———. *El general en su laberinto.* Buenos Aires: Sudamericana, 1989.

———. *The General in His Labyrinth.* Tr. Edith Grossman. New York: Knopf, 1989.

———. "The Incredible and Sad Tale of Innocent Eréndira and Her Heartless Grandmother." *Innocent Eréndira and Other Stories.* Tr. Gregory Rabassa. 1978.

———. "La increíble y triste historia de la candida Eréndira y de su abuela desalmada."
        "Muerte más allá del amor." "El mar del tiempo perdido." *La increíble y triste historia
        de la candida Eréndira y de su abuela desalmada.* 8th ed. Colombia: La Oveja Negra,
        1984. 15–38, 49–60, 83–142.

———. *Love in the Time of Cholera.* Tr. Edith Grossman. New York: Knopf, 1988.

———. *One Hundred Years of Solitude* Tr. Gregory Rabassa. New York: Harper & Row,
        1970.

———. *El otoño del patriarca.* Esplugas de Llobregat: Plaza y Janés, 1975.

Gonzalez, Anibal. "The Ends of the Text: Journalism in the Fiction of Gabriel García
        Márquez." *Gabriel García Márquez and the Powers of Fiction.* Ed. Julio Ortega with
        assistance of Claudia Elliott. Austin: U Texas P, 1988. 61–73.

Guerra, Ruy, dir. "Eréndira." 1982.

Hancock, Joel. "Gabriel García Márquez's 'Eréndira' and the Brothers Grimm." *Studies in
        Twentieth-Century Literature* 3 (Fall 1978): 43–52.

Jaeck, Lois Marie. "*Cien años de soledad*: The End of the Book and the Beginning of
        Writing." *Hispania* 74.1 (March 1991): 50–56.

Jain, Jasbir. "Innocent Eréndira: The Reversal of a Fairy Tale." *García Márquez and Latin
        America.* Ed. Alok Bhalla. New Delhi, India: Sterling Publishers Private Ltd., 1987.

Joset, Jacques. *Gabriel García Márquez, coétaneo de la eternidad.* Amsterdam: Rodopi, 1984.

———. "*La mujer más bella del mundo*: Un narrema constante en la obra de Gabriel García
        Márquez." *Narradores latinoamericanos, 1929–1979.* Vol. 2 of XIX Congreso
        Internacional de Literatura Iberoamericana, Segunda Reunión, Caracas, 29 de julio
        a 4 de a gosto de 1979. Caracas: Centro de Estudios Latinoamericanos Romulo
        Gallegos, 1980. 207–18.

Kermode, Frank. *The Sense of an Ending: Studies in the Theory of Fiction.* NY: Oxford UP,
        1966.

Millington, Mark. "Aspects of Narrative Structure in 'The Incredible and Sad Story of the
        Innocent Eréndira and Her Heartless Grandmother.'" *Gabriel García Márquez:
        New Readings.* Ed. Bernard McGuirk and Richard Cardwell. Cambridge:
        Cambridge UP, 1987. 117–33.

Morello-Frosch, Marta. "Función de lo fantastico en 'La increíble y triste historia de la
        candida Eréndira y de su abuela desalmada' de Gabriel García Márquez."
        Symposium 38.4 (Winter 1984–85): 321–30.

Ortiz, Efrén. "La Candida Eréndira: una lectura mítica." *Texto Crítico* 5.16–17
        (Enero–junio 1980): 248–54.

Pacheco, José Emilio. "Muchos años después ..." *Novelistas como críticos.* Vol. 2. Ed. Norma
        Klahn and Wilfredo H. Corral. Mexico: Fondo de Cultura Económica; Ediciones
        del Norte, 1991. 459–69.

Peden, Sayers Margaret. "Las buenas y las malas mujeres de Macondo." *Explicación de
        Textos Literarios* 4 (Suppl. 1976): 313–27.

Penuel, Arnold M. "The Theme of Colonialism in García Márquez' 'La increíble y triste
        historia de la candida Eréndira y de su abuela desalmada.' *Hispanic Journal* 10.1 (Fall
        1988): 67–83.

Reis, Roberto. "O Fantástico do poder e o poder do fantastico." *Ideologies & Literature* 3.13
        (June–Aug. 1980): 3–22.

Schrade, George. "El arte narrativo de García Márquez en su novela corta 'La increíble y
        triste historia de la candida Eréndira.'" *Thesaurus* (May–Aug. 1977): 374–83.

Sepúlveda Niño, Saturnino. *La prostitucion en Colombia, una quiebra de las estructuras sociales.*
        3rd ed. Bogotá: Tercer Mundo, 1970, 1976.

Siemens, William L. "The Devouring Female in Four Latin American Novels." *Essays in Literature* 1.1 (Spring 1974): 118–29.

Vargas Llosa, Mario. "Hegemonía de lo imaginario." *Historia de un deicidio*. Barcelona: Seix Barral, 1971. 617–40.

Williams, Raymond. "García Márquez y Gardeazábal ante *Cien años de soledad*: un desafío a la interpretación crítica." *Revista Iberoamericana* 47.116–17 (July–Dec. 1981): 169.

RAYMOND L. WILLIAMS

The Autumn of the Patriarch *(1975)*

INTRODUCTION AND PLOT

The publication of this novel about a dictator disappointed some of those readers who had associated García Márquez exclusively with the enchantment and accessibility of Macondo. It does not take place in Macondo and is more difficult to read than any of García Márquez's other novels. Judged strictly on its own instrinsic artistic merit, however, *The Autumn of the Patriarch* is a major book for both García Márquez and the field of the contemporary Latin-American novel. It was one of several Latin-American novels appearing in the 1970s dealing with a dictator.

The novel of the dictator is a venerable tradition in Latin America. The two best known initial novels of this type were *Tirando Banderas* (1926) by the Spaniard Ramón del Valle Inclán and *El señor presidente* (1946) by Miguel Angel Asturias. The decade of the 1970s saw the startling empowerment of military dictatorships in Latin America, particularly in the Southern Cone. As if by tacit agreement, major novelists, such as Alejo Carpentier, Augusto Roa Bastos, and García Márquez all published novels on dictators: Carpentier's *Reasons of State* appeared in 1974 and Roa Bastos's *Yo el Supremo* (*I, the supreme*) in the following year. García Márquez had begun his project at the end of a dictatorship that preceded these sanguine *caudillos* of the 1970s, that of Pérez Jiménez, ruler of Venezuela during the 1950s. Upon arriving in Caracas from Europe in 1958, García Márquez witnessed the downfall of Pérez Jiménez and the concurrent spectacle created by the outburst of a national celebration in Venezuela. The figure of Pérez Jiménez, nevertheless, was just a point of departure. García Márquez began reading histories of dictators, books containing historical anecdotes that can make the most fantastic Latin-American fiction read like stodgy realism. For example, García Márquez has told of reading about a recent Haitian dictator, Duvalier, who ordered all black dogs in the country killed because he believed one of his political enemies had transformed himself into a black dog; Maximiliano Hernández Martinez of El Salvador invented a pendulum to weigh his food before eating to assure it was not poisoned.[1] *The Autumn of the Patriarch* contains anecdotes from these history books. The author explains:

> My intention was always to make a synthesis of all the Latin American dictators, but especially those from the Caribbean. Nevertheless, the personality of Juan Vicente Gómez [of Venezuela) was so strong, in addition to the fact that he exercised a special fascination over me, that undoubtedly the Patriarch has much more of him than anyone else. In any case, the mental image that I have of both is the same. Which doesn't mean, of course, that he is the same character as the one in the book, but rather an idealization of his image.[2]

The protagonist of this novel, of course, is a dictator. A more precise definition of the theme, however, is not dictatorships but power. From those days of Pérez Jiménez's fall García Márquez was intrigued by the "mystery of power," as he called it.[3] He had dealt with this abstract notion in such stories as "Big Mama's Funeral" and several stories written between 1968 and 1972 (see chapter 5). The project on the theme of power was begun in the late 1950s, set aside, and then completed after *One Hundred Years of Solitude*. The result was a stunning and enormously complex performance in the craft of fiction.

One indicator of the change in García Márquez's fiction is the fact that this novel is not located in Colombia. The exact location of the dictator's realm is impossible to establish, although it is a nation in the Caribbean area. Some readers will find themselves locating the imaginary country in Venezuela, while others will envision an island. The text's ambiguities make both possibilities plausible. The problem is that there are references to locations that different readers will associate with specific areas of the Caribbean. García Márquez, who knows all the Caribbean intimately, explains the novel's locale as follows:

Undoubtedly, it is a country in the Caribbean. But it is a Caribbean mixed with the Spanish Caribbean and the English Caribbean. You are aware that I know the Caribbean island by island, city by city. And I've put everything there. What is mine first. The bordello where I lived in Barranquilla, the Cartagena of my student days, the little port bars where I used to eat when leaving the newspaper at four in the morning, and even the ships that at dawn would leave for Aruba and Curazao filled with whores. In it there are streets that are like the Calle del Comercio in Panamá, street corners of the old section of Havana, of San Juan and of Guajira. But also places that belong to the English Antilles, with their Hindus, Chinese, and Dutch.[4]

To speak of a plot is an equally ambiguous proposition, since there is no plot developed in a consistent fashion. The novel involves a series of anecdotes which relate to the life of a dictator identified as the General. The anecdotes do not appear in chronological order; in addition, they sometimes include such gross anachronisms as the presence of Christopher Columbus and American marines in the same scene.

The first chapter begins with the discovery of the General's rotting corpse in the presidential palace. The narrative moves quickly to anecdotes during his lifetime. The central anecdote in this chapter is what is identified as his "first death": his government-appointed double, Patricio Aragonés, dies. The General is able to observe the spectacle of popular celebration over his death. He learns a valuable lesson about the fragility of power, and consequently has those who had taken over his government assassinated, while he rewards those who mourned his death. At the end of the chapter he looks out the window facing the sea of his palace, and he sees that the marines have abandoned the dock and three Spanish ships are arriving.

The action of the second chapter is centered on the woman with whom the General falls obsessively in love, Manuela Sánchez. She is characterized somewhat like Laura Farina in "Death Constant Beyond Love." Manuela, of working-class origins, has a stunning beauty which overwhelms the General, who is rendered helpless at her sight. The relationship between Senator Onésimo Sánchez and Laura Farina is also quite similar to the one between the General and Manuela Sánchez: both men are impotent and childlike figures; both women are more mother figures for these two men than potential lovers. Manuela Sánchez disappears at the end of the chapter, never to be found, despite the rumors

of her having been sighted in different parts of the Caribbean, from
Aracataca to Panama. The General realizes he is condemned to dying
without her love, and envisions a death lying facedown between the ages
of 107 and 232 years.

The third chapter deals with the politics of power. His power seems
limitless, as he is capable of arranging the weather, and signaling with his
finger so that trees give fruit, animals grow, and men prosper. A revealing
scene with respect to the General's politics occurs when an idealistic young
foreigner visits the General to request support. The young man needs
logistic and political support for the conservative cause, for which he
professes his willingness to die. Hearing these words, the General
recommends that the young idealist not be a fool, for he should enjoy the
country while he is alive. The patriarch does not aid this conservative
idealist. One of the novel's most memorable scenes occurs at the end of the
chapter when the General intuits a plot against his government. He decides
the culprit is one of his most intimate friends, General Rodrigo de Aguilar.
The guests wait an inordinate amount of time for Rodrigo de Aguilar's
arrival, but he does finally arrive at the banquet. The chapter ends with his
grand entrance:

> and then the curtains parted and the distinguished Major General
> Rodrigo de Aguilar entered on a silver tray stretched out full
> length on a garnish of cauliflower and laurel leaves, steeped with
> spices, oven brown, embellished with the uniform of five golden
> almonds for solemn occasions and the limitless loops for valor on
> the sleeve of his right arm, fourteen pounds of medals on his
> chest and a sprig of parsley in his mouth, ready to be served at a
> banquet of comrades by the official carvers to the petrified horror
> of the guests as without breathing we witness the exquisite
> ceremony of carving and serving, and when every plate held an
> equal portion of minister of defense stuffed with pine nuts and
> aromatic herbs, he gave the order to begin, eat hearty
> gentlemen.[5]

The General's power begins to wane in the fourth chapter. His ability
to understand either his loss of power or a diminishing contact with reality
seems limited. His aging mother, Bendición Alvarado, becomes the object of
an obsession on the part of the General to have her canonized. The result of
his campaign is her being given the status of "civil sanctity" and being named
patroness of the nation. Near the end of the chapter he initiates an intimate
relationship with his future wife, Nazareno Leticia. The General becomes so

terrorized by the prospect of physical intimacy with her, however, that he defecates in his shorts.

The last two chapters narrate his final demise. The General marries Nazareno Leticia and has a child by her. The wife and child are assassinated and dogs rip apart their corpses in a public plaza. The General hires a smooth and handsome henchman, Sáenz de la Barra, to carry out the sadistic assassinations of the government needs. The supreme dictator celebrates his one hundredth anniversary in power, but thereafter his reign is one of decadence in all senses of the word. He dies unsure of the possession of the power that he exercised and by which he was tormented in the solitude of his dictatorship.

STRUCTURE, THEME, AND NARRATIVE TECHNIQUE

This basic anecdote as described above could be reduced to a nuclear verb: "A corpse is found."[6] This simple anecdote is the point of departure and frame for the actual storytelling. Each chapter begins with this basic anecdote, describing the discovery of the General's corpse in the presidential palace. The total narrative content of the novel, however, is developed beyond this discovery: it relates the General's entire life by transforming this basic anecdote of the framework into a more complete biographical revelation.

The transformation of this anecdotal material to the actual story of the text can be described by considering the novel's six chapters as a system of progressive apertures.[7] That is, the first chapter is developed on the basis of an aperture, the second on another aperture, and so on. The qualifier "progressive" underlines the fact that the apertures occur at an earlier point in each of the six chapters. These apertures occur in each of the six chapters on four levels. It must be noted, however, that each level will be discussed separately only for the clarity of analysis. In the novel's experience these levels occur simultaneously. The four levels of aperture are (1) the opening or the original situation, (2) the opening of the sentence length, (3) the opening of narrative focus, and (4) the opening of a "seen" reality. The structure of progressive apertures provides for a dynamic experience.

The first chapter establishes the basic circumstances involved with the discovery of the General's corpse, the original situation (first level) in the presidential palace. In this first scene an unidentified narrator within the story describes some vultures entering the presidential palace. With this sign, the narrator notes, he and some of his accomplices dare to enter the premises. Upon their entrance, the narrative describes the physical surroundings—for the most part decaying objects in the palace. After an initial two-and-one-half-page description of the physical surroundings, this narrator provides the first description of the General's body, an image that recurs throughout the novel: "y allí lo vimos a él con el uniforme de lienzo sin insignias, las polainas, la espuela de oro en el talón izquierdo, más viejo que todos los hombres y todos los animales viejos de la tierra y del agua, y estaba tirado en el suelo, bocabajo, con el brazo derecho doblado bajo la cabeza para que le sirviera de almohada, como había dormido noche tras noche durante todas las noches de su larguísima vida de déspota solitario"[8] ("and there we saw him, in his denim uniform without insignia, boots, the gold spur on his left heel, older than all old men and all old animals on land or sea, and he was stretched out on the floor, face down, his right arm bent under his head as a pillow, as he had slept night after night every night of his ever so long life of a solitary despot," 9–10). At approximately this point the narration changes from exclusively a description of the immediate surroundings to the telling of the General's story: "Sólo cuando lo volteamos para verle la cara comprendimos que era imposible reconocerlo aunque no hubiera estado carcomido de gallinazos, porque ninguno de nosotros lo había visto nunca ..." (8) ("Only when we turned him over to look at his face did we realize that it was impossible to recognize him, even though his face had not been pecked away by vultures, because none of us had ever seen him ...," 10).

By noting that none of them had ever actually seen the General before his death, the narrator has changed from a description of the physical surroundings to relating *past* circumstances. This is the point in the first chapter that may be identified as the "aperture" in the narrative—an opening of the original situation into a broader story.

Each of the five remaining chapters establishes the original situation as described above and follows it with an aperture to narration of the General's past. In the second chapter the narrator begins to integrate the elements of the General's story almost immediately upon beginning the description of the original situation in the presidential palace. The first sentence of the second chapter reads as follows: "La segunda vez que lo encontraron carcomido por los gallinazos en la misma oficina, con la misma ropa y en la misma posición, ninguno de nosotros era bastante viejo para recordar lo que ocurrió la primera vez, pues siempre había otra verdad detrás de la verdad" (46) ("The second time he was found, chewed away by vultures in the same office, wearing the same clothes and in the same position, none of us was old enough to remember what had happened the first time, but we knew that no evidence of his death was final, because there was always another truth behind the truth," 45). The sentence may be divided into three parts that demonstrate the way the structure of the novel functions. The first part, to the word "posición," refers to the original situation, the corpse. The second part, from "ninguno" to "primera vez," refers to that part of the story already learned by the reader, in addition to the original situation. In the third part, the story opens to present new information—that is, information other than the original situation and what the reader has already learned. By the second page of this chapter, however, the narrator has returned to the original situation, employing a short sentence that makes reference to it: "Tampoco el escrutinio meticuloso de la casa aporté elemento válido para establecer su identidad" (48) ("Nor did the meticulous scrutiny of the house bring forth any valid element to establish his identity," 46). (It is important to note the use of short sentences at the beginning of the chapters and also for reference to the original situation.) Then the narrator describes more of the physical surroundings—Bendición Alvarado's room. After approximately two and a half pages the complete opening can be identified, changing the focus from the original situation to telling the General's story: "Al contrario de la ropa, las descripciones de sus historiadores le quedaban grandes ..." (50) ("Contrary to what his clothing showed, the descriptions made by his historians made him very big ...," 47). From this point in the chapter there is no more description of the physical surroundings, and the narrative opens exclusively to the narration of the General's story. By the third chapter the transformation from the revelation of details concerning the original situation to reference to the known story occurs earlier, and the original situation is less important than in the two previous chapters (again, stressing the "progressive" nature of the structure).

The first sentence refers to the cadaver: "Asi lo encontraron en las vísperas de su otoño, cuando el cadáver era en realidad el de Patricio Aragonés, y así volvimos a encontrarlo muchos años más tarde en una época de tantas incertidumbres que nadie podía rendirse a la evidencia de que fuera suyo aquel cuerpo senil carcomido de gallinazos y plagado de parásitos de fondo de mar" (89) ("That was how they found him on the evening of his autumn, when the corpse was really that of Patricio Aragonés, and that was how we found him again many years later during a moment of such uncertainty that no one could give in to the evidence that the senile body there gouged by vultures and infested with parasites from the depths of the sea was his," 83). In this sentence there is one reference with a scope beyond the original situation: "during a moment of such uncertainty." The second sentence refers to the physical (his hand), and from this point the sentence moves toward the past. By the third sentence (still on the first page of the chapter), there are no references to the immediate physical surroundings, and the chapter has opened up to narration of the General's story. The fourth sentence (first and second page, in Spanish) and the fifth sentence (second, third, and fourth pages) make no reference to the physical environment, and mention the corpse only as a point of departure for relating to the story beyond this situation. These two sentences can be identified as the point of definitive opening of the chapter from the original situation to narration of the General's story. There are no more references to the original situation, and the opening has occurred on the second page of the chapter. The original situation has now become less important, being used more as a technical point of departure.

The first sentence of the fourth chapter deals with the General's story, making no reference to the original situation. The second sentence does refer to the corpse, and then continues beyond this original situation to relate popular opinion concerning the General: "Sin embargo, mientras se adelantaban los trámites para componer y embalsamar el cuerpo, hasta los menos cándidos esperábamos sin confesarlo el cumplimiento de predicciones antiguas, como que el día de su muerte el lodo de los cenegales había de regresar por sus afluentes hasta las cabaceras, que había de llover sangre ..." (129) ("Yet, while the plans for reassembling and embalming the body went forward, even the most candid among us waited without so confessing for the fulfillment of ancient predictions, such as the one that said that on the day of his death the mud from the swamps would go back upriver to its source, that it would rain blood ...," 120). The third sentence makes no reference to the General's physical environment. It continues relating the rumors and versions about his life. At this point on the first page the opening to narration of the General's past takes place.

In the fifth chapter the first sentence refers specifically to the original situation: "Poco antes del anochecer, cuando acabamos de sacar los cascarones podridos de las vacas y pusimos un poco de arreglo en aquel desorden de fábula, aún no habíamos conseguido que el cadáver se pareciera a la imagen de su leyenda" (169) ("Shortly before nightfall, when we finished taking out the rotten husks of the cows and putting a little order into that fabulous disarray, we were still unable to tell if the corpse looked like its legendary image," 157). The second sentence also refers to this original situation; the narrator explains the attempts made to prepare the Generals' corpse. The third sentence functions as a bridge between relating the original situation and opening to the past. It remains within the framework of the original situation, but extends the immediate present (the specificity of the corpse) by relating the meeting of officials in a nearby room ("salón de consejo") in which they begin to decide upon the division of power: "Mientras tanto, en el salón de consejo de gobierno invocábamos la unión de todos contra el despotismo de siglos para repartirse por partes iguales el botín de su poder, pues todos ..." (169) ("In the cabinet room meanwhile we called for the unity of all against the despotism of centuries so we could divide up the booty of his power in equal parts, because everyone ...," 157). The "salón de consejo" is not precisely within the scope of the original situation, and thus serves as a physical link between this situation and the relating of the General's story. The fourth sentence creates the actual opening of this narrative: "Nos encontrábamos inermes ante esa evidencia, comprometidos con un cuerpo pestilente que no éramos capaces de sustituir en el mundo porque él se había negado en sus instancias seniles a tomar ninguna determinación sobre el destino de la patria después de él, había resistido con una terquedad de viejo a cuantas sugerencias se le hicieron desde que el gobierno ..." (170) ("We were defenseless against that evidence, compromised by a pestilential corpse that we were incapable of replacing in the world because he had refused in his senile insistence to take any decision concerning the destiny of the nation after he was gone, with the invincible stubborness of an old man he had resisted all suggestions made to him ever since the government ...," 158). At the beginning of the sentence the narrator makes note of the "pestilential corpse." Then, however, the sentence begins to describe the General's actions (having refused to make any provisions for what was to be arranged after his death) previous to this basic situation, and thus marks the point of opening in the narrative: the chapter continues as the story of the General and there are no more references to the original situation.

In the last chapter, the sixth, the aperture occurs on the first page. Several parts of the sentence refer to the original situation: "Ahí estaba, pues, como si hubiera sido él aunque no to fuera, acostado en la mesa de banquetes ..."; "más temible muerto que vivo con el guante de raso relleno sobre el pecho ..." (214) ("There he was, then, as if it had been he even though it might not be, lying on the banquet table ... "; "more fearsome dead than alive, the velvet glove stuffed with cotton on a chest ...," 203). Toward the end of the first page the narrator changes the focus to a previous discussion, which, in turn, leads to opening the narrative to related matters: "discutíamos palabra por palabra el boletín final con la noticia que nadie se atrevía ..." (219) ("we were discussing the final bulletin with the news that no one dared believe word by word ...," 203).

Both tradition and innovation are descriptive of the effect of this aperture on the first level, or the original situation. The manner in which physical space functions in this novel corresponds in a sense to the realist-naturalist tradition: the beginning of the novel focuses more precisely on the physical space; then, after the physical environment has been described at the outset of the novel, the narrator elaborates the anecdotal material with less background provided for the reader in terms of setting. On the other hand, the reader does not experience place in exactly the same manner as in the traditional novel. García Márquez manipulates physical space to such a degree that the reader finds himself progressively more limited in terms of physical space and background setting, and at the same time progressively more involved in the elaboration of the General's life.

These apertures that function as points indicating change from the original situation to the General's story are supported technically by the use of a progressive opening of the length of the sentence.[9] This is the second level of aperture. The sentences lengthen at approximately the same point in each of the chapters as the noted point at which the transformation from the original situation to the General's story occurs. In each chapter the beginning sentences might be identified as a normal length. The sentences then expand in length as the chapter continues. The progressive nature of this development is evidenced by the fact that each chapter has fewer sentences: chapter 1 has thirty-one sentences; chapter 2, twenty-four sentences; chapter 3, nineteen sentences; chapter 4, eighteen sentences; chapter 5, fifteen sentences; and chapter 6 is a single sentence.

In the first chapter the sentences on the first page might be described as a "normal" length—that is, of eight, eight, and five lines, respectively, in the text. The fourth sentence (ending the first page and beginning the second) expands to twenty-one lines. Throughout the next seven pages (to page 12, in the Spanish text) the length of the sentences varies, but remains approximately within the limits of the sentences on the first two pages, ranging from a few lines in length to a full page (thirty-five lines in the text). Then, on page 12, the first significant opening of the length of the sentence takes place, with the sentence on pages 12 and 13 being sixty-four lines in length. From this point, sentences become progressively longer, or at least tend to maintain the length of the longer sentences observed (about a page or slightly more).

The change in sentence length is abrupt in the second chapter. On the first two pages the sentences tend to be relatively short. As in the first chapter, the first sentence is eight lines. The second sentence, the longest in the beginning pages, consists of thirty lines (slightly less than a page); the remainder of the sentences on the first two pages range from three to twenty-one lines. At approximately the same point where the narrative changes its focus from the original situation to the General's story, the sentence length expands to a page or more. The change from the original situation to past description has been noted on page 50 in this second chapter (in Spanish text). The initial expansion of the sentence also takes place on page 50; the sentence on pages 50–51 is thirty-five lines, or a full page, in length. From this point the narrative opens (both in its circumstance and in sentence length), and the remaining sentences of the chapter tend to be longer than a page rather than shorter than a page.

The progressive nature of the openings in sentence length is equally evident in the third, fourth, and fifth chapters. In the third chapter there are three sentences before the extension of the length, and the fourth and fifth chapters contain two sentences and one sentence of normal length, respectively. The sentences that mark these openings in the three chapters are of twenty-eight lines, forty-nine lines, and twenty-two lines. In each case the change in sentence length is noted at the same place in the text that marked the change from the original situation as discussed.

The last chapter begins "Ahí estaba, pues como si hubiera ..." (219) ("There he was, then, as if it had been ..., 203). This is a reference to the corpse and the immediate situation. Within this same sentence the chapter opens to related matters on the first page ("we were discussing"). The opening in terms of sentence length reaches the extreme; the entire chapter is one sentence of one thousand eight hundred and twenty-five lines (in Spanish text). This change is in accordance with the progressive nature of the structure as it has been discussed. Although more extreme than in the previous chapters, this length is a logical step in the development: sentences have become progressively longer in each chapter.

The progressive and precise manner of organizing the sentence length in correspondence with the opening of the original situation contributes to the formation of the narrative system García Márquez constructs in this novel. Although apparently lacking in punctuation (in the first reading), this novel employs punctuation in a manner different from its traditional function in prose; the specific placement of the period corresponds to the poetic use of textual space. Such technical precision supports García Márquez's contention that this novel is a "poem about the solitude of power."[10]

The third level of aperture, also corresponding to the first two, is the opening of narrative focus. The narrative focus in which each chapter begins is relatively limited; then it opens to other points of view, and in some cases to multiple points of view within the same sentence. This variation of the narrative's focus, by use of the apertures to be described, has various effects and is a particularly important aspect of the experience of the novel.[11]

An unidentified narrator within the story recounts the beginning pages of the first chapter. He and other unidentified accomplices enter the presidential palace to discover the rotting corpse. For this reason this narrator will be referred to as the "narrator-discoverer." Thus, the initial pages are narrated in the first-person plural ("we saw"). The first sentence does not identify a narrator as necessarily within the story, and technically it could be told by a narrator outside the story: "Durante el fin de semana los gallinazos se metieron por los balcones de la casa presidencial, destrozaron a picotazos las mallas de alambre de las ventanas y removieron con sus alas el tiempo estancado en el interior, y en la madrugada del lunes la ciudad despertó de su letargo de siglos con una tibia y tierna brisa de muerto grande y de podrida grandeza." (5) ("Over the weekend the vultures got into the presidential palace by pecking through the screens on the balcony windows and the flapping of their wings stirred up the stagnant time inside, and at dawn on Monday the city awoke out of its lethargy of centuries with the warm, soft breeze of a great man dead and rotting grandeur," 7).

From the beginning of the next sentence the position of the narrator within the story is evident: "Sólo entonces nos atrevimos a entrar ..." (5) ("Only then did we dare go in ...," 7). For approximately the next three pages the narrative remains within the scope of this narrator who enters the palace in the company of others. By the fourth page, however, the narrative begins to open to other speakers. The first change occurs on page 9 in the Spanish text (page 11 in English text) in which the narrator inside the story is relating details about the physical environment, and suddenly the narrative changes to several words that originate from another speaker: "y una tarde de enero habíamos visto una vaca contemplando el crepúsculo desde el balcón presidencial, imaginese, una vaca en el balcón de la patria, qué cosa más inicua, qué pass de mierda" (9) ("and one January afternoon we had seen a cow contemplating the sunset from the presidential balcony, just imagine, a cow on the balcony of the nation, what an awful thing, what a shitty country," 11). The "just imagine" interrupts the original narrator's account through the use of this conversational style. In this case the narrative has changed from pure narration to inferring a live dialogue. This point in the narrative, noted as the opening of the narrative focus (transcending the limits of the narrator-discoverer), occurs in the same sentence already discussed, changing from the original situation to the story of the General. Later in the chapter, as the sentences lengthen, the length of the communications by other speakers is extended.

The second chapter begins once more with the relatively "closed" narrative focus of the narrator-discoverer. The first change in this focus, an expansion beyond the limits of this narrator, occurs in the place identified as the point of aperture on the two other levels, on the fourth and fifth pages of the chapter (page 50–51; pages 47–48 in English text). Here, the narrator changes his scope from a general knowledge to the specific words of the General. The key sentence in which this change takes place reads as follows: (I quote it through the first change in narrative focus): "Esta certidumbre parecía válida inclusive para él, pues se sabía que era un hombre sin padre

como los déspotas más ilustres de la historia, que el único pariente que se le
conoció y tal vez único que tuvo fue su madre de mi alma Bendición Alvarado
a quien los textos escolares ..." (51) ("That certainly seemed valid even for
him, as he knew that he was a man without a father like the most illustrious
despots of history, that the only relative known to him and perhaps the only
one he had was his mother of my heart Bendición Alvarado to whom the
school texts ...," 48) The words "se sabía" ("it was known") exemplify the
level of communication identified as general knowledge—that which
everybody (or all the inhabitants) knows.[12] Later in this sentence the first
opening beyond the limits of this narrator and general knowledge is noted
with the word "mi," either the actual speech of the General or the narrator's
imitation of his words. Three additional parts of this sentence express a focus
beyond general knowledge. First, the narrator states: "a quien él proclamó
por decreto matriarca de la patria con el argumento simple de que madre no
hay sino una, la mía, una rara mujer de origen incierto ..., (51) ("and whom
he proclaimed matriarch of the land by decree with the simple argument that
there is no mother but one, mine, a strange woman of uncertain origins ...,"
48). Later in the same sentence the first longer opening of narrative focus in
the chapter takes place in the voice of the General's mother:

> ni podía soportar que había dicho en una fiesta diplomática que
> estoy cansada de rogarle a Dios que tumben a mi hijo, porque
> esto de vivir en la casa presidencial es como estar a toda hora con
> la luz prendida, señor, y lo había dicho con la misma verdad
> natural con que un día de la patria ... (51)

> nor could they bear the fact that at a diplomatic party she had said
> I'm tired of begging God to overthrow my son, because all this
> business of living in the presidential palace is like having the
> lights on all the time, sir, and she had said it with the same
> naturalness with which on one national holiday ..., (49).

At the end of the sentence another phrase changes to the mother's actual
words, and the last two words are of the General. From this point in the
chapter the focus of the narrative has been opened, and the voices continue
to vary as the chapter proceeds, such changes becoming more frequent and
lengthy.

 In accordance with the progressive nature of the structure, the opening
of focus occurs at an earlier point in the third chapter than in the first two.
The narrator-discoverer who begins the chapter has entire control of the
narrative for only the first page. In the fourth sentence the chapter opens in

sentence length and likewise into the past beyond the original situation. It is also this fourth sentence that opens the narrative to speakers other than the narrator-discoverer. This takes place on the second page of the chapter and in the words of Palmerston (page 90 in Spanish; page 84 in English). Palmerston's voice continues for eighteen lines: at this point in the novel the opening of narrative focus not only occurs earlier than in the previous chapters, now there is an *extensive* opening from the beginning of the chapter. The sixth sentence, the longest of the chapter (207 lines in Spanish), contains numerous changes in speaker.

The fourth chapter is structured quite similarly to the third, contains approximately the same number of sentences, and does not vary significantly from the procedures noted in the third chapter. The chapter opens, in sentence length, in the third sentence (forty-nine lines, in Spanish). With the fourth sentence, of forty lines, the focus expands with the use of short phrases in the voices of characters other than the narrator-discoverer. Thus, on the third page of the chapter (page 131; page 122 in English) a character says "adiós" to the General, and later in the same sentence we find the short phrase: "al pasar con un pañuelo blanco, adiós mi general, adiós, pero él no oía nada desde los lutos crepusculares ..." (131) ("with a white handkerchief when he passed, hello general sir, hello, but he didn't hear, he had heard nothing since the sunset mourning rites ...," 122). From this point, the sentence that opens the narrative focus, the fourth chapter continues with at least short interruptions of the narration of the narrator-discoverer. The opening of the narrative focus takes place slightly earlier in the fifth chapter than in the fourth. The opening to the General's story has been seen in the fourth sentence, and this is the point at which the narrative focus opens beyond the narrator-discoverer. This chapter also contains another of the rare, extensive uninterrupted monologues by the General (thirteen lines on pages 201–2; pages 187–88 in English). It is significant both in theme and structure: (1) the subject of this monologue is his "mar," an object very important to the General's power, and (2) as in the extensive monologue in the previous chapter, it occurs near the end of the chapter where the length of the sentence is extended and in the second longest sentence of the chapter (214 lines).

The last chapter carries the progressive nature of the structure to its extreme by opening to the General's story on the first page and extending the sentence to constitute the entire chapter. The use of various speakers also takes place earlier than before, beginning immediately after the first page of the chapter: "un teniente que iba de puerta en puerta ordenando cerrar las pocas tiendas que empezaban a abrirse en la calle del comercio, hoy es feriado nacional gritaba ..." (220) ("a lieutenant going from door to door ordering people to close the doors of the few shops that were beginning to open on the commercial street, today is a national holiday they shouted," 204). Other brief changes in the narrative voice follow on the same page and immediately thereafter. The variety of narrative voices present in this one-sentence chapter makes it the most complex of all. These speakers appear more frequently and their communication is more extensive than in the preceding chapters. At the beginning of the chapter the first extensive change in narrative focus is communicated in the words of an adolescent girl whom the General seduces, an act described by her in a monologue of twenty-seven lines (page 222; page 206 in English). The second monologue on the following page is by another of his lovers. It also describes the General's sexual preferences from the point of view of a woman, a monologue of nineteen lines (page 223; page 207 in English). Afterward and throughout the chapter, there are numerous short dialogues by the General and other characters, such as José Ignacio Sáenz de la Barra, Commander Kitchener, Consul Macdonnal, Bendición Alvarado, Ambassador Kipling, unidentified officials close to the General, and unidentified citizenry.

One function of the changing narrative focus is to provide a more complete characterization of the General, which, in turn, is responsible for humorous effects in this characterization. A common technique is to place emphasis on the General's omnipotence (usually the "exterior" view of the General) in contrast with his fundamental simplicity (usually the "interior" view of him). Power is expressed from the first page as something intangible but perceived by all under the General's rule. The narrator-discoverer reveals the generalized perception of the General's power by professing to believe in the General's power to order trees to bear fruit: "power was still not the shoreless bog of the fullness of his autumn but a feverish torrent that we saw gush out of its spring before our very eyes so that all he had to do was point at trees for them to bear fruit and at animals for them to grow and at men for them to prosper ..." (87). As this passage suggests in both its content and style, according to the "exterior" and distanced view, the General is a God-like figure.[13]

The inside view of the General and his power supports this God-like characterization, and also creates humor by showing the pettiness of his conception of power (in contrast with the grandiosity of the God figure), and his paranoia and puerility. Once the first chapter has opened beyond the generalized view, an omniscient narrator communicates the General's God-like understanding of his capacity to decide "destiny." When he justifies the assassination of officials who betray him, he does so with a God-like expression of being their creator (page 116; page 109 in English).

In contrast with the God-like power that he manipulates both in the view of the citizenry and in his own self-esteem, the inside view consistently emphasizes his pettiness and puerility. Throughout the novel the General carefully and repetitively locks an elaborate combination of "the three crossbars, the three locks, the three bolts" in his room, thus underlining his paranoia. Despite his God-like self-confidence, his friend Rodrigo de Aguilar is the only person "authorized" to defeat him in dominoes. The General's simplicity is an aspect of his characterization not revealed by the narrator-discoverer. The General is characterized as such after the narrative focus has opened to other speakers beyond the voice of the citizenry. In the first chapter, after the narrative opens beyond the narrator-discoverer, an omniscient narrator explains that the General oversees the milking of the cows each day in order to measure the exact amount of milk the presidential carts carry to the city, providing a humorous contrast with the grandiose figure seen by the citizenry, and even with the interior view of himself as a God figure. When the General decides to find his love, Manuela Sánchez, his search for her resembles an adolescent experience: he looks for her in the neighborhood, nervously asks various people for directions to the home he describes, and after introducing himself to her mother, waits anxiously in the living room while her mother knits.

His characterization as a child figure is developed from the beginning of the novel when he is described as a "decrepit child." At one point he joyfully plays with his live siren, wind-up angel, and giant shell. In general, the relationship between the mother and son tends to be a mother–child relationship. For example, she reprimands him about his health and informs him that he must stay home for dinner. After his mothers death, he marries Leticia Nazareno and she assumes the mother role. She teaches him to read and write, the important factor here being the infantile methodology she uses: he recites children's songs.

The technique of contrasting the exterior and interior views of the General is particularly effective in certain passages in which a particular anecdote changes from the exterior to the interior focus within one sentence. For example, an attempted assassination is foiled by the General when, as the potential assassin holds him at gunpoint, he confronts the man and screams: "atrévete cabrón, atrévete" ("I dare you you bastard, I dare you"). When the assassin hesitates, the General attacks him, calls his guards, and orders the victim tortured. After the narration of this anecdote by an omniscient narrator (with occasional interjections by the General), the story is completed by providing at the very end of the sentence the interior focus (of which those who saw him were not aware): "desapareció en la sala de audiencias como un relámpago fugitivo hacia los aposentos privados, entró en el dormitorio, cerró las tres aldabas, los tres pestillos, los tres cerrojos, y se quitó con la punta de los dedos los pantalones que llevaba ensopados de mierda" (123) ("he disappeared into the hearing room like a fugitive lightning flash toward the private quarters, he went into the bedroom, shut the three crossbars, the three bolts, the three locks, and with his fingertips he took off the pants he was wearing that were soaked in shit," 115). Until the narrator reveals the General's reactions in the last three words, the reader's view has been exterior and similar to that of the people observing the General's reactions. The last three words provide the interior contrasting characterization of the General and thus creates the humor.

The fourth, and final, level of aperture in the structure of *The Autumn of the Patriarch* is the opening to a "seen" reality; or one could say that this fourth level is an opening of the dimensions of reality experienced in the novel. Each chapter begins with defined limits of reality—that which can be seen. The reader experiences this manipulation of visible and invisible reality in conjunction with the three other levels of aperture.

In the first scene of the novel, vultures are entering the presidential palace". The first suggestion that the General is dead is thus provided by visual means. From this sentence and throughout the novel, it becomes apparent that only that which is seen may possibly be believed: the General, the citizenry, and the reader learn to believe only what they can see.[14] This problem of visible and invisible reality is fundamental to the main theme of the novel—the General's power—and to the reader's experience. After the description of the vultures, the visible sign of death, the narrator-discoverer emphasizes the importance of what can be *seen*: "y las cosas eran arduamente visibles en la luz decrépita ..." (5) ("and things were hard to see in the decrepit light," 7). He follows with an elaboration of his realm of the visible, using the verb "to see" repetitively (pages 5–6 in Spanish; pages 7–8 in English). The final use of the verb "to see" at the beginning of the chapter takes place when they discover the General's corpse. Appropriately, upon describing this visible image of the General, the narrative opens to beyond what this narrator can see—the point of aperture in the chapter. In the sentence following the description of the General, for example, the conjugated verbs are "comprender" ("to understand") and "saber" ("to know"). The narrative changes from what can be seen to what is understood, and to what has been related.

The first sentence of the second chapter sets forth the actual theme—the problem of the visible versus illusion—thus discussing the experience of living under the General's power and the process elaborated by the novel's structure: "La segunda vez que to encontraron carcomido por los gallinazos en la misma oficina, con la misma ropa y en la misma posición, ninguno de nosotros era bastante viejo para recordar to que ocurrió la primera vez, pero sabíamos que ninguna evidencia de su muerte era terminante, pues siempre había otra verdad detrás de la verdad. Ni siquiera los menos prudentes nos conformábamos con las apariencias ..." (47) ("The second time he was found, chewed away by vultures in the same office, wearing the same clothes and in the same position, none of us was old enough to remember what had happened the first time, but we knew that no evidence of his death was final, because there was always another truth behind the truth. Not even the least prudent among us would accept ...," 45). After this initial suggestion of one of the novel's fundamental themes, the narrator-discoverer once more describes the experience of entering the palace by relating exclusively what he sees: "vimos un sillón de mimbre mordisqueado por las vacas ... vimos estuches de pinturas de agua ... vimos una tinaja ..." (48) ("we saw a wicker easy chair nibbled by the cows ... we saw watercolor sets ... we saw a tub ...," 46). When they enter the General's bedroom the verb employed is "to find" ("encontramos"), rather than "to see," but stress continues to fall on the tangible. At this point in the chapter the emphasis changes from what is actually seen to what has been said.

In the third chapter the opening takes place on the first page of the chapter. The verb "to see" is not employed, but the verb "to find" functions similarly, indicating something tangible. The narrator-discoverer describes the General in the first sentence of the chapter: "y así volvimos a encontrarlo muchos años más tarde en una época de tantas incertidumbres que nadie podía rendirse a la evidencia de que fuera suyo aquel cuerpo senil carcomido de gallinazos y plagado de parásitos de fondo de mar" (90) ("and that was how we found him again many years later during a moment of such uncertainty that no one could give in to the evidence that the senile body there gouged by vultures and infested with parasites from the depths of the sea was his," 83). The second sentence also describes the strictly visible. The next sentence changes the emphasis from the visible: the narrator explains what it seemed like and what they doubted.

The first sentence of the fifth chapter refers to the problem of the visible versus the invisible General, the latter being the one that has been imagined, the one that has been created through general knowledge, that is, "se dice" ("it is said") or "se contaba" ("it was told"): "we were still unable to tell if the corpse looked like its legendary image" (157). In this instance the narrator-discoverer is in the presence of the visible General, but an attempt is being made to change him so that he might correspond to the reality—his legend—that has superseded the real and tangible. The second sentence involves the actual physical process through which reconciliation of these two realities is attempted. The theme of the visible versus the invisible reality is abandoned by the third sentence and the chapter opens beyond this problem to a meeting of officials after the General's death.

Just as in the previous chapters, the last chapter uses as its point of departure the theme of the visible General versus the popular legend. The first words of the first line emphasize his visual image: "Ahí estaba, pues como si hubiera sido él aunque no to fuera ..." (203) ("There he was, then, as if it had been even though ...," 203). At this point the theme of the visible versus the invisible has become problematical: it appears to be the General even if it is not, and it is impossible to make any definitive statement concerning the matter. Later in the first page there is another direct reference to the problem of the visible General versus the invisible, in this case affirming the importance of the visible within this fictional world. By the last chapter the characterization of the General only affirms the observation made concerning the reiteration of the verb "to see" in the beginning chapters of the novel: only the visible offers the possibility of being believable, although it certainly does not assure credibility.

This fourth level of the structure is fundamental to the novel's experience not only because this experience is based considerably on the manipulation of the visible and the invisible, but also because the General controls power and the image he projects by manipulating what is visible. Thus, there is a correlation between characterization and character and also between them and technique. When the General actually sees his own death (that of his double) in the first chapter, the experience changes him profoundly. This anecdote is described by means of a repetition of the verb "to see." The intensity of this experience is based on the fact that he sees death. Just as death becomes a reality for the General after he sees it, he confides only in reality as he can observe it, and becomes a victim of the circumstances he has created through his power. When he falls in love with Manuela Sánchez, he attempts to attract her with the visible manifestation of his power. Logically, the maximum gift for his maximum love, then, is the most impressive visual spectacle possible. Thus, his gift for Manuela Sánchez is a comet.

Maintenance of power is determined by the General's ability to manipulate the visible and the invisible. After a potential assassin fails to kill him, the General not only orders the man put to death, but more significantly in the context of his own understanding of the importance of the visible, he orders that the different parts of the assassin's body be exhibited throughout the country, thus providing a visible manifestation of the consequences of questioning the General's power. When he feels the necessity for exerting maximum control of his power, he visibly observes its functioning. This also explains the General's bizarre insistence in observing the milking of the cows each morning. On the other hand, when his power is threatened by the church (it denies sainthood to his mother), the General takes direct control of the situation, declares "civil sainthood" for his mother, and, given the seriousness of the situation, visibly oversees the fulfillment of his orders. In one description the General is portrayed as most content when he has a complete view of his country through his window. Similarly, he considers himself less responsible for that which he does not see. He feels no compunction about ordering the massacre of two thousand children, because he does not observe the actual killing, and the brutal maneuvers of Sáenz de la Barra are of little consequence to him because they are covert. Being aware of this importance of the visible, one of the General's officials suggests that Sáenz might be eliminated from the government if there were some way the General could see the atrocities taking place.

The question of the visible and the invisible and its relation to the novel's main theme, power, is also elaborated through the presence of the sea ("mar") in the novel. As the superb visible object in the General's daily life, the "mar" is his most treasured possession. The "mar" is first mentioned in the first chapter when, after a reiteration of the verb "to see," the narrator-discoverer ends a sentence on the third page of the novel as follows: "vimos los cráteres muertos de ásperas cenizas de luna de llanura sin término donde habia estado el mar" (7) ("we saw the dead craters of harsh moon ash on the endless plain where the sea had been," 9). Early in the novel such a reference to the "mar" seems inexplicable. In the context of the novel and the General's concept of power, it is understood that, since the General conceives of his "mar" as lost, it is naturally perceived as such by the citizenry, which is totally indoctrinated by him. In the first chapter the "mar" also becomes closely associated with his window, and from this point his window and his "mar" are inseparable in the novel. Technically, this association is established through the use of the preposition "de" ("of"): "oyó por la ventana abierta del mar los tambores lejanos las taitas tristes ... (25) ("through the open windows facing the sea he could hear the distant drums ...," 25–26). When the General condemns some political prisoners to death, international pressure is placed upon him to annul the order. In such moments of crisis, he contemplates from his window. As he gradually loses control of his power, he turns to his window more often. At the end of the fifth chapter, decrepit and in his hundredth year of power, he goes to his window and watches the sea, seemingly observing his very loss of power: "iba viendo pasar el mismo mar por las ventanas ..." (216) ("he went along seeing as he passed the same sea through the windows ...," 201).

His window, his "mar," and his power become so intimately associated that the General insists upon maintaining possession of his window and "mar" as persistently as he does with reference to maintaining his power. When he is in the process of losing his power, he is adamant about not losing his "mar." In one of his extensive dialogues with an ambassador, he defends his position concerning the sea:

> trying to explain to him that he could take anything he wanted except the sea of my windows, just imagine, what would I do all alone in this big building if I couldn't look out now as always at this time at what looks like a marsh in flames, what would I do without the December winds that sneak in barking through the broken windowpanes, how could I live without the green flashes of the lighthouse, I who abandoned my misty barrens and enlisted to the agony of fever in the tumult of the federalist war, and don't you think that I did it out of patriotism as the dictionary says, or from the spirit of adventure, or least of all because I gave a shit about federal principles which God keep in his holy kingdom, no my dear Wilson, I did it all so I could get to know the sea.... (187–88)

He has a similar response later for Ambassador Stevenson. When yet another ambassador attempts to make a deal, the General once more refuses. The sign that the General has lost his power is the selling of his sea at the end of the novel: "I granted them the right to make use of our territorial waters in the way they considered best for the interests of humanity and peace among peoples, with the understanding that said cession not only included the physical waters visible from the window of his bedroom to the horizon but everything that is understood by sea in the broadest sense, or, the flora and fauna belonging to said waters ..." (230–31). The General has lost his maximum view and all that was significant for him: "they carried off everything that had been the reasons for my wars and the motive of his power ..." (231).

The four levels of the novel's structure as described above are functional in the elaboration of the novel's themes. The opening of the original situation into the General's story provides a complete characterization of the General not limited by traditional subordination of the narration to the requirements of space and time. The latter are subordinate, in *The Autumn of the Patriarch*, to the act of narrating itself. The opening of the sentence supports this first opening technically, and is a specific device that provides for a progressively more elaborate textual presentation of the story. The opening of the narrative focus provides for a multiplicity of views of the General, and this is significant not only in the complexity and completeness of the characterization of him, but also in establishing the novel's tone—the humor that is fundamental to the experience of the novel. On the final level, the opening of a seen reality into a confluence of the visible and the invisible, the experience of the novel becomes similar to the principle theme it develops: the illusion of reality and power. To a considerable extent, the universalization of this theme through specific techniques creates the reader's experience. Although the cycle of novels focused on Macondo is finished, the universal experience created in *The Autumn of the Patriarch* is a continuation of the transcendent regionalism so evident in García Márquez's previous work, especially *One Hundred Years of Solitude*.

NOTES

1. *El olor de la guayaba*, 88.

2. Ibid., 86.

3. Ibid., 85.

4. Ibid., 89.

5. *The Autumn of the Patriarch* (New York, 1977), p. 119; all quotations in English are from this edition.

6. This reference to Gérard Genette is explained in "Discours du récit" which appears in *Figures III* (Paris: Sevil, 1972). *In the introduction Genette suggests the possibility of considering a story on the basis of the expansion of a verb. He notes that for the Odyssey the verb would be "Ulysses returns to Ithaca" and for A la Recherche du temps perdu, "Marcel becomes a writer."*

7. This structure was originally delineated in my article "The Dynamic Structure of García Márquez's *El otoño del patriarca*," *Symposium* 32, no. 1 (Spring 1978): 56–75. The analysis in this article contains more textual references than the length of this chapter allows.

8. *El otoño del patriarca* (Buenos Aires, 1975), 8; all quotations in Spanish are from this edition.

9. José Miguel Oviedo has noted the progression in sentence length. See "García Márquez: la novela como taumaturgia," *American Hispanist* 1, no. 2 (October 1975): 7.

10. *El olor de la guayaba*, 87.

11. John M. Lipski discusses the changes in narrative perspective in "Embedded Dialogue in *El otoño del patriarca*," *American Hispanist* 2, no. 14 (January 1977): 9–12.

12. Julio Ortega discusses the implications of impersonal expressions such as "se sabía" in "*El otoño del patriarca*: texto y cultura," *Hispanic Review* 46 (1978): 421–46.

13. George McMurray discusses the characterization of the General as a myth in *Gabriel García Márquez*, pp. 129–56.

14. Seymour Menton has suggested that even what is seen cannot be believed. Yet only that which is seen offers the possibility of being believed. See "Ver para no creer: *El otoño del patriarca*," *Caribe* 1, no. 1 (Spring 1976): 7–27.

JO LABANYI

Language and Power in
The Autumn of the Patriarch

Language and power are closely linked. We use language to persuade, that is, to manipulate others into acquiescence. We call a statement true if it has power over us. The authority of language derives from the notion of authorship, the assumption that language is the direct expression of a central, unified voice. The statement which does not have a clear relationship to the voice that speaks it does not have authority. Reported speech is less authoritative than direct speech because its relationship to its source has become adulterated. Writing, as Derrida has shown, is frequently regarded as an extreme form of reported—and therefore adulterated—speech.[1] As a novel about power, *The Autumn of the Patriarch* is inevitably concerned with the expression of power via language, and particularly via the written word. It is a disconcerting novel, because it depicts a dictator who is not directly responsible for his commands, but becomes their prisoner. García Márquez's creation of a powerless tyrant looks, at first sight, politically naive. The novel can be read, however, not as an attempt to exonerate dictators of their crimes, but as an exploration of the relationship between power and language. This relationship is shown to work in two directions. On the one hand, language is the patriarch's principal instrument of power. On the other, it is his increasing delegation of power to language that brings about his

From *Gabriel García Márquz: New Readings*, Bernard McGuirk and Richard Cardwell, ed. © 1987 Cambridge University Press.

downfall. García Márquez shows that language can undermine power as well as enforce it.

The power of speech is referred to at the beginning of the novel. 'We did not have to force an entry, as we had thought, because the main door seemed to yield to the mere force of the human voice' (p. 7).[2] The patriarch's authority resides in his voice: 'he spat out a lethal blast of authority with his words' (p. 73). But, for most of the novel, the patriarch exercises his power via reported speech. His voice is not heard directly, but his commands are relayed at second hand from an invisible centre of power. He is a dictator in the literal sense of the word, someone who dictates his words to others. To be more precise, the 'autumn' of his reign is inaugurated by the transition from direct to reported speech. Decadence sets in when he ceases to be a presence and becomes a legend, heard but not seen. The dependence of the patriarch's authority on hearsay is underlined by the repeated ironic use in the novel of the phrase 'we saw', when what is meant is that the people see only what legend has told them.[3] They see the dead patriarch not as he actually died, but as the prophecy had said he would. They have no way of checking the authentic identity of the corpse, because they can measure what they see only against a remote chain of verbal accounts:

> Only when we turned him over to see his face did we realize there was no way of recognizing him ... because none of us had ever seen him and although his profile was on both sides of all the coins ... we knew they were copies of copies of portraits which were deemed unfaithful at the time of the comet, when our parents knew who he was because they had been told by their parents, as they had been told by theirs. (p. 8)

Seeing has been replaced by hearing.

The patriarch's reliance on reported speech strengthens his power in the sense that his existence via second-hand verbal repetitions leads to the attribution to him of a superhuman ubiquity. What this really means is that he is nowhere, except in the form of words. In effect, the replacement of the patriarch's presence by hearsay adulterates his authority, inasmuch as it leads to a usurpation of his voice: 'On many occasions it was held that he had lost his voice from so much speaking and had ventriloquists posted behind the curtains pretending he was speaking' (p. 49). The first chapter of the novel specifies that the patriarch's 'autumn' begins with his recourse to a double, who replaces him on most of his public appearances. García Márquez points out that the one area where the double is not able to provide an exact replica of the original is that of speech: '"That's me damn it", he said, because it was, indeed, as if it were he, except for the authority of his voice, which the double had never learnt to imitate properly' (p. 14). The linguistic nature of the usurpation is emphasized by the fact that the double has a name (Patricio Aragonés), while the patriarch has none. The patriarch's voice has passed to a substitute; language has become independent of its source.

The patriarch's recourse to reported speech creates a power vacuum, as authority comes to reside increasingly in the words themselves rather than in the voice from which they originate. The more he conceals his presence, the more absolutely his commands are obeyed, to the extent that they begin to be obeyed without him even voicing them: 'all in accord with an order he had not given but which was an order of his beyond any doubt my general because it had the imperturbable firmness of his voice and the incontrovertible style of his authority' (p. 178). The mere thought that it would be preferable for his wife and son to be dead rather than live daily with the fear of their death leads to their murder. 'It was like a thunderous command not yet articulated when his aides burst into his office with the ghastly news that Leticia Nazareno and the child had been torn to pieces and devoured by the dogs' (p. 199). Language, having become independent of its master, has turned against him.

From this point on, the patriarch's role as the absent centre of command makes him increasingly dependent on the reports of the outside world that he receives from his informers. Since these reports reflect back at him the commands he had previously issued, he becomes trapped in a series of mirror-reflections: 'a captive monarch ... dragging his heavy feet through the dark mirrors' (pp. 215–16). In the same way, he comes to rely on information extracted under torture which, again, reflects back at him what he wants to see. The ironic leitmotif 'we saw' is paralleled by the equally ironic 'he saw'. Like the people, the patriarch does not see reality but hears his own legend. 'He had seen this and many other things in that remote world although not even he could be sure whether they really were memories or tales he had heard' (p. 173). By the end of the novel, the patriarch has become symbolically deaf to the outside world—'deaf like a mirror' (p. 131)—able to hear only the noise of the silence inside his own head.

The ironic confusion of seeing with hearing is at its most amusing when the patriarch notices outside his window the three caravels of Christopher Columbus which his informers have told him about. In this scene, something important has happened: the three caravels are derived indirectly from a written text—Columbus's diary—from which García Márquez quotes to reinforce the point. Seeing here has become confused not just with hearing but also with reading. The patriarch is forced to rely on second-hand oral reports, because at this stage in the novel he is still illiterate. The absurd logic of this scene implies that, if the written word has the authority with which the patriarch credits it, then he has been living all this time in an undiscovered—indeed non-existent—world. The patriarch's 'invention' of the nation in his patriotic speeches—'The fatherland is the best thing that's ever been invented, mother' (p. 22)—pales into insignificance in comparison with the ability of the written word to 'invent' the whole continent of America, himself included. The patriarch is, of course, ironically unaware that he is indeed the creation of a written text, that his invention by García Márquez means that he exists only in words.

A key point in the novel, when the patriarch is for the first time confronted directly with the power of the written word, is the recital given by the poet Rubén Dario. The recital makes such a strong impact because the written word is combined with the speaking voice of the author. Dario's reading of his poem 'Marcha triunfal' (from which García Márquez again quotes) reveals to the patriarch a verbal power which transcends that of any mortal ruler and whose authority is absolute:

> He saw the heroic athletes... he saw the ranks of warlike youths [fighting for] the eternal splendour of an immortal fatherland greater and more glorious than any he had ever imagined ... he felt impoverished and diminished ... dazzled by the revelation of written beauty. (pp. 194–5)

What attracts the patriarch in Dario's poetry is his attempt to create an eternal, universal poetic language that transcends the limitations of human existence. For the patriarch, writing has the value of memory; it is an attempt to perpetuate through repetition that which otherwise is condemned to oblivion. After the recital, he takes to 'writing the verses on the lavatory walls, trying to recite the whole poem from memory' (p. 195). His second-hand repetitions inevitably fail to reproduce the power of the author's original rendition. The futility of the attempt to immortalize reality via the written word is underlined by García Márquez's ironic application to the decaying palace of the euphemisms and mythological references which characterize Dario's poetic language: 'in the calid Olympus of the cowshit in the dairy' (p. 195). The choice of Dario as the patriarch's literary mentor is appropriate, not only because of his reputation as the doyen of Spanish American letters, but also because a major theme of his later poetry is the fear of death.

The early part of chapter 5, where Dario's recital is narrated, describes the efforts of Leticia Nazareno to teach the patriarch to read and write. Even at the beginning of his 'autumn', while still illiterate, the value attached by the patriarch to the ability of writing to preserve human life could be seen in his choice of two ministers, 'his private doctor and another who was the nation's best calligrapher' (p. 37). The adulteration of authority that began with the transition from direct to reported speech is completed with the patriarch's initiations in the later part of the novel, into writing. The delegation of his power to the written word leads to his mythification, in the sense that the manifestations of his existence become increasingly remote from their source. An image of the mythical prestige of the written word, as the trace of an absent voice, can be seen in the description, in that chapter in which the patriarch discovers writing, of the patriarch's footprint: 'In that imprint/trace [Sp. *huella*] we saw power, we felt the contact of its mystery with a greater sense of revelation than when one of us was chosen to see him in person' (p. 187). The religious terminology used here is no accident. The discovery of writing allows the patriarch to play God. He refuses to admit God to his presence—' "let no one into the house, come what may, he ordered ... not even God, if he turns up"' (p. 264)—because he has learnt his secret, that omnipotence depends on absence. Only if the speaker is invisible do his words attain the status of Scripture. From now on, the patriarch stops appearing in public altogether. It is not for nothing that he recognizes in the church his main rival for power. At the same time, he is bound to be an agnostic, since he knows that God is all powerful because he does not exist except in terms of written texts.

The patriarch's scepticism about the existence of God, however, logically leads him to have doubts about his own identity as the mythical product of words: 'One night he had written my name is Zacarías, had reread it by the fleeting glare of the lighthouse, had read it over and over again, and with so many repetitions the name ended up looking remote and alien' (p. 132). The written word, as the repetition of an absent original, does serve as a form of memory, but the memory becomes detached from its source. The patriarch's last years are spent recording his own power in graffiti in the palace lavatories and hiding away written reminders to himself which he cannot remember writing. The written word does not give him eternal life, but condemns him to living in terms of memories of the past: His activity as head of state becomes limited to the commemoration of anniversaries.

The patriarch looks to the written word not only to immortalize himself but also to preserve his links with the outside world: 'At that time his only contacts with the reality of this world were a few loose fragments of his most important memories', written appropriately in the margins of the volumes of official records (p. 132). Here again, writing fails him. The written word does not connect him with the outside world, but becomes a substitute for it: 'He checked the truths stated in the documents against the misleading truths of real life' (p. 161). Writing mythifies not only its author but also its subject matter, inasmuch as it supplants, and ultimately suppresses, the original it represents. By the end of the novel the patriarch is relying for information entirely on his own censored newspapers. His written reminders to himself are rendered worthless, despite their permanence, by the fact that he forgets what they refer to. His last act before dying is to return to its hiding place the note he had written recording 'some anniversary or other of the illustrious poet Rubén Dario', whose identity he has now forgotten (p. 267). Writing perpetuates neither its author nor the outside world, but only itself. The patriarch's obsession, in his later years, with writing traps him in an unreal world beyond the looking glass, where 'the light of the mirrors has been turned inside out' (p. 234.). 'In the trail of yellow leaves of his autumn he became convinced that he would never be master of all his power, that he was condemned to know life the wrong way round/from the other side [Sp. *por el revés*]' (p. 270). The written word does not hold a mirror up to reality, but turns reality into a mirror-image.

The image of the trace—the 'trail of yellow leaves of his autumn'—is an apt metaphor for writing.[4] The displacement of the patriarch's power from speech to writing converts it into a trail of words referring back to an absent source. The implication is that, like myth, writing separates man from a source with which at the same time it seeks to reestablish contact. Writing is a circular, counter-productive process, in that it causes the problem it sets out to solve. The patriarch's recourse to written expressions of his authority aggravates the power vacuum he is trying to overcome. He attempts to secure a papal edict grounding his power in his genealogical origins by canonizing his mother, but the papal envoy's efforts to trace his ancestry reveal only that he is the son of an unknown father and a mother of uncertain name and reputation, who used to make a living by painting birds (falsifying nature). The people also attempt to establish an authoritative account of the patriarch's life by piecing together vestiges of a past that becomes more elusive the more they inquire: 'it would have been all too easy to let oneself be convinced by the immediate signs'; 'neither in that room could we find any clue', 'every trace of his origins had disappeared from the textbooks' (pp. 48–50). The patriarch's power becomes reduced to the peripheral trace of a remote and intermittent central source of light: 'the flurry of dust of the trail of stars of the gold spur in the fleeting dawn of the green flashes of the shafts of light of the turns of the lighthouse' (p. 69). At the end of the novel, with the sale of the sea to the United States, the patriarch orders the lighthouse—his metaphorical centre of power—to be put out of action. With this symbolic act, designed to conceal the power vacuum left by the absence of the sea, he destroys the last remaining vestiges of his power, and dies. The loss of the sea can be seen not only as an allegory of imperialism, but also as a metaphor for the loss by the 'ship of state' of its foundations. Prior to the sale of the sea, the palace is described as a ship that has broken free of its anchor and is floating in the air: 'The house of power [...] looked like a steamboat sailing in the sky' (p. 185). A similar image is used to describe the effect on the patriarch of his discovery, at Dario's recital, of the written word: '[it] lifted him clean out of his place and time and left him floating' (p. 194). The patriarch dies drowned in his own efforts to immortalize himself in words, 'a solitary corpse floating face down in the lunar waters of his dreams' (p. 13).

The image of the trace which has lost touch with its source, repeatedly applied to the patriarch, invites comparison with the description of the comet, which returns every hundred years, as a 'trail of radiant dust of astral residues and dawns prolonged by tar moons and ashes of craters of oceans prior to the origins of time on earth' (pp. 83–4). The implication is that the comet, as part of nature, is in touch with a source to which it can return, in order to renew itself. The patriarch, by contrast, loses contact with his origins through his delegation of power to words, and his attempts at repetition—again through words—lead to exhaustion. When he orders a repeat of the comet, he gets an eclipse. The transition from speech to writing cuts him off from nature. The loss of the sea provides an appropriate image of the final phase of this process of alienation.

The notion that writing is the trace of an absent source is reinforced by García Márquez's use of narrative perspective. It is important that the novel should start with the end, the patriarch's death. The patriarch is thus an absence throughout the novel. It is also important that García Márquez should, within the flashback that is the whole novel, narrate chronologically only the events of the patriarch's 'autumn'. The heyday of his power, when he was still a presence, becomes a flashback within a flashback, narrated via a double chain of hearsay. By making it clear that the text of the novel refers back to an absent source, García Márquez shows how writing is untrustworthy because it mythifies reality. The distance of the written word from its source undermines its authority. The patriarch's most authoritative acts are narrated in the least authoritative way.

Conversely, the moments in the novel which appear to give a direct, authoritative insight into the patriarch's mind, unmediated by hearsay, are those which reveal his inner doubts. When we are given a description of the thoughts he silently addresses to his mother—'thinking dearest mother Bendición Alvarado, if only you knew that this world is too much for me, that I want to run away but I don't know where to, mother, away from all this misery, but he didn't even show his private sighs to his mother' (p. 25)—we assume that the omniscient author is speaking, since no character can see inside the patriarch's head. We again assume the omniscient author is responsible for the narration of the patriarch's dream of Manuela Sánchez (pp. 70–1) and of his encounter with death (pp. 268–9), particularly since he is locked alone in his bedroom at the time. In these last two instances, the illusion of objectivity is heightened by the fact that the patriarch's mental states are narrated as if they were events. But, in fact, all the apparently omniscient insights into the patriarch's mind are contained in a narrative which, in each chapter, clearly starts as the uninformed collective voice of the people who discover the patriarch's corpse. What looks at first sight like an authoritative/authorial account of what the patriarch is really like is, it seems, hypothetical speculation on the part of the uninformed collective narrator, in other words, another part of the legend. By tricking the reader into thinking that what he is reading is the work of an omniscient author, and subsequently making him realize it is the product of an unreliable intermediary narrator, García Márquez calls into question the authority of the written word. Just as the patriarch discovers that he is not in control of the words that are designed to perpetuate his power, so the reader discovers that there is no omniscient author in control of the text he is reading.

What is more, the text is the product not of one unreliable intermediary narrator, but of a bewildering profusion of intermediary narrators, all of them unreliable. It is impossible to know at how many removes we are from the original version; all we know for sure is that the version we have is adulterated. The collective voice that narrates the beginning of each chapter, and which we therefore presume is responsible for the whole text, contains within it a multiplicity of individual voices which report events at second hand, and in turn are reported at second hand. Whenever we have something that looks like a factual account we suddenly come across a term of address which shows that it is a story told by one character to another. The intercalation 'my general' appears throughout, revealing that what we have been reading is a second-hand report made to the patriarch. In the same way, the intercalation 'Sir' reveals that what looks like objective narration is spoken by the patriarch's mother, who constantly uses this term of address. To add to the confusion, it is not always clear whether she is speaking to an interviewer or to God, since the Spanish *Señor* could also be translated as 'Lord'. The frequent interruption of the narrative by the expletive 'damn it' (Sp. *carajo*), or the interjections 'mother' or 'poor man', likewise indicates that the patriarch is speaking, despite the absence of any other indication to that effect. The army chief is always referred to as 'my old pal General Rodrigo de Aguilar', raising the possibility that the patriarch may be speaking even when this seems unlikely. There are several moments when we are made aware that what we are reading is spoken by a character, without being sure who the speaker is. The end of chapter 4 is addressed to the patriarch as 'general', despite the fact that he is also referred to in the third person—'and yet he forgot her, he was left alone in the dark searching for himself in the salty water of his tears general' (p. 168)—but it seems unlikely that this is spoken by Leticia Nazareno who is the only person present (and who is also referred to in the third person). The episode with the three caravels of Columbus again provides the most amusing example of this ambiguous use of narrative voice, with the patriarch's informers slipping anachronistically into the language of Columbus's diary that ought to be reserved for the newly arrived conquistadors (p. 45). This kind of narrative inconsistency makes it impossible to attribute the text to anyone in particular.

Not only do all the apparently factual accounts in the novel turn out to be reported speech, but so do all the passages which appear to be narrated as direct speech. The first-person narrative voice which characterizes direct speech is usually taken, despite its partiality, to give an authoritative account of events second only to that of the omniscient author, inasmuch as it gives an eye-witness description, unmediated by an external narrator. In *The Autumn of the Patriarch*, nothing can be regarded as authoritative, because everything is mediated. The absence of any punctuation indicating speech in the passages narrated in the first person is a clue to the fact that what we have is a disguised form of reported speech. The first time in the novel that direct speech appears, it is made quite clear that it is really reported speech: 'Someone had told how I saw the sad eyes' (p. 8). In subsequent examples, we have to wait for some time before discovering that what we have been reading is not genuine direct speech. The first-person account by Francisca Linero of her rape by the patriarch ends with the sentence, 'They were images of his power which reached him from afar' (p. 100), implying the whole story is a dramatization of legend. We frequently find an inconsistent mixture of direct and reported speech, suggesting that nothing is uncontaminated by hearsay. The patriarch issues orders to his servants in what starts as direct speech but lapses into reported speech: 'Take that door away for me and put it over there ... the belfry clock was not to strike twelve at twelve but at two' (p. 12). The first and third persons that correspond to direct and reported speech respectively occur in the same sentence: 'They had intimidated them with all manner of threats and that was why we did it' (p. 39); 'Bendición Alvarado spurned the crown jewels which make me feel like the Pope's wife' (p. 52). This technique is used most effectively in the patriarch's repeated invocations of 'his mother of my life', 'his mother of my soul', 'his mother of my death' (pp. 137–9), implying that what looks like a direct rendering of the patriarch's words is in fact relayed to us indirectly. The patriarch's voice is absent even when it appears to be present. Conversely, the people's voice is present even when it appears to be absent, inasmuch as all the individual voices in the novel are presented indirectly via popular legend.

The most extreme case of this confusion of direct and reported speech occurs, appropriately, in the episode in which the patriarch's informers reconstruct the efforts of the papal envoy to reconstruct the patriarch's origins. Within the illusion of direct speech that is the informers' report to the patriarch we have the illusion of direct speech of the informers' earlier conversations with the envoy:

> ... my general, if you could only see him in the midst of the human debris of the weatherbeaten sloops ... packed with their cargo of teenage whores for the glass hotels of Curaçao, bound for Guantánamo, father ... remember how strange we felt when the boat had left ... the distant drums, life, father, this god-awful life, boys, because he talks like us my general. (p. 149)

The confusion of distinct conversations taking place at different times and places leaves the reader unsure where he stands. A similar effect is produced by the use of a number of anonymous first-person-singular voices—an ex-dictator (pp. 21, 42), a fortune-teller (pp. 95–6), the revolutionary (p. 107), a schoolgirl (pp. 220–3), a prostitute (pp. 226–7), a palace decorator (p. 227), a leper (p. 251)—whose identity cannot be established with any precision. It is, of course, important that the major individual voice in the novel—that of the patriarch—should belong to this category of anonymous narrators. On several occasions, these first-person-singular voices fade into the anonymous first-person-plural voice of the collective narrator, so that we begin to think that the collective narrator perhaps comprises the sum of the individual voices, rather than being a separate group of people recording their stories at a remove.

The reader is reluctant to abandon his assumption that the first-person-plural narrator who relates the beginning of each chapter is responsible for the whole novel, because the existence of a frame-narrator gives at least some coherence to the text, by locating it within the framework of a single perspective. But the collective narrator turns out, on inspection, to be even more inconsistent than the individual voices it appears to contain. The very existence of a first-person-plural narrator confronts us with a disconcerting mixture of the apparent authority of the first-person voice and the plurality—and probable divergence—of a collective voice. The authority of this first-person-plural narrator is undermined in the opening pages, which show that the 'we' who is speaking is superstitious and ignorant. The initial impression that the text emanates from a fixed source, given by the fact that at the beginning of each chapter the collective narrator is clearly identified as the people who find the patriarch's corpse, is quickly dispelled as the 'we' that narrates the subsequent passages starts, like the patriarch's palace, to drift free of its anchor. It is not that we cannot attribute the text to a source, but that this source constantly shifts. The impression that the text is floating, ungrounded in a fixed source, is reinforced by the fact that this shifting first-person-plural narrator is always anonymous. First of all we find that the 'we' frequently refers to the patriarch's subjects at the time of events, such as the landing of the Marines (p. 51) or the appearance of the comet (p. 84), which the 'we' of the opening pages has told us took place many years before their birth. Then the 'we' begins to pass, at increasing speed, from one group of characters to another. The successive identities assumed by the first-person-plural narrator include the following (in order of appearance): the national baseball team (p. 40), the ex-dictators of other Latin American countries (p. 42), the witnesses of Columbus's landing (pp. 44–5), successive generations of army generals (pp. 60, 126–7, 196–7, 207), marauding pirates (p. 95), various army officers (pp. 109–11, 248), government advisers (p. 170), merchants (p. 188), the audience at Dario's recital (p. 193–4), schoolgirls (p. 202), economists (p. 224), security guards (p. 226), cadets (p. 240), lepers and cripples (p. 251), the police looking for Columbus (p. 258), palace servants (p. 264). To add to the confusion, the patriarch sometimes uses the royal 'we'.

Our first reaction is to explain this proliferation of first-person-plural narrators in the same way as we had initially explained the first-person-singular narrators, as being voices contained within the narrative of the 'we' who, at the beginning of each chapter, find the patriarch's corpse. But the view that the people who find the corpse provide a narrative frame to the novel appears to be contradicted by the fact that on two occasions, at the beginning and end of the novel, the people who find the corpse are referred to in the third person. The first time, this can be explained by the fact that the reference includes the different group of people who previously found the corpse of the patriarch's double, even though 'we' plus 'they' normally adds up to 'we': 'but not even then did we dare believe in his death because it was the second time they had found him in that office' (p. 20). But when at the end of the novel we read, 'although those who found the body were to say that it was on the office floor' (p. 269), no such explanation is available. Either there is no frame-narrator, or else the people who find the corpse are characters in someone else's story. If there is a frame-narrator, it can only be the 'we' who narrates the last two pages of the novel. This final 'we' appears to represent a different group of people from the 'we' that starts each chapter, because the people who find the corpse are uninformed and submissive, whereas the first-person-plural narrator of the closing pages utters a clear rejection of everything the patriarch stands for. This is the one authoritative statement in the novel. All we know about this final 'we' is that they live 'on this side of reality in the world of the poor' (p. 270). If they are responsible for reporting the stories of all the other narrators in the novel, the fact that they are entirely absent until the last two pages means that they do not provide the coherence of a genuine frame-narrator, like Scheherezade in the *Arabian Nights*, whose presence is made clear at the very beginning in order to ground the ensuing proliferation of narrative voices in a single perspective. There is, in fact, no evidence to suggest that the narrator of the end of the novel is responsible for the rest of the text. The reader has to face the disquieting fact that the story he has been reading is, like an Escher drawing, depicted from an entirely inconsistent, indeed impossible, perspective. The fact that the collective narrator can be identified only as the sum of all the individual points of view confronts the reader with the optical illusion of a narrator that is the voices it appears to report. The impossible nature of the narrative voice is underlined at the end of the novel, when the patriarch's dead mother and death itself speak in the first person. The implausibility of the voice that speaks destroys the authority of what is said.

The critic Julio Ortega has suggested that García Márquez's use of a collective narrative voice represents a vindication of democracy, since the dictator is placed in the power of the masses who narrate his story.[5] This is an attractive interpretation, but it presents problems. The most noticeable feature of the collective narrative voice is that, with the exception of the last two pages, it shows remarkably little political awareness. Indeed, it is often highly hagiographic in tone. García Márquez is not suggesting that the patriarch's tyranny is justified by popular support, for the point is that the collective voice of the people is unreliable. The fact that it is anonymous, uninformed and inconsistent means that it cannot be seen as an alternative source of authority. I would suggest that García Márquez's use of narrative perspective does not represent a vindication of popular power, but an attempt to subvert the concept of language as an instrument of power. The absence in the novel of a central, coherent narrative voice is a warning to the reader that he should not look to the text for an authoritative account of events. García Márquez's writing is subversive because it is unashamedly fictitious. He is not mythifying dictatorship, but using language ironically in order to expose the ways in which it mythifies reality. By using language to undermine its own mythifications, he demonstrates that the unreliability of fiction, when used critically, can be a strength as well as a weakness. His use of an anonymous, uninformed and inconsistent narrative voice suggests that writing has an advantage over speech precisely because it is not the voice of authority.

García Márquez has, on several occasions, talked of his self-identification with the patriarch as a prisoner of power. By this, he is referring not only to the power that comes with fame but also to that of the creator. To quote one interview:

> On the one hand, as you say, the solitude of fame is very like the solitude of power ... on the other hand, there is no profession more solitary than that of the writer, in the sense that at the time of writing no one can help you, no one can tell you what you want to do. When you are faced with the blank page, you are on your own, totally on your own.[6]

The writer, like the dictator, chooses to play God but, at the same time, if he succumbs to the temptation to do so he is lost. García Márquez's depiction of a dictator who becomes the prisoner of the power of words shows an understanding of the pitfalls that await the writer who lets his power go to his head. García Márquez's delegation of responsibility for the text of his novel to an anonymous, unreliable collective voice can be seen as an act of authorial self-effacement. It is also an affirmation of the value of human error and limitation. In its one authoritative pronouncement at the end of the novel, the collective narrator rejects the dictator's search for divine status, in favour of 'this life which we loved with an insatiable passion that you never even dared imagine for fear of knowing what we knew so well that it was brief and cruel, but there was no other' (pp. 270–1). The patriarch's concern with language as an instrument of power leaves him speechless when it comes to expressing his love for Manuela Sánchez. 'He overwhelmed her in silence with those crazy gifts with which he tried to tell her what he could not say in words, because the only way he knew of expressing his deepest desires was through the visible symbols of his monstrous power' (p. 79). The language of *The Autumn of the the Patriarch* lays no claim to authority. García Márquez opts for the more modest aim of depicting human fallibility.

NOTES

1. See J. Derrida, *Of Grammatology*, trans. Gayatry Chakravorty Spivak (Baltimore and London, 1976). A lucid analysis of Derrida's ideas on language can be found in Jonathan Culler's article in *Structuralism and Since*, ed. J. Sturrock (Oxford, 1979), pp. 154–80.

2. All references given in the text are to the first edition of *El otoño del patriarca* (Barcelona, 1975). The translations are my own.

3. The ironic references in the novel to seeing have been pointed out by Seymour Menton in his article 'Ver para no creer: *El otoño del patriarca*', in *García Márquez*, ed. P. Earle (Madrid, 1981), pp. 189–209.

4. The metaphor of the trace is also used by Derrida to describe language. García Márquez's view of language, however, differs from that of Derrida in an important respect. Derrida rejects the view that writing is a decadent form of speech inasmuch as it is the indirect expression of a voice which is absent, as opposed to speech which is assumed to be the direct expression of the speaker's voice. For Derrida, both speech and writing are the trace of an absent source. García Márquez retains the traditional notion of the decadence of writing with regard to speech.

5. See J. Ortega, '*El otoño delpatriarca*, texto y cultura', in *García Márquez*, ed. P. Earle, pp. 214–35.

6. Plinio Apuleyo Mendoza, *El olor de la guayaba* (Barcelona, 1982), p. 127.

ISABEL ALVAREZ-BORLAND

From Mystery to Parody: (Re)readings of García Márquez's Crónica de una Muerte Anunciada

Crónica de una Muerte Anunciada presents the critic with a text which, by way of a complex system of narrative and temporal levels, explores why an entire town allows a senseless murder to occur in the name of hypocritical honor codes. A sociological reading of *Crónica* traces the backward mentality of small towns in Latin America and elsewhere. The rich system of *presagios* and the biblical symbolism in the names of the main participants would support the interpretation of the story as a biblical myth, Santiago Nasar as its Christ figure, a scapegoat for the town's bloodthirstiness.[1] Although helpful in the understanding of the text's didactic message, these interpretations only look for solutions in the mimesis of the text, leaving the reader with many unanswered questions regarding the direct references to the creative process contained in Márquez's tale. Analysing these allusions from the standpoint of the detective story as the perfect model of the "hermeneutic tale,"[2] the present study envisions this novel as a questioning structure rather than as an answer-providing construct. An analysis of the detective conventions as well as of their aesthetic effect is necessary in the appraisal of a work which has been labeled by reviewers as a "simplistic murder mystery," inferior in quality to the author's previous writings.[3]

García Márquez's text is indeed a detective story which subverts the conventionality of its genre,[4] but which at the same time takes advantage of

From *Symposium* Vol. 38, No. 4 (Winter 1984–85). © 1985 by the Helen Dwight Reid Educational Foundation.

the genre's inherent traits. *Crónica* exhibits what, according to Frank
Kermode, makes the detective novel the perfect hermeneutic tale: a
hermeneutic preoccupation at the expense of depth, undifferentiation of
characters, a turbulent temporal flow, and an ambiguity of clues.[5] In fact,
Kermode's descriptive categories become extremely important in García
Márquez's subversion of the genre as they invite the reader to make
inferences about an entirely new system of interpretation.

The tale centers around an unnamed *cronista*, who early on announces
his intentions to "recomponer con tantas astillas dispersas, el espejo roto de
la memoria."[6] There seem to be no secrets left to discover in this so-called
mystery. The reader is told who killed Santiago Nasar twenty-seven years
before, the manner in which he was killed, and even the exact time of the
murder. The reader's first impression is one of confusion: if this is a mystery,
what exactly is the narrator looking for? The book's investigative structure
thus convinces the reader that he, along with the narrator, is on a hunt—
although the reason for the search is never expressed.

Further confusion is introduced when the narrator dramatizes the
recollections which more than fifty witnesses have of the murder. The ironic
language used to narrate the events surrounding Nasar's death serves to hide
rather than to reveal facts, and functions exclusively to distance the reader
from the events he is seeking to resolve. The potentially illuminating function
of language is constantly undermined, as is illustrated by the *cronista*'s
description of Bayardo San Román, an enigmatic figure who exhibits "una
manera de hablar que más bien le servía para ocultar que para decir" (p. 37).
The contradictions in the townspeople's versions, as well as their simplistic
evaluation of the events as predetermined acts of fate, are manifested by a
narrator who himself is guilty of the same fatalistic line of reasoning. Faced
with a multiplicity of accounts lacking any kind of specificity and coherence,
the reader is forced to surmise, to read between the lines, careful not to
interpret the townspeople's declarations in a literal fashion.

The text's discourse changes, however, in those passages which advance
the action as well as provide the background of the protagonist. Here the
language is transparent, straightforward, and gives the text its direct, mimetic
quality. The text's linguistic duality causes the reader to be at once distanced
from the events he is seeking to resolve, and seduced by the apparent clarity
and simplicity of the tale unfolding before him. As demonstrated by the
investigation, this dual language reveals *Crónica* as a two-tiered novel, with
simultaneous plots metaphorically related by the conventions of the
detective story.

At least two temporal levels can be distinguished in the narrator's
account: the time contemporaneous with the murder, that is, twenty-seven

years before, and the present of the *crónica*, the time in which the narrator decides to reconstruct these events. The first temporal level involves the declarations of the witnesses recorded in the instructor's summary as well as the memories the *cronista* has of the events, for he was in town the day of the murder. The second temporal category includes the retrospective memories of the multiple witnesses, as well as the narrator's own reminiscences of the crime. The intermingling of these two temporal levels is unsettling to the reader, since the narrator never distinguishes one from the other.

For further temporal ambiguity, we have only to look at the order in which the narrative events are reported. The text of the chronicle is divided into five unnumbered segments which reveal the events of Santiago Nasar's death in a most peculiar manner:

1. Recreation of the events immediately before Santiago Nasar's death.
2. Background of Angela Vicario and Bayardo San Román (the defiled virgin and the wronged husband).
3. Background of the bride's twin brothers, the perpetrators of the crime.
4. Morbid description of the autopsy of Santiago Nasar's body.
5. Recreation of the events immediately before Nasar's death. Graphic rendition of his death. Poetic description of his death.

A traditionalist analysis of these five segments would indicate that if the first three can be considered the exposition of the murder and the background of its main perpetrators, parts four and five could be interpreted as the implied author's[7] indictment of the townspeople (including the narrator). The gloomy descriptions of the autopsy and the murder can thus be viewed as a motivation for the reader to realize, with the implied author, the dire consequences of stale and hypocritical honor codes. The fact that the point of view in the fifth segment changes from 'I' to 'We' can be taken as further evidence of the condemnation by the author of the narrator *and* the townspeople, thus presenting a scathing comment on the corruption of their moral values as well as their institutions. After this interpretation, however, many questions remain unresolved, two of which are fundamental to our investigation: What is the relationship between the narrator and his reconstructive sources, especially the instructor's text? Why is the narrator interested in revisiting the scene of the crime in the last segment; why the double rendition of the death of Santiago Nasar?

These two questions constitute the premise for an interpretation of *Crónica* based on the understanding by the reader of the text's narrative patterns. To begin to understand this text is to accept the book's process, and to move beyond what may seem to be the centers of the book—a parody of rigid conventions, even a tragedy.

As has been suggested by my comments regarding the narrator's categories of order and the ambiguity of his language, the overall pattern of this text strives against satisfactory closure of the issues that it raises. If at the mimetic level the reader is involved in the injustices of the gratuitous murder of Santiago Nasar, then on the level of discourse the reader must exert his own interpretative role. Viewed in this manner, the questions created by the text become incentives for the reader to examine its narrative process further. The complex relationship between the narrator and his written sources is a crucial aspect of this examination.

In addition to the reports of the townspeople as well as his own first-hand knowledge of the events narrated, the *cronista* uses as his reconstructive sources the official records of the Summary. These documents were recorded by a *juez/instructor* who does not appear on the scene but who, nevertheless, becomes an important presence in this text. The instructor's *sumario* becomes important to the *cronista* not for its contents—which many times are not different from the meaningless utterances remembered and quoted by the narrator—but for the record's literariness, the way in which the *cronista* 'reads' the instructor's language. For instance, when the record mentions the fateful door, which could have been Nasar's salvation, the *cronista* dwells on the instructor's style: "la puerta estaba citada varias veces con un nombre de folletín: *La puerta fatal*" (p. 21). On other occasions, the *cronista* seems to forego the contents of the record only to comment on the marginal notes of the instructor (p. 21), and even on the drawings which the instructor made of the knives used in the murder (p. 79). Moreover, in the last segment of the text, the instructor is described by the *cronista* as, "un hombre abrasado por la fiebre de la literatura," as the *cronista* continues to ponder over the enigma of his marginal notes: "Las notas marginales, y no sólo por el color de la tinta, parecían escritas con sangre. Estaba tan perplejo con el enigma que le había tocado en suerte, que muchas veces incurrió en distracciones líricas contrarias al rigor de su oficio. Sobre todo, nunca le pareció legítimo que la vida le sirviera de tantas casualidades prohibidas a la literatura, para que se cumpliera sin tropiezos una muerte tan anunciada" (p. 130). The instructor's *distracciones líricas* mentioned in the above passage also extend to his special liking for proverbs (pp. 99, 147), a fact which might imply that the proverb appearing at the beginning of the text, "La caza de amor es de altanería," could be the work of either the *cronista* or the instructor. Intentional blurring of identities is suggested here, one which will be of crucial importance in our understanding of the role of the *cronista* as the reader of the *pliegos* as well as the author of this chronicle.[8]

Of additional interest in the above citation is the analogy the *cronista* makes between literature and the story's main events. The confounding of life and art clearly indicates a commentary on the author's craft, and makes the reader aware of the text's conscious fictionality. Similar allusions can be found interspersed throughout the text, such as the *cronista*'s description of Angela Vicario, 23 years after the murder: "Al verla así, dentro del marco idílico de la ventana, no quise creer que aquella mujer fuera la que yo creía, porque me resistía a admitir que la vida terminara por parecerse tanto a la mala literatura" (p. 116). Such comparisons between the text's reality and the literary reality indicate a playful subversion of the concepts of life and art, and point towards the impossibility of ever arriving at factual truth—in this case the truth behind Santiago Nasar's murder.

Coupled with the *cronista*'s unusual interest in the literary quality of his reconstructive sources is the important issue of the *sumario*'s fragmented condition, for he found these *pliegos* in the disordered and abandoned archives of his hometown: "Yo mismo exploré muchas veces con las aguas hasta los tobillos aquel estante de aguas perdidas, y sólo una casualidad me permitió rescatar al cabo de cinco años de búsqueda unos 322 pliegos salteados de los más de 500 que debió tener el sumario" (p. 129). The fact that the *pliegos* are incomplete not only parallels the unfinished quality of the *cronista*'s text (our text) but also points towards the possible origin of yet another *pliego*, a mysterious piece of paper mentioned only twice in the narrative. In the first segment, this piece of paper is mentioned as a forgotten document, which, had it been found by the victim, could have prevented his death: "Alguien que nunca fue identificado había metido por debajo de la puerta un papel dentro de un sobre, en el cual le avisaban a Santiago Nasar que lo estaban esperando para matarlo, y le revelaban además el lugar y los motivos, y otros detalles muy precisos de la intriga" (p. 23). The use of the word *intriga* is of extreme importance here, as is the fact that, in a manner reminiscent of the Melquíades manuscripts in *One Hundred Years of Solitude*, this paper contains the story of Santiago Nasar, that is, a replica of our text. Actually, it is not until the last segment of the narrative, when the narrator revisits the scene of the crime, that the paper is mentioned again: "Plácida Linero vio entonces el papel en el suelo, pero no pensó en recogerlo, y sólo se enteró de lo que decía cuando alguien se lo mostró más tarde en la confusión de la tragedia" (p. 151). This piece of paper, like the marginal notes of the instructor, never figures directly at the level of the anecdote, although both play an important role in revealing the text's insistence on its literary nature. The paper also serves to thematize literary self-consciousness and functions to call attention to the repetitive, un-lifelike nature of the story. Because it contains the details of the plot, it can be considered a duplication of our text, a perfect example of what Dällenbach defines as a *mise en abyme*.[9] This curious mirroring effect is not limited to just one incident, but can be encountered in other instances within the story. A good example is the equal but contradictory relationship between the twin brothers Vicario who, consistently, assume opposite physical and ideological postures throughout the tale.[10]

Mirrors also function within the story as devices which enhance the characters' perspectives. For instance, they play a crucial role in the encounter between Angela Vicario and Bayardo San Román many years after the tragedy: "Pura Vicario pidió un vaso de agua en la cantina. Se lo estaba tomando, de espaldas a la hija, cuando ésta vio su propio pensamiento reflejado en los espejos repetidos de la sala. Angela Vicario volvió la cabeza con el último aliento, y to vio pasar a su lado sin verla, y lo vio salir del hotel" (p. 120). In this instance, the mirror serves to reveal a new perspective, one that will lead Angela Vicario to the man she has loved for so many years. Sadly, the reflection of Bayardo is all she obtains, for the real Bayardo had gone by without really seeing her.

Mirrors have always been crucial to self-conscious texts as novelistic devices enhancing the problematic relationship between reality and its literary representation. In *Crónica*, the narrator is not only our mediator between the facts and his *crónica*, but he also seems to mirror a multiplicity of fictional roles going beyond his explicit task of reporting the facts. If the *cronista* becomes the reader and thus the interpreter of the *pliegos* and of the mysterious piece of paper, his role is also that of an author. He is our link between the events and the townspeople's declarations, and he is the only one who has control of the information we receive as readers. Indeed, the *cronista* plays with narrative truth (p. 116), tells us that his *crónica* is only his personal impressions (p. 132), introduces playful intertextual references such as the names of Aureliano Buendía and Gerineldo Márquez as his relatives, and lastly mentions Wenefrida Márquez, his aunt, as one of the last persons to have seen Santiago Nasar alive.

This invitation to equate the *cronista* with García Márquez is further complicated by the similarities between characters since the *instructor* and the *cronista* also share a common penchant for literary descriptions. For instance, the *cronista*'s description of Angela Vicario (p. 116) and that of Alejandrina Cervantes (p. 86) are clear products of a literary rather than a detectivesque mind. Even the witnesses seem to be well versed in the language of literature, for when Angela Vicario is questioned about Santiago Nasar's culpability, she answers with an enigmatic: "Fue mi autor" (p. 131). Thus, while narrating an apparently objective account of a murder, the chronicle is permeated with literary allusions and with descriptions which betray any desire to present a faithful account of the facts.

The *cronista*'s literary penchants become more evident when he revisits the scene of the crime in the last segment of the text. His recreation deserves close attention because it points to the literary theme while demanding that the reader reflect upon the book's artistic process.

At the anecdotal level, the morbid description of Nasar's stabbing, as well as the stylized description of this 'double' death, can be interpreted as repetitions or amplifications of the same event mentioned in the text's first pages. In a very general sense the first segment of the text (Part 1) is not different from the last (Part 5). If at the literal level this description does not advance the action, or shed new light on the story, then its purposes must be interpreted as artistic. The reader knows Nasar is dead; he has known it since the very first lines. Nevertheless, he is presented once again with a naturalistic, gloomy account of the stabbing: "En realidad Santiago Nasar no caía porque ellos mismos lo estaban sosteniendo a cuchilladas contra la puerta. Desesperado, Pablo Vicario le dio un tajo horizontal en el vientre y los intestinos completos afloraron con una explosión.... Santiago Nasar permaneció todavía un instante apoyado contra la puerta, hasta que vio sus propias vísceras al sol, limpias y azules, y cayó de rodillas" (p. 154). The information that follows is crucial because it is out of character with the somber, grotesque mood pervading the account of the stabbing of Nasar. After his brutal experience, Santiago Nasar "se incorporó de medio lado, y se echó a andar en un estado de alucinación, sosteniendo con las manos las vísceras colgantes" (p. 155). The character continues to walk and manages to greet Wenefrida Márquez, who becomes the final reporter of his death: "contó que Santiago Nasar caminaba con la prestancia de siempre, midiendo bien los pasos, y que su rostro de sarraceno con los rizos alborotados estaba más bello que nunca .... Tropezó en el último escalón, pero se incorporó de inmediato. 'Hasta tuvo el cuidado de sacudir con la mano la tierra que le quedó en las tripas,' me dijo mi tía Wene" (p. 156). Nasar's second death, although tied to the book's events by the important detail of the fatal door, can be considered totally unnecessary from a mimetic or anecdotal perspective. This passage represents García Márquez's right to artistic selection, and his power over his textual reality. The segment could thus be interpreted as a playful ending, an invitation for the reader to experience the book's essentially artistic nature.[11]

If the reader is perpetually led away from closure as he grapples with the facts presented to him, then we must remember that, even at the anecdotal level, the book is not about *what* happened, but about arriving at an *understanding* of what happened (*why* a town became the silent accomplice to a murder committed by the brothers of a defiled virgin). Taking into consideration the important questions raised here regarding the narrator's sources as well as the text's artistic finale, a parallel emerges between the anecdotal and the artistic readings of this text, for they both become an invitation to *understanding* rather than knowing. Facts, temporality, events become muddled, for they are not important even if we have them. Ironic parody, the main impediment to a comfortable reading of this slippery text, can thus be seen on two levels: as a parody of the institutions and morals at the textual level, and as a parody of the classic detective structure at the artistic level. The text suggests multiple readings and should be viewed as a structure seeking pluralism. Thus it is possible to appreciate not only the meanings indicated by the narrator, but also the meanings implied by the novel's narrative discourse. Just as the text's ironic language forces the reader to read between the lines, so the narrative's duality invites him to understand the acts of reading and writing better by means of an intentional blurring of the three fictional components: the author, the reader, and the text.

NOTES

1. William Siemens, "Structures of Rage in García Márquez's *Crónica de una muerte anunciada*," Unpublished paper read at the Eleventh Annual Conference on Twentieth Century Literatures, University of Louisville, Louisville, Kentucky, 1983. Also see: Edith Grossman, "Truth is Stranger than Fact," *Review* 30 (1981), 72–73.

2. Wolfgang Iser, "Indeterminacy and the Reader's Response to Prose Fiction," in J. Hillis Miller, ed., *Aspects of Narrative* (New York: Columbia University Press, 1971), p. 285. According to Iser, the hermeneutic aspect of reading consists in detecting an enigma (a gap), searching for clues, forming hypotheses, trying to choose among them, and constructing a finalized hypothesis. In detective stories these features are so crucial and central as to become the very pivot of the reading process.

3. Numerous book reviews have appeared of *Crónica de una muerte anunciada*. A few which seem to hold the view that *Crónica* does not represent an important contribution to García Márquez's *oeuvre* are the following: Brian Morton, *TES*, 24 September 1982; Bill Buford, *TLS*, 10 September 1982, p. 965; Julio Marzán, *The Village Voice*, October, 1981, pp. 20–21; Salman Rushdie, *London Review of Books*, 4, 17 (1982), p. 3.

4. Critics have devised several typologies for detective fiction. Two of the best are: Tzvetan Todorov's "Typologie du roman policier," in *Poétique de la prose* (Paris: Éditions du Seuil, 1981), pp. 55–65; John G. Cawelti, *Adventure, Mystery and Romance: Formula Stories as Art and Popular Culture* (Chicago: University of Chicago Press, 1976).

5. Frank Kermode, "Novel and Narrative," in Glenn W. Most and W. W. Stowe, eds., *The Poetics of Murder* (New York: Harcourt, Brace, Jovanovich, 1983), pp. 175–97.

6. Gabriel García Márquez, *Crónica de una muerte anunciada* (Bogotá: Editorial La Oveja Negra, 1981). All parenthetical page references are to this edition.

7. Wayne Booth, *The Rhetoric of Fiction*, 2nd ed., (Chicago: The University of Chicago Press, 1982) pp. 243–71. More than just a textual stance, Booth's implied author

is often designated as "the author's second self." According to this view, the implied author is the governing consciousness of the work as a whole, the source of the norms embodied in the work. The implied author of a particular work is conceived as a stable entity and is different from the narrator. See also: Seymour Chatman, *Story and Discourse* (Ithaca, N.Y.: Cornell University Press, 1978).

8. On the subject of readers and authors "encoded" in texts see Christine Brooke-Rose, *Thru* (London: Hamish Hamilton, 1975). Also see Walter J. Ong, "The Writer's Audience is Always a Fiction," *PMLA*, 90 (1975), 9–21. In *Crónica*, the *cronista* parallels the reactions of the "real" readers as he abstracts the story from the *pliegos* and constructs the characters from various indications dispersed along the text.

9. Lucien Dällenbach, *Le Récit spéculaire: Essai sur la mise en abyme* (Paris: Éditions du Seuil, 1977). Dällenbach's extensive study of this reflexive modality explains how the mirroring image is central to the concept of the *mise en abyme*.

10. Other examples of the mirror motif can be found on pages 3–56, 83–84, 160–61.

11. Robert Alter, *Partial Magic. The Novel as a Self-Conscious Genre* (Berkeley: University of California Press, 1975). In this study, Alter traces the phenomenon of the self-conscious narrator to its Cervantine roots and discusses the reasons for its popularity in the contemporary novel.

ROBIN FIDDIAN

A Prospective Post-Script:
Apropos of Love in the Times of Cholera

*L*ove in the Times of Cholera is the first novel by García Márquez to be published since the award of the Nobel Prize for Literature in October 1982. As abundant publicity surrounding the book's appearance in December 1985 revealed, the author was already working on a sequel to *Chronicle of a Death Foretold* (1981) when the Nobel committee's decision was announced; with the award there came numerous public commitments which obliged García Márquez to interrupt the progress of his project until January 1984, when he resumed work on the existing material. *Love in the Times of Cholera* was eventually completed in August 1985 and published three months ahead of schedule in a first edition of 1,200,000 copies for distribution in Spanish America and a further 250,000 reserved for the Spanish market.[1]

Initial critical response has taken the form of summary notices and reviews, the most enthusiastic of which asserts that *Love in the Times of Cholera* is 'one of the great living classics of the Spanish language'.[2] It is not my intention to debate that claim here. In the absence of any properly established critical guidelines, my role will be restricted to providing a brief description of the essential features of *Love in the Times of Cholera* and to indicating possible avenues of approach which readers may decide to explore at greater length in the future.

From *Gabriel García Márquz: New Readings*, Bernard McGuirk and Richard Cardwell, ed. © 1987 Cambridge University Press.

Love in the Times of Cholera is an accomplished work which exhibits many aspects of interest, including a dynamic discursive form. Its six chapters, ranging from 71 to 98 pages in length, progress smoothly along a linear axis punctuated by frequent parentheses and reprises. The story is told by a single narrative voice which recounts certain events in duplicate in order to represent the overlapping experiences of its multiple protagonists. In terms of narrative design, the novel incorporates three temporal perspectives, the most immediate of which focuses on a period of slightly less than two years during which a seventy-six-year-old romantic, Florentino Ariza, courts and finally consummates a lifetime's love for Fermina Daza who had broken their engagement 'fifty-one years, nine months and four days previously' (p. 418)[3] and married a handsome young doctor whose accidental death, narrated in chapter 1, eventually leaves her a widow at the age of seventy-two. The events set in motion by Doctor Juvenal Urbino's fatal fall are overlain by a second level of the narrative which extends some sixty years back into the past in order to account for Florentino, Fermina and Juvenal's family backgrounds; at the same time, it registers the principal social developments which shape the life of their community during the period concerned, and surveys the political history of Colombia since that country achieved independence in 1819. A still more remote perspective encompassing the period of Spanish colonial rule completes the range of temporal references in the book.

The spatial setting of *Love in the Times of Cholera* concentrates on the social and racial microcosm of a formerly prosperous community situated at the mouth of the Magdalenas River in northern Colombia. The city, which had been 'the habitual residence of the viceroys of the New Kingdom of Granada' (p. 35), is in fact a composite image of Cartagena de Indias, Santa Marta, Barranquilla and other locations on the Caribbean coast.[4] The story line also takes in several points along the Magdalenas River, as well as some countries in Western Europe which Fermina Daza and her husband visit on their honeymoon (chapter 3) and again some years later (chapter 4); other journeys along the river, related in chapters 2 (Fermina in the company of her father, Lorenzo Daza), 3 (Florentino, alone), 5 (Fermina, alone), and 6 (Fermina and Florentino, together), reinforce the novel's expansive spatial projection, thereby setting it strikingly apart from previous works by García Márquez, including *Leaf Storm, No One Writes to the Colonel* and *Chronicle of a Death Foretold*.

The generic status of the novel is of particular interest here. In effect, *Love in the Times of Cholera* masquerades as a nineteenth-century work; on García Márquez's own admission, he had set out 'to write a nineteenth-century novel as examples of the type were written in the nineteenth century, as if it were actually written at that time'.[5] His text displays many conventional features of realist or naturalist fiction, 'as exemplified by the schools of Emile Zola or Gustave Flaubert';[6] in its documentation of social custom and historical fact, it partakes of the qualities of a chronicle; above all, it draws conspicuously on a type of nineteenth-century writing to which other Spanish American novelists, including Manuel Puig and Mario Vargas Llosa, have also turned for creative inspiration, that is, the 'folletines de amor' (p. 220) and 'folletines de lágrimas' (pp. 101 and 117) (sentimental and lachrymose love stories, or *feuilletons*) which enjoyed wide popularity with nineteenth-century readers in Europe and America, appearing in serialized form in the newspapers on a weekly or monthly basis (see pp. 207 and 426). It is not the first time that the *folletín* is cited in García Márquez's work: the *juez-instructor* (or official investigator) in *Chronicle of a Death Foretold* had been unable to cast off the influence of the *folletín* when reporting on the circumstances of Santiago Nasar's death. Imitation of the *folletín*, arguably an embryonic and incidental feature of that text, becomes the basis of *Love in the Times of Cholera*, where Florentino Ariza models himself, from the earliest years of his adult life, on the romantic stereotypes associated with the genre.

During the 'medicinal journey' (p. 205) which Florentino takes up the Magdalenas River in search of a cure for the sickness of love,

> At night, when the boat was tied up and most of the passengers walked disconsolately up and down the deck, he would reread the illustrated stories that he knew almost off by heart, by the light of the carbide lamp in the dining room, the only one which stayed alight throughout the night. The stories charged with drama which he had read so often would recover their original magic when he substituted people whom he knew in real life for the imaginary protagonists, and reserved the roles of lovers thwarted by circumstances for himself and Fermina Daza. (p. 211)

The very first love letters he writes to Fermina incorporate 'entire paragraphs from the Spanish Romantics, undigested'; as the narrator explains, 'By then he had moved one step closer to the tear jerking serial stories and other even more profane prose writings of his times' (a reference to a well-known volume of poetry published in 1896 by the Nicaraguan *modernista*, Rubén Darío) (p. 117).[7]

Fermina Daza is not immune to the infectious appeal of the *folletín*. The picture which she forms of the young Florentino and his mother bespeaks a naivety fostered by the commonplaces of a facile culture:

He was the son of a hard-working and serious woman who had
not married but who displayed the irremediable mark of a fiery
stigma which had its origins in a single false step she had taken in
her youth. [Fermina] had discovered that he was not the
telegraphist's messenger boy, as she had assumed, but a well-
qualified assistant with a promising future ... (p. 104)

Although soon displaced by the down-to-earth pragmatism typical of so
many of García Márquez's women characters (for example, Úrsula Buendía
and the colonel's anonymous, asthmatic wife), Fermina's attraction to the
stylized and improbable world of the *folletín* is revived in the early days of
widowhood when she would 'fill her empty hours with tear jerking serial
stories transmitted on the radio from Santiago de Cuba' (p. 460).

García Márquez draws as systematically as his characters on the
conventions of the *folletín*. He fashions a novel which, besides featuring the
stock figure of the solitary, love-sick poet who, like many a Romantic hero,
finds refuge, as though he were the victim of a fateful shipwreck (p. 258), in
the remote seclusion of a light-house (p. 144), also reproduces the stereotype
of a three-cornered love relationship. In this the more passionate male plays
a serenade beneath the window of the woman he adores, writes her
interminable love letters, and, when she cuts short their engagement,
distraughtly returns a lock of her hair which he had displayed 'like a holy
relic' in a glass case hanging on his bedroom wall (p. 157). A no less familiar
chord is struck by the scene in which Florentino 'planted a clump of roses on
[his dear mother's] grave' (p. 318) and transplanted a cutting to that of a
lover, Olimpia Zuleta, who died violently at the hands of her jealous,
cuckolded husband (p. 318).

The author introduces into the story-line of *Love in the Times of
Cholera* a number of 'unlikely coincidences' (p. 200) of the sort which
'were common currency in the novels of the time, but which nobody
believed actually happened in real life' (p. 387). See, for example, the
'exceptional' occurrence, on the day of Pentecost, of 'two extraordinary
events: the death of one of Doctor Juvenal Urbino's friends and the silver-
wedding celebrations of an eminent pupil of his' (p. 25); and, the unlikely
arrival of a telegram informing Florentino of the death of América
Vicuña—an adolescent school-girl put in his charge—as he cruises along
the Magdalenas River with Fermina, oblivious to the banalities of life (p.
485). The arbitrary intrusion here of an adverse element of fate is at once
reminiscent of the world of the *folletín* and of the classic nineteenth-
century novel, *María*, written by García Márquez's fellow Colombian,
Jorge Isaacs.[8]

In *Love in the Times of Cholera*, some of Florentino's statements are culled directly from the pages of the *folletín*, as when he exclaims that 'There is no greater glory than to die for love' (p. 127), or when he confides to Fermina that 'I kept my virginity for you' (p. 490). The narrator imitates this hackneyed language, describing Florentino on one occasion as 'prostrate with grief' p. 217), using variants of the word 'desgarrado' ('heart-rending') to the point of excess, and frequently employing stilted metaphors: at a delicate stage of Fermina and Juvenal Urbino's love-making on their honeymoon voyage, the doctor 'realized that they had rounded the Cape of Good Hope' (p. 233); Lorenzo Daza's progress in fulfilling his ambition to 'make Fermina into a fine lady' had been pictured earlier as a journey along 'a long and uncertain road' to social acceptance (p. 125).

The verbal clichés, character types and narrative situations illustrated here are evidence of a clear intent on García Márquez's part to write a pastiche of the *folletín*. His description of *Love in the Times of Cholera* as 'practically a "telenovela" [television soap opera]'[9] encourages the view that the book is a recreation of the sentimental episodic melodramas of a previous age, as perceived through the prism of late-twentieth-century generic equivalents such as 'Dallas' and 'The Colbys'. Arguably, the resulting form of a literary telenovela provides an ideal mould for the hyperbolic style characteristic of much of García Márquez's writing. The story of Florentino Ariza's uncle, León XII, who out of necessity 'kept spare sets of dentures everywhere, in different places throughout the house, in the drawer of his desk and one set in each of the three ships belonging to his business' (p. 385), rests comfortably within the bounds of the narrative, as does the extravagant account of the Olivella silver-wedding celebrations which are attended by 122 guests, and the description of the huge breakfast which the Gargantuan Diego Samaritano devours on the last morning of the period covered in the story.

García Márquez's personal brand of humour, including elements of bathos and ridicule and an acute sense of irony, also acquires appropriate expression through the vehicle of an up-dated *folletín*. *Love in the Times of Cholera* contains many comic ingredients which make it at times hilarious (see the episode of the scalding of Juvenal Urbino's parrot in chapter 1), at times black and tragicomic in the manner of *Belarmino y Apolonio* by Ramón Pérez de Ayala. In keeping with this design, García Márquez presents Florentino Ariza both as a pathetic character whom adult female citizens regard compassionately as 'a solitary person in heed of love and affection' (p. 226), and as 'a squalid, timid and insignificant [wretch]' (p. 93) whose 'vigil' in the park attracts Fermina's attention more than it does her sympathy. The 'cagada', or bird-shit, that soils a love letter he sends her (p. 97) is a typical instance of the author's deflationary procedures which serve to ridicule Florentino's idealistic pretensions. To the same end, García Márquez endows his protagonist with defective eyesight, makes him prone to 'chronic constipation' (p. 86), and imposes on him the affliction of premature baldness, a characteristic not generally associated with his type.

In this way, the topoi and values of a lachrymose and implausible romanticism are subjected to sustained debasement, their excesses kept in check by an author who maintains a humorous detachment from a world of melodrama rooted in literary convention. García Márquez's strategy in this regard carries resounding echoes of that of Gustave Flaubert in *Madame Bovary*, a text with which *Love in the Times of Cholera* bears numerous resemblances, as it does with *L'É'ducation sentimentale* by the same author, and *Don Quixote* by Cervantes. Many of the representative themes of traditional and nineteenth-century fiction are superimposed on the *folletín*-esque framework of *Love in the Times of Cholera*. They include the problematic relationship between essence and appearance, the conflict between an individual's private aspirations and the established norms of public life, the view of reading as an 'insatiable vice' (p. 116) which distorts our perception of ourselves and the world and, lastly, the theme of disillusionment, illustrated most strikingly in the experience of Doctor Juvenal Urbino who, on the very last day of his life, discovers distressing truths about his friend, Jeremiah de Saint-Amour. According to García Márquez, 'Juvenal Urbino discovers the fraudulent foundation of his love for Jeremiah. And he is deeply disillusioned. He comes to realize on the very last day of his life only hours before he dies, that he had given his affection to someone who was not quite the person he thought he was.'[10] Florentino Ariza's acknowledgement of 'the fallacy of his own life' (p. 292) two years later is a similarly chastening admission of error. As happened regularly in the classical novel, the experience of *desengaño* (i.e. of being disabused of one's illusions) heightens a character's 'sense of reality' (p. 35) and forces a retreat from naive idealism of the sort indulged in by the *folletín*. On this evidence we observe how García Márquez employs the themes and conventions of one literary genre to undermine assumptions implicit in another, thereby providing an interesting illustration of the principle, enunciated in one of Jorge Luis Borges's fictions, that 'A text which does not incorporate its counter-text is considered to be incomplete.'[11]

Desengaño and the consequences of an unstable view of reality are concerns which are articulated throughout García Márquez's work. Other themes characteristic of his writing also reappear in *Love in the Times of Cholera*. Foremost among them are: dreams, memory and nostalgia, personal identity, sex and solitude, death, fate and destiny (with associated imagery of chess and card games), the historical experience of Colombia and Spanish America, social and sexual emancipation, patriarchy and the family, and the nature of—and relations between—the sexes. Such a broad range of interests promises to stimulate a variety of critical responses. In the remainder of this essay a number of themes and issues are considered which may prove likely to figure prominently in criticism of *Love in the Times of Cholera*. Three complementary readings of the novel are advanced from standpoints which may loosely be defined as 'humanist', 'feminist' and 'Americanist'. Needless to say, in choosing these categories there is no pretence that the interpretative possibilities of a many-sided text have been exhausted.

Love in the Times of Cholera is susceptible to a humanist reading of the sort illustrated in Giovanni Pontiero's study of *No One Writes to the Colonel*.[12] The narrative highlights the themes of love, marriage and old age, and promotes the value of human dignity, happiness, compassion, and (sensual) pleasure in defiance of cultural constraints, the strongest and most insidious of which is a sense of shame and remorse. In his mature writings Florentino Ariza develops his own ideas about 'life, love, old age and death' (p. 433) which challenge 'the conventional beliefs of his times' (p. 378) and are a source of 'prodigious consolation' to Fermina in her hours of grief (p. 459). Florentino insists on the propriety and dignity of love in old age, a belief shared by Fermina's daughter-in-law who counters the puritanical intolerance of Ophelia Urbino Daza with 'a serene justification of love at any age'. Ophelia, Fermina's daughter, 'was unable to conceive of an innocent relationship between two people of the opposite sex at the age of five, let alone at the age of eighty' and, in a heated family exchange, exclaims indignantly to her older brother, Urbino: 'Love is ridiculous at our age, but at [Florentino and Fermina's] it is disgusting' (p. 467). Her attitude offends Fermina to such an extent that she bans Ophelia from the family house, in an episode which secures our sympathy and admiration for her and elicits our firm disapproval of all forms of mean-minded moralism.

Heterosexual love, irrespective of age and in an almost infinite variety of forms, is García Márquez's single most important concern in *Love in the Times of Cholera*. He remarked to a journalist that 'What interests me most in the novel is the analysis it conducts of love at all ages.'[13] Arguably, some of Florentino Ariza's experiences as, alternately, a shy and vulnerable idealist and a selfish, calculating 'night-time prowler', who in his relations with several women 'gave nothing and wanted everything in return' (pp. 316–17), are less than exemplary and result in the most trite of revelations: see, for example, his discovery that 'one can be friendly with a woman without going to bed with her' (p. 276). But, his unfaltering devotion to Fermina and 'his infinite capacity for sustaining hope' (p. 336) are eventually rewarded by an author who is convinced that 'If we persevere, our bodies persevere. I think that we persevere if there is love. Always.'[14] Without underestimating the claims of the body, the novel proposes an idealistic conception of love as 'a state of grace which [is] not a means to anything but, rather, a beginning and an end in itself' (p. 425), and celebrates its realization in Fermina and Florentino's relationship:

> They carried on in silence like an old couple whom life has taught to act warily, beyond the range of the pitfalls of passion, beyond the range of the unkind tricks played on us by our hopes and by our failure to learn from our disappointments: beyond the range of love. For they had shared enough experiences to know by now that love is love in any period and in any place, but that it increases in intensity the closer we are to death. (p. 499)

The fulfilment of the couple's desires provides *Love in the Times of Cholera* with a narrative conclusion which several reviewers have interpreted as an affirmation of hope, life and love. Fermina and Florentino's dogged achievement may indeed be seen as a victory over the rigours of old age; the obstacles of fate and the prejudices of an unsympathetic society. Yet, the ending of the novel is deliberately left open and cannot be said unequivocally to be a happy one. The couple's position on the *New Fidelity* ('Nueva Fidelidad') which is destined to sail up and down the Magdalenas River (i.e. the river of life) as long as they remain alive, strikes us as being not only an acute form of social isolation—or quarantine, as it is termed in the symbolic idiom of the book—but also a wilfully artificial situation. García Márquez implicitly acknowledges this in an interview with Françesc Arroyo, in which he carefully evades the issue of whether his novel ends on an affirmative or negative note and confesses, instead, to 'a great curiosity': 'How do they end up? I mean, how do they really end up? What eventually happened to them?' In effect, García Márquez admits to providing a rhetorical denouement for his novel, which, he declares, '[is] a problem for the critics to solve'.[15] A brief examination of the scenes which immediately precede the conclusion may help to reveal the full implications of the final chapter.

In the period which leads up to the consummation of their love, Fermina and Florentino have to contend with a series of set-backs and obstacles to their happiness. First, Florentino breaks his ankle in a fall on a flight of stairs and is prevented from seeing Fermina for four months. When he recovers and invites her to take a cruise on the *New Fidelity*, she brushes aside her children's open opposition to her romance with Florentino and embarks with him, but the sound of the ship's horn as the *New Fidelity* sets sail damages her left ear, leaving her hearing permanently impaired. Finally, just as the couple begin to experience a fragile happiness, a telegram arrives bringing the disturbing news of América Vicuña's suicide. Now, it is possible to explain Florentino's accident merely as a comic narrative device and to attribute the onset of Fermina's deafness, which nicely matches Florentino's physical deficiencies, to a perverse symmetry. But, América Vicuña's suicide resists a reductive interpretation of this kind and requires to be accounted for at a deeper level of analysis which involves renewed consideration of the themes of love, happiness, moral responsibility, and death.

Leona Cassiani's telegraphic message attributes the suicide to mysterious causes: 'América Vicuña died yesterday cause unknown' (p. 485). The reader, however, is left in no doubt that the girl kills herself because she cannot bear the pain and humiliation caused by Florentino's abandoning her for Fermina Daza. Some three years previously, Florentino had wasted no time in seducing América when, as a teenager, she had been placed in his care by distant relations; now, still standing *in loco parentis*, he treats her with peremptory indifference and is to be held largely responsible for her death. In the book's final chapter the sudden announcement of América's suicide thereby signifies the intrusion, into Fermina and Florentino's idyll, of disturbing realities of selfishness, cruelty and death. The central importance of these ideas is enhanced by a newspaper report about an elderly couple who are battered to death by a boatman as he ferries them to the location where they had enjoyed their honey-moon forty years before (pp. 460–1). Fermina is haunted by this story which provides an approximate but telling reflection of her position with Florentino on the *New Fidelity*; it is also a compelling intimation of mortality. The old folk's murder, coupled with América Vicuña's suicide, thus modifies the mood of the narrative at a climactic point and persuades us that García Márquez's vision of humanity is best understood in nuanced terms, not simply as generous and humane, but, fundamentally, as 'a fatalistic brand of humanism' (p. 23) which rests on a mature recognition of 'the certainty of death' (p. 35).

The relationship between feminist ideology and the values of liberal humanism is at once intricate and controversial; as Toril Moi observes in a recent critical survey,[16] some feminist positions in fact reproduce the aesthetic and philosophical assumptions of patriarchal humanism, while others engage in a radical critique of them. By virtue of its ideological complexity, *Love in the Times of Cholera* is sure to attract the attention of egalitarian and radical feminists alike.

The questions of marriage and the curtailment of personal freedom preoccupy García Márquez in this novel. *Pace* José Font Castro, who sees *Love in the Times of Cholera* as a *roman à clef* designed to pay homage to García

Márquez's own parents and their marriage,[17] I discern in the book substantial evidence of an indictment of that particular institution. For, if on one occasion Fermina and Juvenal's marriage is credited with certain positive achievements (see p. 328), on countless others it is presented as a form of 'sterile captivity' (p. 296) and 'servitude' (p. 405) endured by Fermina. Her experience of married life testifies emphatically to the dehumanizing effect of an institution which traps women 'in [a] web of conventions and prejudices' (p. 305), forcing them to compromise their individuality and, ultimately, to sacrifice their personal identity to their husband's will. In a singular passage, the narrative records the disappointment which Fermina feels as a mature housewife:

> about never having become what she had dreamt of becoming when she was young, in the Park of the Evangelists, but instead, something which she did not dare to admit even to herself a high-class serving maid ... She always felt as if she were living a life that was being leased to her by her husband: with absolute control over a vast empire of happiness established by him and for him alone. She knew that he loved her above all else, more than anyone else in the world, but only for himself she was at his beck and call. (p. 323)

A later reference to Juvenal Urbino's 'patriarchal demands' (p. 434) adds a conclusive touch to the picture of her entrapment by the insidious mechanisms of 'benevolent' patriarchy.

It is no surprise that Fermina finds in widowhood a source of liberation and an opportunity to recover 'all that she had had to give up in the course of half a century's servitude which unquestionably had made her happy but which, in the wake of her husband's death, left her without the slightest trace of an identity' (p. 405). We note that her experience is representative of that of a wider community of women who, in striving to adjust to their new circumstances, 'would discover that the only honest way to live was as their bodies dictated, eating only when they felt hungry, making love without the need to tell lies, sleeping without having to pretend to be asleep in order to avoid the indecency of a conjugal routine' (p. 297). In the guise of a general statement about widowhood, this quotation reiterates condemnation of the constraints placed on women in marriage, and conveys a message of protest which has relevance beyond the boundaries of Colombian society in the late nineteenth century.

García Márquez's attitude to the position which women occupy within the broader framework of society is expressed indirectly through recurrent images of 'maternal manatees' (p. 488). These sea-cows 'with huge breasts for suckling their young, and plaintive voices like those of disconsolate women' (see pp. 211 and 497) are symbols of motherhood; according to legend, they are also 'the only creatures without a male in the animal kingdom' (p. 479), and thereby embody an ideal of sexual self-sufficiency which institutionalized patriarchy is bound to regard as an unnatural form of independence. Whenever he sees a manatee, Diego Samaritano, the ship's captain, is reminded of 'women whom society has condemned for having taken a false step in love' (p. 479); he thus conveys his society's hostility towards behaviour which does not conform to established norms. Manatee imagery also acts as a vehicle for García Márquez's denunciation of the predatory spirit of the male. His story of 'a huntsman from North Carolina who had disobeyed regulations and shot a mother manatee in the head with a bullet from his Springfield rifle' (p. 480) indicates the extremes of cruelty and abuse to which the female of the species is exposed within a supposedly civilized world.

Seen in this light, *Love in the Times of Cholera* stands out as a novel which passes strong censure on the order of patriarchy. However, García Márquez's reliance on the image of woman as a vulnerable mother-figure betrays a conservative sexual ideology which, in its perpetuation of given assumptions about the function of gender in social relations, may actually further that system's interests. If we assume that the narrative voice in the novel embodies overall the attitudes of an implied author, then it is possible to identify certain moments in *Love in the Times of Cholera* which reveal a suspect essentialism in García Márquez's account of the nature of the sexes. An early description of Juvenal and Fermina's house as a place which displays throughout 'the good judgement and careful attention of a woman who had her feet firmly on the ground' (p. 37) raises the spectre of a sexist mystique which attributes *a priori* one set of characteristics (for example, pragmatism and reliability) to women, represented here by Leona Cassiani as well as by Fermina Daza, and another quite distinct set to men, who are depicted as helplessly idealistic and impractical. A subsequent portrayal of Fermina disembarking at Riohacha, 'looking radiant, every inch a woman' (p. 191), increases our sense of unease, as does a statement to the effect that 'Women think more about the meanings behind the questions than about the questions themselves' (p. 417). The same narrator goes on to attribute Juvenal's dependence on his wife, not so much to personal psychological peculiarities, as to the fact that 'He is a man and weaker [than she is]' (p. 328). Such statements may possibly ring true to certain readers, but we cannot help but dispute the essentialist foundations on which they appear to rest; future commentators will almost certainly wish to undertake a systematic deconstruction of García Márquez's position on this issue which is of profound concern to several types of feminist inquiry.

This reading of *Love in the Times of Cholera* concludes with some reflections on the theme of America. This important area of García Márquez's writing embraces considerations of history, politics, class, race and culture, expressed here in literal, symbolic and allegorical terms. From a detailed historical vantage point, the narrative evokes the era of Spanish colonial rule as a time of prosperity for the local *criollo* merchant class and, on a wider scale, as a period of slavery and abuse by the Inquisition in 'the sinister palace where the Holy Office's prison was located' (p. 197). Hazardous open sewers 'inherited from the Spanish' (p. 27) are a pungent image of the colonial heritage of a city which 'had now existed on the margins of history ... for four hundred years'; during that time 'nothing had happened except that it had grown old slowly midst its withered laurel trees and putrid cess pools' (p. 33). This vision of secular inertia holds true for the postcolonial era, as the experience of Juvenal Urbino's family illustrates: 'Independence from Spanish rule, followed by the abolition of slavery, precipitated the circumstances of honourable decline in which [Juvenal] was born and grew up' (p. 34). According to García Márquez, at this juncture in their history those 'families that had been influential in days gone by' (p. 34) cultivated a fatalistic acceptance of 'the sad and oppressive world which God had provided for them' (p. 163) and sought refuge in an artificial order of social snobbery, racial prejudice and political mystification.

In this respect, Juvenal Urbino exemplifies the contradictions of his class. His conciliatory liberal views, which he holds 'more out of habit than conviction' (p. 74), are at variance with the inflexible moral stance of an 'old-style Christian' (p. 68). On an innocent reading, the name 'Juvenal Urbino' connotes qualities of youthful dynamism and commitment to a civilizing mission which are echoed in the narrator's remark about Juvenal's 'spirit of renovation and his maniacal civic sense' (p. 164); yet, we learn that in private the doctor displayed 'a narrow-mindedness which did not conform to his public image' (p. 56). On his death, the Urbino dynasty is shown to be a spent force which leaves no significant political legacy: the narrative describes Juvenal's children by Fermina as 'two mediocre tail-ends of a race' and attests to his status as 'the last bearer of a surname doomed to extinction' (p. 75).

García Márquez deliberately contrasts *criollo* decadence with the instinctual vitality of 'the impoverished mulattoes' (p. 33). In an image of visionary proportions, the masses of mixed racial origins 'infused the dead city with a frenzy of human jubilation smelling of fried fish: [they infused it] with new life' (p. 34). This affirmation is redolent of the author's Nobel speech which celebrates the vital potential of the people of Latin America.

However, in neither context is that belief translated into any clearly outlined philosophy of political action which might lead to an improvement in the people's lives. In fact, at a level of significance to which we now turn, *Love in the Times of Cholera* recounts not the revival but the death of America in the allegorical figure of América Vicuña, whose name identifies her as an emblem of the natural and political life of the subcontinent (recalling that the vicuña is a mammal peculiar to some parts of South America).

As already stated, responsibility for América Vicuña's death may be imputed to Florentino Ariza, who is pictured in symbolic terms 'leading her by the hand with the gentle cunning of an apparently well-meaning grandfather towards a hidden place of slaughter' (p. 396). This image, which evokes a famous story, *The Slaughterhouse*, by the nineteenth-century Argentinian writer, Esteban Echeverría, provides graphic confirmation of Florentino's involvement in the death of América, and opens up the possibility of an allegorical reading of their relationship as a re-enactment of the treacherous destruction of young America by the Florentine (i.e. the Columbus Renaissance) spirit of Europe. The killing, by a huntsman from North Carolina, of a second species of mammal indigenous to the Caribbean (the manatee) further enhances the novel's figurative dimension and contributes to the projection of a poetic image of Latin America as a living body which European and American interests have courted and stalked as prey since the colonization of the New World began in the sixteenth century. Western readers may feel that they have a particular obligation to examine the view of Latin American history which, on this interpretation, is implied in the narrative of *Love in the Times of Cholera*.

These observations on García Márquez's representation of Latin America bring this study of his most recent novel to a close. In this essay I have attempted to convey a sense of the generic and ideological complexity of *Love in the Times of Cholera*, by demonstrating its capacity to accommodate various readings. My reluctance to impose a reductive or unitary interpretation on the book reflects a belief in the principle, expressed by Mario Vargas Llosa, that 'The richness of a work of art derives from the diversity of elements which it comprises and from the number of readings which it admits.'[18] In my view, *Love in the Times of Cholera* affords generous opportunities to future commentators who may wish to extend appreciation of a richly allusive and open work beyond the confines of this introductory study.

NOTES

1. Information on the circumstances of the novel's composition and publication is provided by Antonio Caballero, 'La increíble y divertida historia de la novela de García

Márquez', *Cambio* 16, 736 (Madrid, 6 January 1986), 102–3, and in a special report entitled 'El amor en los tiempos del Nobel', published in *Semana*, 187 (Bogotá, 3–9 December 1985), 28–35.

2. See Carlos Monsiváis, 'García Márquez, al margen del Nobel', in *Culturas* (Suplemento semanal de *Diario* 16), 38 (Madrid, 29 December 1985), i–ii.

3. Gabriel García Márquez, *El amor en los tiempos del cólera* (Barcelona, Bruguera, 1985). All page references cited in the text of this study are to this edition. All translations of material into English are mine.

4. As confirmed by García Márquez and reported in 'El amor en los tiempos del Nobel', p. 29.

5. See García Márquez's declarations to Françesc Arroyo, reproduced in 'El amor, la vejez, la muerte: un paseo con Gabriel García Márquez por la trama y la historia de su última novela', *El País* (*Libros*), Year 7,321 (Madrid, 12 December 1985) 1–3 (p. 1).

6. Ex-President Dr Alfonso López Michelsen referred to this and other properties of *Love in the Times of Cholera* in a public address celebrating the book's publication in Bogotá, in December 1985. The text of Dr López Michelsen's address, entitled 'El amor en los tiempos del cólera', was supplied by Sr Mario Ramirez of the Colombian Embassy in London. I wish to take this opportunity of thanking Sr Ramirez and his staff for providing a wide range of bibliographical information connected with this project.

7. Other echoes of Dario are to be found in this novel as well as in the pages of *The Autumn of the Patriarch*.

8. In 'El amor en los tiempos de cólera', Dr López Michelsen reminded his Colombian audience that *María* 'was obligatory reading' in the age of Romanticism.

9. See Antonio Caballero, 'La increíble y divertida historia de la novela de García Márquez', p. 103.

10. See García Márquez's declarations to Françesc Arroyo, mentioned in note 5 above, p. 2.

11. Jorge Luis Borges, 'Tlön, Uqbar, Orbis Tertius', in *Ficciones*, 11th ed. (Madrid, 1982), P. 28.

12. Gabriel García Márquez, *El coronel no tiene quien le escriba*, edited with an introductory study by Giovanni Pontiero (Manchester, 1981).

13. See García Márquez's declarations to Françesc Arroyo, p. 2.

14. *Ibid.*, p. 3.

15. *Ibid.*, p. 2.

16. Toril Moi, *Sexual/Textual Politics: Feminist Literary Theory* (London and New York, 1985).

17. Font Castro documents numerous similarities in the experience of the characters in *Love in the Times of Cholera* with the courtship and marriage of García Márquez's parents, in 'Las claves reales de *El amor en los tiempos del cólera*', *El País* (Domingo) (Madrid, 19 January 1986), 14–15.

18. See Vargas Llosa's remarks on the film 'Furtivos', by the Spanish director, José Luis Borau, in *Vuelta*, 9 (Mexico City, August 1977), 44–8 (46).

LOIS PARKINSON ZAMORA

Apocalypse and Human Time
in the Fiction of Gabriel García Márquez

For all our days are passed away in Thy wrath: we spend our years as a
tale that is told.

Psalms 90:9

The fiction of Gabriel García Márquez presents an extended
consideration of temporal reality, of the beginnings and ends of individual
human beings and humanity as a whole. García Márquez's perspective is
mythical and eschatological: Temporal movement in his novels is neither
aimless nor endless but successive and purposeful, advancing on an end to
which significance can be assigned, if not by the characters in the novel, then
by the novelist and the reader. The history of Macondo, presented whole by
García Márquez in *One Hundred Years of Solitude* (1967), is a monumental
fiction of succession and ending, of communal and narrative fulfillment.
Much of the rest of García Márquez's fiction is also impelled by a powerful
eschatological impulse. In *The Autumn of the Patriarch* (1975), the apocalypse
is political. Moral and social degeneration become a function of the political
travesties of the general in this novel, his dictatorship an image of the last
loosing of Satan, his prolonged domination suggestive of the reign of the
Beast which in Revelation signals the end of time. In *Chronicle of a Death
Foretold* (1981), the end is neither social nor political but individual, and
wholly inevitable. Alfred J. MacAdam has asserted quite correctly that "the

---

From *Writing the Apocalypse: Historical Vision in Contemporary U.S. and Latin American Fiction.*
©1989 by Cambridge University Press.

essential problem of [*One Hundred Years of Solitude*] structurally and in its attitude toward history is duration."[1] My discussion here will amplify that observation to include the proposition that in much of García Márquez's fiction, the essential problem is how duration ends.

García Márquez uses the patterns of apocalypse to structure and direct his temporal fictions, and to relate human time to the time of the universe. Frank Kermode observes in *The Sense of an Ending* that the relationship between the individual human span and the span of history has become increasingly problematic with the modern lengthening of the scale of perceived history, an observation immediately applicable to García Márquez's fiction, as is Hannah Arendt's discussion of the absence of a beginning and end in our modern conception of history.[2] If the individual's relation to the beginning and end of time now seems impossible to imagine, it is precisely the temporal patterns of apocalypse which provide for García Márquez the mythological and narrative means to do so. Though the author bases his novels on the specific historical and cultural conditions of Colombia and Latin America, events of the actual past repeatedly adhere to the mythic shape of apocalyptic history. In accordance with much contemporary Latin American narrative, García Márquez engages historical fact the better to assert the primacy of historical fable.[3] Gregory Rabassa, translator of García Márquez, has commented with regard to *One Hundred Years of Solitude*, "The broadest tale of a people, and therefore of an individual, is more often than not elegiac or apocalyptic. Beowulf's funeral pyre is also sensed to be that of all the Geats...."[4] Whether individual and collective ends coincide, as at the end of *One Hundred Years of Solitude*, or whether the end is a measure of individual solitude, as in *Chronicle of a Death Foretold*, García Márquez's vision of history is like a tale that is told, a tale that presses steadily toward conclusion.

I.

The title of *One Hundred Years of Solitude* suggests its central concern with the nature—and the limits—of human time. In 100 years, the history of the Buendía family and their town is chronicled from beginning to end. Like a biblical apocalyptist, García Márquez's narrator, Melquíades, recounts the past, present, and future of Macondo from a point beyond the future. He constantly relates past events to subsequent events in a retrospective future tense, because the fates which await the characters are already known to him: For Melquíades, the future is past. He also relates past events to an even more remote past, revealing the lifespan of Macondo and its inhabitants with sweeping totality. Thus, in a room of the Buendía house where it is always

March and always Monday, Melquíades unifies past, present, and future by means of his narrative art. Melquíades is linked early in the novel with Nostradamus, the sixteenth-century French astrologer and mystic whose books of apocalyptic predictions were divided into 100 rhymed quatrains called centuries. We learn at the end of the novel that what Melquíades has been writing is another kind of apocalyptic century: Macondo's history is "written by Melquíades, down to the most trivial details, one hundred years ahead of time"; in it, he concentrates "a century of daily episodes in such a way that they coexisted in one instant. "5

The temporal structure of *One Hundred Years of Solitude*, like apocalypse, is rectilinear rather than cyclical. Of course, human temporal reality can never be described as merely flat or linear: García Márquez manages to convey the temporal vagaries that make moments seem endless and ages like moments, and that make Macondo's history seem to double back upon itself and describe circles in time. Several critics have commented on the cyclical movement inherent in Macondo's structure. Ricardo Gullón and G. D. Carillo emphasize the repetition of the Buendías' names and personalities, the recurring events and activities from one generation to another; the seemingly endless series of futile civil wars that involve one character after another; Carmen Arnau describes Macondo as cyclical in the Spenglerian sense that the town participates in birth, growth, maturity, decline, death, and rebirth.6 This is certainly so during the course of Macondo's 100-year history, but those 100 years do come to an end, and a rebirth ultimately fails to occur. García Márquez concludes his novel on this very point: "races condemned to one hundred years of solitude did not have a second opportunity on earth" (384).

Mikhail Bakhtin, in his *Esthétique et théorie du roman*, raises the interesting question of whether cyclical temporal patterns can ever provide the structural principle of the novel. Discussing *Madame Bovary*, he contrasts "la vie quotidienne" to progressive temporal structures, recognizing that the life of the "petite ville de province" seems nothing but repetition. Time appears bereft of any historic movement: In its repetitive sameness, one day is never only one day but every day, all days, and one life is by definition endlessly multiplied in the undistinguished sameness of all of the lives in the town. Despite the enormous distance of Yonville from Macondo, Bakhtin's comments about the temporal stasis of daily routine in *Madame Bovary* may nonetheless be applied to *One Hundred Years of Solitude*: "Time here is without event and therefore, seems almost to stand still. Here there are no meetings, no partings! It is a viscous and sticky time that drags itself slowly through space."7 For this reason, continues Bakhtin, repeating cycles cannot sustain a novelistic structure, though the novelist may use such cycles as the contrasting background for "energetic and eventful temporal series"—as do both Flaubert and García Márquez. The seemingly endless generational cycles of the Buendías and the recurring sequences of events in Macondo are set against the progressive temporal structure of the myth of apocalypse. They do eventually reach their end: "the family was a machine with unavoidable repetitions, a turning wheel that would have gone on spilling into eternity were it not for the progressive and irremediable wearing of the axle" (364). José Arcadio Buendía's city of mirrors, with its seemingly infinite self-reflections, proves in fact an unrepeatable mirage: "It was foreseen that the city of mirrors (or mirages) would be wiped out by the wind and exiled from the memory of men ..." (383). The end of the Buendía line is anticipated from its beginning.

Eschatological pressure is inherent in the temporal organization of the narrative. The phrase "many years later" begins the novel and is repeated frequently by Melquíades. As the narrative progresses, "many years later" becomes "some years later," "a few years later," and then "a few months later": The end of the history of Macondo approaches relentlessly. The decline of Macondo, which begins with the banana boom, is filled with reminders that the "banana company hurricane" is an anticipation of "the prophetic wind that years later would wipe Macondo off the face of the earth" (305). The events that destroy Macondo—the oppression of the banana company, the strike and massacre of the banana company workers, the ensuing flood—lead to the inevitable moment when Macondo will be blown away, and the tropics will reclaim its territory. The cataclysm occurs at the same moment that the last surviving Buendía, Aureliano *Babilonia*, completes the deciphering of Melquíades's coded history of his family. He understands that the family's history has been fulfilled, that the child with a pig's tail, long predicted, has arrived. The end of the apocalyptic manuscript and the end of time coincide.

Just as the whole history of Macondo is revealed, so is the whole history of the characters, their beginnings constantly related to their ends by Melquíades from his point of view beyond the end. Colonel Aureliano Buendía's career is summarized before it is dramatized, and long before his death is described, Melquíades tells us that all that remains of his illustrious life is a street bearing his name. Meme, one of the ill-fated Buendías, experiences a tragic love affair as a young girl, and the rest of her life is quickly recapitulated in terms of that tragic love. She enters a convent, thinking about her lover, "and she would keep on thinking about him for all the days of her life until the remote autumn morning when she died of old age, with her name changed and her head shaved and without ever having spoken a word, in a gloomy hospital in Cracow" (275). Meme's individual span is related to the collective span as she leaves Macondo: From the train window, she glimpses the carbonized skeleton of the Spanish galleon which José Arcadio had encountered as he entered the pristine world of Macondo almost a century earlier.

All of the characters in *One Hundred Years of Solitude* feel the pressure of time from two directions: Past and future, memories and premonitions burden their present and separate them from one another. Unlike many modern fictional characters who, in existential (and archetypically American) fashion, leave their pasts behind in order to remake themselves according to their own design, García Márquez's characters are inextricably bound to their pasts and, at the same time, long for the future. Georges Poulet, in *Studies in Human Time*, discusses "romantic nostalgia," which seems to describe the situation of the inhabitants of Macondo. "It is as if duration had been broken in the middle and man felt his life torn from him, ahead and behind. The romantic effort to form itself a being out of presentiment and memory ends in the experience of a double tearing of the self."[8] The characters in *One Hundred Years of Solitude* constantly search on both sides of the moment for an escape from their solitude. Their futile search for release in the passionate present of sex only emphasizes the compelling necessity of this process.

Memories are important to the Buendías because they offer the illusory possibility of transcending the momentary, or as Poulet puts it, the possibility of participating in duration. It is thus poignantly ironic that throughout the novel memories are associated not with duration but with death. The characters' most vivid memories are recounted as they realize that they are about to die. The novel begins with Colonel Aureliano Buendía's first memory as he awaits death before a firing squad. The memories of Arcadio, Aureliano Segundo, Meme also irrupt as they face death. José Arcadio Segundo sees a man shot—the only memory he retains of his childhood. Memories become an especial source of isolation for José Arcadio Segundo, who later remembers with painful clarity the slaughter of the workers by the forces of the banana company, a fact which everyone else has been induced by those very forces to forget. Facing death, the characters' memories only serve to heighten their realization that the past is irretrievable and incommunicable. The wise Catalan bookstore owner speaks for most of the Buendías when he insists that "the past was a lie, that memory has no return, that every spring gone by could never be recovered, and that the wildest and most tenacious love was an ephemeral truth in the end" (370). Memory accentuates, rather than mitigates, each Buendía's isolation in the time capsule of his or her own history.

Premonition, like memory, leads the characters to the inevitable fact of death. Amaranta has a "premonition of her own end; she sees death, a woman dressed in blue with long hair and an antiquated look: "Death did not tell her when she was going to die or whether her hour was assigned ... but ordered her to begin sewing her own shroud on the next sixth of April" (260). Like Penelope in *The Odyssey*, Amaranta devises ways to prolong her task and thus her life, but her resignation to the truth of her presentiment of death is absolute. As she painstakingly stitches her shroud, she understands why Colonel Aureliano spent his last years making little gold fishes, melting them down, and making them again. She knows that the vicious circle of little gold fishes, like her intricate embroidery, reduces the world to a surface and temporarily denies annihilation. Úrsula, the matriarch of the Buendías, also knows with certainty when she will die. After the banana company massacre, it rains for four years, eleven months and two days: When the rain stops, she expects death. In the "clairvoyance of her decrepitude," she perceives a progressive breakdown in time itself. She knows that "the world is slowly coming to an end" (176), and there is nothing in the future to assuage her solitude.

García Márquez provides an anterior comic version of Úrsula's death, as he has of several of the apocalyptic elements in *One Hundred Years of Solitude*.[9] In his short story, "Big Mama's Funeral" (1962), García Márquez parodies the hyperbole of apocalyptic description and the magnitude of its terminal vision with his own fantastically exaggerated account of the end of Big Mama; she and Macondo are coterminous, but her funeral is a comic saturnalia rather than a *dies irae*. The carnival atmosphere surrounding the death of Big Mama is replaced in the novel by the monotonous sound of rain as the end approaches. Not only Úrsula but the whole town of Macondo as well is waiting for the rain to stop in order to die. One of the Buendías observes that Macondo's inhabitants no longer divide the years into months, or the days into hours. This sense of endless, hence meaningless, duration is the subject of another of García Márquez's early stories about Macondo, "Monologue of Isabel Watching It Rain in Macondo" (1955). In this story, García Márquez's geographical and historical cipher of the world—Macondo—is already visible: the intolerable heat, the relentless rains, the tropical ennui of habit and unpunctuated time. Isabel describes time as viscous (also Bakhtin's word), as a physical, jellylike thing, and the people as paralyzed, waiting for the rain to stop. Waiting is also the subject of *No One Writes to the Colonel* (1961), the account of an aged colonel who fought with Aureliano Buendía on the losing side of the civil wars, and who has waited decades for the pension promised him by the victorious generals. The colonel's hope turns to self-delusion as nothing happens, nothing concludes. His expectations are never realized: They serve only to delineate the shape of human impotence in a realm of fated history. These last two stories describe the violence with which the apocalypse fails to occur; as in the epoch of the flood in *One Hundred Years of Solitude*, undifferentiated time stretches before the characters. In García Márquez's tropics, temporal resolution, even cataclysmic resolution, comes to seem welcome. In accordance with apocalyptic convention, all that can be anticipated is the end of time itself.

Waiting is inherent in apocalypse, and the biblical apocalyptists conceived the need to wait in terms of eschatological conviction. The goal of time was understood to be God's perfect realm, and waiting implied the realization of history and the fulfillment of providential plan. The Book of Daniel presents patience as an apocalyptic policy. Rejecting political involvement, Daniel argues that waiting itself represents an ideological commitment, that refusal to wait represents a failure of faith and a repudiation of the divine plan for history.[10] This policy is based on an understanding of secular history as separated from sacred history, an understanding that was institutionalized by Augustine; it is not until the twelfth century, with Joachim of Fiore and the subsequent growth of popular millenarian movements, that apocalyptic visions began to inspire impatience, and hence revolutionary ideologies (an eventuality dramatized by Carlos Fuentes in *Terra Nostra*). García Márquez does not, of course, reject political involvement, but his character in *No One Writes to the Colonel* does. In this story, all of García Márquez's characters are caught in webs of circumstance they cannot influence. So are most of the inhabitants of postdiluvian Macondo, in *One Hundred Years of Solitude*: Only the inheritors of Melquíades's manuscripts, particularly Aureliano Babilonia, are capable of doing anything other than waiting, arms folded, for the end. The apocalyptic narrators' textual deciphering is the sole activity of import in the drenched and dying Macondo.

But time was not always an unbearable and seemingly endless burden in Macondo, nor did memory and premonition always reinforce the solitude of the characters' present. In prelapsarian Macondo, the past and the future were scarcely distinguished from the present, for time was unified in innocence. Then, memory and premonition enhanced the present, and allowed the earliest Buendías to participate in duration. José Arcadio Buendía finds in the original Macondo a paradise which calls up ancient memories of archetypal realms. For him, the most intriguing of the gypsies' inventions are the apparatus to make a person forget his bad memories, and a poultice to assuage the effects of time; indeed, suggests the narrator, José Arcadio must have wanted to invent a memory machine in order not to forget all of the things brought by the gypsies to Macondo. In fact, the young and innocent town survives the plague of forgetfulness by labeling everything and describing its use. José Arcadio's premonitions are not about death but, on the contrary, about the existence of the Buendías *per omnia saecula saeculorum*: He is a prophet who guides his people to the promised land which, like Israel, represents the fulfillment of their history.

It is not long after the founding of Macondo that José Arcadio's prophetic vision is replaced by the apocalyptic vision of his heirs, as I have already suggested. This shift from prophetic to apocalyptic eschatology reiterates that of Hebrew history. The biblical prophets' vision of their history as moving toward the establishment of a blessed community seemed less and less likely in view of their contemporary historical situation of exile and oppression. By the second century before Christ, their prophetic vision began to be replaced by an apocalyptic vision which insisted on a radical change or break in history as the only possible remedy for existing evils.[11] Early in Macondo's history, José Arcadio prophesies an eternal city with great glass houses, a luminous new community separated physically and morally from the old world of temporal decay. After all, he has left the old world behind, arriving full of insight into the possibilities of moral freedom in a new world. In him, we recognize initially the Latin American counterpart to what Earl Rovit calls the "seminal image" of U.S. literature, "man against the sky, the lone figure in an infinite cosmos, trying either to come to terms with tho cosmos or force the cosmos to come to terms with him."[12] For a brief moment, Macondo remains balanced between the terms of the cosmos and those of José Arcadio, but death, war, pestilence, and the banana company intrude upon his arcadia, tainting the future he has conjured. His dream of history becomes a nightmare of politics, a progression that makes the novel's critical perspective inevitable.

It is the breakdown of the patriarch's perpetual motion machine that heralds the shift, early in the novel, from prophetic to apocalyptic eschatology. Its failure forces José Arcadio to recognize that time is discontinuous, that Macondo is no longer paradise. Clocks appear, and so does an old man with white hair. He is Prudencio Aguilar, whom José Arcadio has killed years before, and who signals the irruption of the past, and death, into Macondo. Prudencio's appearance initiates Macondo's apocalyptic history, just as the appearance of a man whose "hairs were white like wool" (Rev. 1:14) initiates the apocalyptic events recounted in Revelation. It is José Arcadio's realizations about time that drive him crazy. He is tied to a chestnut tree and there he remains, insensible to the apocalyptic decline and destruction of the city that he prophesied would endure forever.

If, as I have said, memory is the source and confirmation of the Buendías' solitude, it is above all one particular memory, that of the paradisal Macondo, which isolates José Arcadio and alienates the rest of the characters from their present time and place. In *The Labyrinth of Solitude*, Octavio Paz proposes that the Latin American sense of solitude originates as a longing for the idealized time and place in the mythical past—whether a paradise or a holy center, an omphalos of the universe. To this longing, Paz relates a nostalgia for the divine body from which, he argues, humanity senses itself separated. He points to the idealized history which all mythologies describe, "a time when time was not succession and transition, but rather the perpetual source of a fixed present in which all times, past and future, were contained.... As soon as reality was divided up into yesterday, today, and tomorrow, into hours, minutes, and seconds, man ceased to be one with time, ceased to coincide with the flow of reality."[13] With clocks in Macondo, the rhythms of nature are replaced by those of empire: rise and fall, beginning and end, institution and catastrophe. Like the Latin American history which it epitomizes, Macondo's history begins as an idyll, degenerates into an imperial epic, until—we understand at the end of the novel—it is reconstituted by the mythic vision of Melquíades's text.

II.

If One Hundred Years of Solitude is about the cataclysmic history of the Buendías and Macondo, it is also about the deciphering of the manuscript that records and preserves their history, and about the narrative equivocations inherent in the process. It is this aspect of the novel that most clearly connects García Márquez to his "maestro," William Faulkner. García Márquez has repeatedly acknowledged his great appreciation of Faulkner's fiction, most recently in his speech accepting the 1982 Nobel Prize for literature; for García Márquez, Faulkner is the most influential of Latin America's literary predecessors. He describes his own affinity for Faulkner's fiction in terms of shared worlds and world views, saying that "Yoknapatawpha County has Caribbean shores; thus, in some sense Faulkner is a Caribbean writer, in some sense a Latin American writer."[14] It is tempting to stop and explore this expanded map of the Caribbean, and if we did, we would find that it has been charted in similar ways by the Cuban writer, Alejo Carpentier.[15] In Carpentier's special understanding of the idea of America, in his development of the concept and techniques of magical realism, even in the green wind that sweeps Haiti away at the end of his apocalyptically titled novel, *The Kingdom of This World* (1949), we would find important sources of the contemporary Latin American fiction I discuss here. However, my own comparative aims will be more broadly served by relating Macondo to Mississippi, rather than to Cuba; in fact, I will return to the issue of the affinities between Southern U.S. fiction and Latin American fiction in my discussion of the fiction of Walker Percy. Here, I only begin to trace the lines of intersection.

Carlos Fuentes describes one point where the lines converge in these terms: "Until recently, American writers never had the chance to deal with a national failure. The American ideal of success has done a great deal to standardize American art forms. That's why I think that for many years the most original American writing has come from the South, where there had been a real sense of regional tragedy and where there was a need to reexamine the things that had been taken for granted."[16] Fuentes singles out Faulkner to exemplify his contentions: "Suddenly there is the spectre of failure facing a country based on success. Then you can write *Absalom, Absalom!* and all the other great novels of Faulkner."[17] Fuentes overstates his case here. There have of course always been U.S. writers (and not just Southerners) who have known that one can suffer from the past: Consider Saul Bellow or Bernard Malamud or, perhaps the greatest example of the type, a New Englander—Nathaniel Hawthorne. But this does not obviate Fuentes's assertion that contemporary Latin American writers have found in the literature of the U.S. South, and especially in Faulkner's work, elements kindred to their own national experience: the guilt of the colonist who had profaned his pristine land, the decadence of an irrelevant aristocracy, the injustice and racial cruelty of the white-skinned usurper.[18] I will not explore the provocative question of Faulkner's influence on Latin American literature. Rather I want to juxtapose novels by Faulkner and García Márquez, and point to similar apocalyptic thematic and narrative structures which illuminate a shared comprehension of America and a shared mode of narrating its history.

It is in *Absalom, Absalom!* (1936) and *One Hundred Years of Solitude* that Faulkner and García Márquez are most closely aligned.[19] The history of the Sutpens, like that of the Buendías, reiterates the archetypal American experience of leaving the past behind and striking out to create an innocent new world in the timeless wilderness; it reiterates, furthermore, the equally American experience of discovering that virgin territory can be the site of evil as well as innocence. And because it is the memory of the narrators, however fallible, upon which these stories rest, they are not only about the Sutpens and the Buendías but also about the nature of historical truth, about how we remember and how we create the past with our words and our literary forms. Faulkner, like García Márquez, depends for the elaboration of his essentially American tale upon an apocalyptic perspective from which his narrators view the beginnings and ends of the world that they describe. Their accounts of the disparity between the original potential of America and its imminent ruin combine nostalgia and violence in an apocalyptic tone which both Faulkner and García Márquez recognize as altogether appropriate for telling secular tales of paradise lost.

As I have said in my introduction, apocalypse is an emphatically inclusive mythical history: Christ's statement, "I am Alpha and Omega, the beginning and the end, the first and the last" echoes throughout Revelation. Speaking from a point beyond the future, the narrator of Revelation senses himself compelled to write his history, for God has ordered him: "Write the things which thou hast seen, the things which are, and the things which shall be hereafter" (Rev. 1:19). Addressed to early Christians at a time of political persecution, John's apocalyptic narrative attempts to make sense of present suffering by seeking a design in history, by ascribing teleological significance to events. Of course, such paradigmatic history has more to do with fictional narration than with experience, for temporal progression is not intrinsically coherent or significant, nor can we relate cause to effect, origin to ending, so readily in our own worlds. Historiographer Hayden White has written about the process of creating explanatory history out of experienced data, of "fashioning human experience into a form assimilable to structures of meaning."[20] In order to comprehend reality, White argues, it is necessary "to narrativize" it, to impose the form of a story, with its well-marked beginning, middle, and end, upon experience: "The events must be not only registered within the chronological framework of their original occurrence but narrated as well, that is to say, revealed as possessing a structure, an order of meaning, which they do not possess as mere sequence" (9). This narrativizing impulse is present in the explanatory histories of individuals as well as larger political and social groups. In his discussion of Freud's case history of the Wolfman, Peter Brooks shows that narrative ordering, the constitution of a coherent order of events with an intelligible beginning and end from inchoate psychological data, is basic to Freud's achievement.[21] The narrativizing of history, the emplotting of the raw material of experience, is relevant here because *Absalom, Absalom!* and *One Hundred Years of Solitude* dramatize this very activity in their narrative techniques: The narrators of these novels use the explanatory structures of apocalypse to give comprehensible—and comprehensive—shape to the histories they survey.

Like José Arcadio Buendía, Thomas Sutpen dreams the peculiarly American dream of creating out of primal territory a world which he may endow with his own stamp and image. For that purpose alone, he rides into Yoknapatawpha County, Mississippi, in the shape of "man-horse-demon" with his "dream of castlelike magnificence," a band of "wild niggers" and a French architect.[22] José Arcadio Buendía also leads an expeditionary force into a new world, and he too dreams an urban dream oddly out of keeping with the surrounding wilderness, a foreshadowing of the inevitable gap between nature's promise and man's fulfillment. Seeing a dazzling city with houses having mirror walls, and hearing the name of the city spoken with a supernatural echo, he orders his men to make a clearing beside the river at the coolest spot on the bank, and there to found Macondo. Both Sutpen and José Arcadio foresee the establishment of a line that will continue forever; both are oblivious to the fact that their histories press steadily toward apocalypse.

Whereas José Arcadio immediately evokes the Judaic patriarch who leads his people into a promised land, Sutpen's aims seem purely selfish. Despite appearances, however, their motives are remarkably similar. Like many of the settlers of the New World, both Sutpen and José Arcadio are fleeing the exhaustion and corruption of an old world. Each is hoping to forget his past and begin history again, for both are convinced that in a world without a past, the future can be molded to their historical design. As stubborn and strong as they are in holding to their visions of historical renewal, they learn that the moral burdens of the past are not so easily sloughed off. The curse of incest, that classical sin against nature which is laid upon the Buendías in Riohacha, is ultimately realized in the once-arcadian Macondo. (Modern usage has narrowed the application of the word "incest," which derives from the more general Latin word, *incestus*, meaning unclean, tainted.) Incest also follows Sutpen into his new world in the shape of Charles Bon, the mulatto son who will not be repudiated along with the rest of his father's past. In both Macondo and Jefferson, the realities of civil war, economic exploitation of the land by alien usurpers, family tragedy, and crushing personal loneliness eventually overwhelm paradisal visions. Although the generational cycles of the families and the sheer staying power of Úrsula and Judith would seem to offer the promise of continuity, the promise is false. Sutpen's Hundred is consumed in a holocaust, the fire reeking of "slow protracted violence with a smell of desolation and decay as if the wood of which it were built was flesh" (366). Macondo, overgrown and almost deserted, is blown from the face of the earth, the Buendía predicted from the first swept away with the last. The promised land of America, it would seem, has been irrevocably cursed.

Miss Rosa, Mr. Compson, Quentin, and Shreve in *Absalom, Absalom!*, and Melquíades and Aureliano Babilonia in *One Hundred Years of Solitude*, like the biblical apocalyptists, survey the story of an entire civilization from an atemporal point beyond its end. There is an ironic disjunction between Sutpen's and José Arcadio's initial optimism and the apocalyptic hindsight of those who tell their stories. For the narrators, the worlds which to their founders seemed endless have in fact ended. The uncharted future has become a schematized and unyielding past. Their apocalyptic narrative perspectives telescope time, mocking intentionality by juxtaposing the youthful optimism of beginnings and the harsh reality of cataclysmic ends. Here, then, they depart from apocalyptic convention, for these narrators' accounts of historical endings are not tempered with countervisions of new beginnings, or their cataclysmic visions with millennial ones. There are, at most, vestigial memories of innocence betrayed, of opportunity wasted. Nevertheless, it is the temporal scope of their apocalyptic perspective, their ability to see history whole, which allows them to confer meaning upon both history and biography.

In *Absalom, Absalom!*, Miss Rosa initiates the narration of Sutpen's history, and her cataclysmic vision dominates the novel. It is she who draws Quentin into that history, and she who causes Mr. Compson to expand on her version to his son. Standing beyond the end of her story, she and her auditor are always visible. Just as John in his Revelation frequently begins his sentences with "And behold, I John saw ...," so Miss Rosa begins hers with the slightly more subdued but equally obtrusive phrase, "I saw," or concludes with, "That's what I found." Medieval apocalypse tapestries and manuscripts often place the figure of John at the side of the scene which he describes, an expression of distress upon his face as he watches the terrors of history (and God's will) unfold. Time is the vehicle of divine purpose, but in Miss Rosa's history, there is no reward—only retribution—at time's end.[23]

Miss Rosa's self-imposed exile in the "dim coffin-smelling gloom" of her "office" is consonant with her apocalyptic narrative stance. The biblical apocalyptist is always an outsider. He deplores the world he describes, and yet also has an urgent moral stake in that world and in its collective end. This ambivalence is reflected in the mediating and distancing devices of the apocalyptic text, devices intensified by the narrator's sense that he is the medium of forces beyond his own ability to understand or control. Messengers speak through other messengers, sealed scrolls must be opened, signs interpreted, phrases revised and reiterated. The apocalyptist's is thus an ambiguous kind of omniscience, for he disavows all personal claims to knowledge, describing only what has been told to him. History is at once an open and a closed book, a tension embodied in the historical narrative which he in turn creates. Miss Rosa and Mr. Compson in *Absalom, Absalom!* are also distanced from and yet desperately involved in the history they tell; and their strategies of indirection may be understood in terms of apocalyptic narrative. Because they seek in the history of Sutpen (and the South) some ultimate moral and ethical significance, the difficulties in historical decoding and recoding are magnified and intensified, as is the importance of their role as narrator, which they sense to be charged with responsibility far beyond that of mere historian.

Like Miss Rosa, Mr. Compson is constantly visible beyond the end of the story he tells, filtering his account of the degeneration and destruction of Sutpen's historical ideal through his own philosophical despair. His apocalyptic perspective is also fundamentally dualistic and deterministic. Human history is impelled by a moral dialectic between opposing forces, both personal and cosmic in character, which vie for control of this world. The progression of events may vary from one apocalypse to another—from Miss Rosa's version to Mr. Compson's—but it is controlled by this moral dialectic. Speaking from a point beyond the end of time, the apocalyptist reveals the predetermined schedule for the rest of time, over which humanity has little or no control. Thus Sutpen's "innocence" of historical necessity— his belief that he could manipulate history by the exercise of his own indomitable will—jars against Mr. Compson's and Miss Rosa's deterministic view of an essentially retributive history. For Mr. Compson, the historical "innocence" upon which Sutpen's Hundred is founded is the very cause of its destruction. Historical necessity—the pressure of time itself—is Sutpen's invincible adversary: Mr. Compson tells Quentin that General Compson hears Wash Jones's granddaughter, in labor with the last possible heir to Sutpen's name, scream "steady as a clock"; shortly afterward, Sutpen is killed with a scythe, his history abruptly truncated with the symbolic tool of Father Time. Mr. Compson's apocalyptic perspective allows him to probe the relation between freedom and historical necessity, to weigh human desire against human limitation and find the scale steeply pitched toward the latter.

Although there are elements of tragedy in Sutpen's history, and Mr. Compson often employs the metaphors of Greek tragedy in his narration, the tale he tells is less tragic than apocalyptic, because tragedy sees a future arising out of the violence of the past, a moral order reasserted and even invigorated after the terrible turbulence of tragic events.[24] Whereas the future envisioned in apocalypse exists by virtue of a radical break with the present, in tragedy, the world is carried on by the exhausted survivors. Such a future as tragedy envisions is nowhere evident in *Absalom, Absalom!*. The howls of Jim Bond, Sutpen's only surviving offspring, heard above the roar of the flames that destroy Sutpen's house, serve to emphasize the irrefutability of the end. And if Quentin's desperate need to understand and communicate Sutpen's history might seem to make *him* a survivor of that history, his survival is only temporary: within six months Quentin will drown himself in the Charles River at Cambridge, Massachusetts. (Only Shreve, the Northerner who bears no relation to Sutpen's world, is granted a future which promises continuance.[25]) Furthermore, apocalypse, unlike tragedy, implies the death not of an individual hero, but of a people, a world. When Mr. Compson, like Miss Rosa, links the destruction of Sutpen's

Hundred to the destruction of the South and the New World, we are hardly surprised.[26]

The primary chronicler of Macondo's 100 years of solitude is Melquíades. He too stands beyond the end of the world he describes, surveying its entire history from his apocalyptic perspective. Like Miss Rosa in her "office," Melquíades removes himself from history to his "timeless room," escaping death in order to record the mortal condition of the Buendías and their world. His narrative is an enunciation, at once successive and cumulative, of all that has been and all that will be in Macondo. He both predicts and remembers events, proposing in advance the contents of the future. The novel begins, "Many years later, as he faced the firing squad, Colonel Aureliano Buendía was to remember that distant afternoon when his father took him to discover ice" (11).[27] The presumed present of the firing squad, itself an apocalyptic moment that would seem to obviate Aureliano's future in any case (but does not, for we learn that the Colonel survives that moment and dies of old age), quickly gives way to the narration of events long preceding the presumed present, the founding of Macondo and before. Melquíades's continual shifts through time, like Miss Rosa's and Mr. Compson's, weight the present with wistful anticipation or mournful recall; the remote past and the distant future intrude on the running present; the generations of Buendías reflect one another forward and back until the end of Melquíades's narrative, which is also the end of the world he narrates.

The importance of Melquíades's narrative record of Macondo is suggested early on, in the incident of the insomnia plague. The loss of sleep is not the most serious effect of this plague, but rather the loss of memory that accompanies it. Whoever was afflicted forgot "the identity of people and even the awareness of his own being, until he sank into a kind of idiocy that had no past" (50). In this pristine new world, which would seem to lack a past in any case, such a threat might be inconsequential were it not that Visitación and Cataure, the Indian servants in the Buendía household, identify the illness, even before its effects are evident. They have suffered from this illness already, having forgotten their own cultural past with the pressures of the colonization of Macondo; the Indians' loss presages Macondo's loss of its own Edenic past in the turbulence of civil war and economic colonization by the Yankees. A temporary antidote to the plague is discovered, however. It is the written word. Every object is labeled and its use recorded: "Thus they went on living in a reality that was slipping away, momentarily captured by words, but which would escape irremediably when they forgot the values of the written letters" (53). Obliteration is forestalled. José Arcadio understands that the very existence of Macondo depends upon words, and he decides to build a memory machine which would review the totality of knowledge acquired during one's lifetime, "from beginning to end" (54). It is precisely as José Arcadio struggles with his spinning dictionary that Melquíades returns to Macondo and begins to record 100 years of solitude.

Whereas we are constantly aware of the presence of the narrators who unravel Sutpen's history, we learn only in the final paragraph of *One Hundred Years of Solitude* that it is Melquíades, rather than an omniscient narrator as we have been allowed to believe, who has preserved the history of Macondo beyond its cataclysmic end. Aureliano Babilonia, the last of the Buendías, realizes just before Macondo is swept off the face of the earth that Melquíades's parchments are both history and prediction. The novel ends with this realization: "it was foreseen that the city of mirrors [or mirages] would be wiped out by the wind ... at the precise moment when Aureliano Babilonia would finish deciphering the parchments ..." (383). That the narrator is revealed to be a character in the novel, one who is obliterated with the town and the family that his parchments commemorate, suggests an indissoluble mixture of lived and written orders in Macondo, a suggestion which in turn emphasizes the totality of this world of words. Whereas an omniscient narrator is everywhere and nowhere in his narration, his existence presupposing another reality—that of the author—outside of the narration, the fiction that encompasses its own narrator and destroys him with the destruction of the fictional world no longer admits a context that is external to it, or that survives it. That García Márquez withholds the identity of his narrator until the final moments of Macondo's 100-year history serves to heighten our sense of the inevitability of individual and collective ends, and of the necessity of fictions to oppose oblivion.

If the narrators' words describe the annihilation of Macondo and Sutpen's Hundred, their words also defy time's destruction. Language is for the apocalyptist the sole remaining defense against historical chaos. His hermetic symbols and series testify to the conviction that language may yet order and communicate important, even saving truths to those who can read and interpret them. Melquíades retires to his room in the newly enlarged Buendía house, spending hours on end "scribbling his enigmatic literature" on the parchment that is brought to him. He tells José Arcadio: "I have found immortality" (68), by which he means that his verbal embodiment of the Buendías—not the Buendías themselves—will endure per *omnia saecula saeculorum*.[28] José Arcadio misunderstands him completely; it is left to the last Buendía to perceive the significance of Melquíades's statement, as it is left to Quentin to perceive significance in the various versions of Sutpen's history.

Miss Rosa, like Melquíades, is destroyed in the final destruction of the world she describes. She dies as a result of the holocaust that consumes

Sutpen's decaying house and his barren offspring in December, 1909, her death nearly simultaneous with that of the last vestige of Sutpen's historical design. Thus to Quentin, her elected audience, is left the artist's task of opposing oblivion with words. At night in the "tomblike" air of his "icebox" room at Harvard, where time itself seems frozen, as it is in Melquíades's room, Quentin attempts to the fullest extent of his narrative power to elucidate Sutpen's world from its origin to its end. One thinks of Roland Barthes's description of myth as "frozen speech," "arrested speech": "On the surface of [mythic] language something has stopped moving."[29] Faulkner's evolutionary history is set against his narrator's impulse to arrest time: So Quentin both describes the decay and destruction of Sutpen's world and preserves it forever. The narration of history in these novels represents a gesture toward eternity even as apocalypse unfolds.

It is Aureliano Babilonia, the decipherer of Melquíades's parchments, who, more than Melquíades, shares Quentin's artistic burden. Both Aureliano and Quentin look backward upon worlds that have been created and then destroyed; from the fragments of those shattered worlds, both narrators strain to construct new orders with their verbal artistry. Both are obsessed by the histories they survey, at once observers and reluctant participants; both search desperately, as it is said of Aureliano, for "an entrance that went back to the past" (379). Melquíades chooses Aureliano, as Miss Rosa has chosen Quentin, to translate the past into art, charging him with the responsibility of decoding his parchments. Like the biblical apocalyptist, Quentin and Aureliano must decipher multilayered texts which are mediated by other narrators, distanced by time, and shrouded in seemingly impenetrable series of events.

Aureliano, the illegitimate child of Meme Buendía and Mauricio Babilonia, has spent his life in captivity, incarcerated by his puritanical grandmother in a "decadent paradise." Nevertheless, he has wide knowledge of the world beyond Macondo, is a medieval scholar like Melquíades, and is, like Quentin, infinitely dedicated to his task of deciphering the past, of narrativizing it into coherence. Furthermore he, like Quentin, understands clearly the economic exploitation and moral abuses that have subverted the original potential of the land, for Aureliano alone believes José Arcadio Segundo's true version of the banana company's massacre of the workers. Thus, Aureliano withdraws to Melquíades's room, much as Quentin encloses himself in his room at Harvard, nailing the doors and windows shut in order to immerse himself in his art. And though their narratives will conserve the communal histories they tell, neither Aureliano nor Quentin deludes himself about his own individual permanence. Aureliano knows that the apocalypse about which he is reading in the past will soon engulf him in the present, and

Quentin asks his father why Miss Rosa is so obsessed with Sutpen's destruction, when he knows that they all will be destroyed in any case. Even his Canadian roommate, Shreve, understands that the story Quentin has constructed must somehow lead to holocaust. He says that his account "clears the whole ledger, you can tear all the pages out and burn them ..." (378). Shreve's conclusion has been foreshadowed by a similar image: Faulkner's omniscient narrator says of the roommates' narrative endeavors, "All that has gone before just so much that had to be overpassed and none else present to overpass it but them, as someone always has to rake the leaves up before you can have the bonfire" (316). The narrators' imposition of an order and an end upon history (their raking of leaves, as Faulkner has it) is the source of the meaning. imputed to Sutpen's blazing mansion. Conclusion is first a fact of narration, then, perhaps, of history.

The biblical apocalyptists distinguish very specific patterns in the flow of time and infer meaningful connections among events in their desire to assign significance to history. In Revelation, the Beast reigns for forty-two months, the messianic kingdom lasts exactly 1,000 years, there is silence in heaven after the breaking of the seventh seal, "about the space of half an hour" (Rev. 13:1). Without a pause in the narrative flow, John describes event after event in series of sevens—the seven seals, the seven trumpet woes, the seven vials of wrath: That God should impose such orderly chaos upon the wicked world is cause for reassurance. Apocalyptic narrative achieves its authority by plotting a comprehensive explanation which traces effects to causes and enchains events along the way.

Similarly, in their attempts to create an explanatory narrative structure, Quentin and Aureliano schematize the events and characters of memory, as have Miss Rosa and Melquíades before them. The generational repetition of the Buendías, the alternation of Aurelianos and José Arcadios, the cycles of civil wars, the unrequited loves take their place in a schematized and structured history. Indeed, Aureliano only makes sense of his own relationship to that history when he sees simultaneously the origin and end of Macondo, the completed whole. The italicized epigraph which concludes the apocalypse provides a fullness that is rarely provided by unauthored temporality: "*The first of the line is tied to a tree and the last is being eaten by the ants*" (381). Quentin too identifies patterns of repetition and duplication within time's forward movement, which link him to the past: Shreve and Quentin *become* Bon and Henry as they create them with their narration, and Quentin suggests that he and Shreve are in fact *all* of the people to whom they have given substance by their verbal retrospection. More than any of the other narrators, Quentin knows that the self is bound in illusory relations, and that his only hope is to situate himself within the symbolic order of the apocalyptic history he both observes and creates. So the individual allies himself to the grander design he intuits, giving significance to his own history by linking it to a history that is intelligible because it is complete.

If the individual gains support from this alliance, so does the community. The biblical apocalyptist sees himself as providing a communal service in mediating between the source of his text and its audience, between God and his believers. He conveys divine voices, texts, scenes to a select audience so that they may hear or read or see and thereby maintain their communal identity, ensure their communal salvation. Quentin and Aureliano Babilonia are also motivated by their sense of community, not so much wishing to warn the community or save it as to understand it themselves, and pass that understanding on to others. In their secular history of a family and a town, each conveys the accumulated voices and actions of generations. The individuals in their stories are described in relation to the community, and their individual fates are largely determined by that relation. It may be because they tell stories of *failed* communities that Quentin and Aureliano feel so strongly moved to attempt their recapitulation of the collective. Ironically, Quentin's communal history centers on a man unable to join (or create) the community that he desperately desires, and Aureliano describes a community that is ultimately united by nothing but the common solitude of its inhabitants. Indeed, their immediate audiences also exist in ironic relation to their communal ideals: Shreve is not a part of the community that Quentin addresses, and Aureliano speaks only to the absent Melquíades, one of the few outsiders ever to have been allowed entry into the Buendías's world.[30]

This relation between individual vision and communal destiny is also central to the narrative structure of García Márquez's novel, *Chronicle of a Death Foretold*.[31] Although the narrator of this novel tells the fated history not of an entire world but of an individual, Santiago Nasar, like Quentin and Aureliano Babilonia, his perspective and tone are that of the apocalyptist. Twenty-seven years after Santiago's murder, he hopes to make sense of the "senseless" death by means of his narration. Though Santiago's death does not imply the end of a community or a family, it is nonetheless a group drama. The narrator's concern, even beyond questions of the moral responsibility of murderers or victim, is the role of the community in the death, and the nature of their communal guilt. It is precisely *because* Santiago's death is foretold, *because* everyone shares the foreknowledge of his imminent murder, that the narrator is moved to undertake his investigation. Why did no one prevent his death? Could no one intercede in the "announced" scenario of events leading to catastrophe? Does announcement imply irrevocability? And will the narrator's written account (the death "aftertold") modify the future, even if it cannot undo the past? These tensions—between foreknowledge and human volition, between individual responsibility and communal history—are inherent in all apocalyptic narration, and García Márquez's investigative narrator places them in the foreground as Aureliano Babilonia does not.

The biblical apocalyptist assumes that his narration will affect his listeners' beliefs and behavior, even as he shows that it is too late, that individual and communal destinies are foretold and hence presumably final. Yet his emphasis on the reforming power of language (in Revelation, Christ is imaged *as* the Word) implies that his own verbal account may yet modify the history it foretells. This too is the implication of the narrator's account in *Chronicle of a Death Foretold*. If Aureliano Babilonia's and Quentin's narrations survive the end of Macondo and Sutpen's Hundred and mitigate their tragic finality, so the narrator's "chronicle" is the mitigating circumstance of Santiago's murder. His dedicated effort to confer meaning on the events he recounts is in fact rewarded. Through the process of returning, researching, ordering, telling Santiago's history, the narrator understands what he has suspected all along, that the murder was inevitable and that it cannot be justified—only accepted. The meaning of Santiago's death lies in this acceptance—an acceptance reflected in the narrator's final, powerful description of the murder. So he writes the ending that the facts will not concede, and concludes Santiago's history with his own text.

Others of García Márquez's narrators are less fortunate. Despite mythic alliances and communal aspirations, the past eventually weighs too heavily on both García Márquez's and Faulkner's appointed apocalyptists. We are told that Aureliano becomes "unable to bear in his soul the crushing weight of so much past" (381) and Quentin, calling himself a ghost, says, "I am older at twenty than a lot of people who have died" (377), and "I have heard too much" (207). Aureliano is described, and Quentin might well be also, surveying "the last that remained of a past whose annihilation had not taken place because it was still in a process of annihilation consuming itself from within, ending at every moment but never ending its ending" (371). But the end does arrive, despite the seemingly interminable decline and decay which they describe. For both Aureliano and Quentin, there is simultaneously a sense of prescience and déjà vu, the ends of their narrations revealing what was suspected from the beginning. Both are caught in the destruction of the worlds they decipher and describe, worlds that their narrative efforts have in some sense created.

The narrators of these novels understand too well the fragility of the words with which they forestall the inevitable apocalypse. Each is greatly burdened by the pressures and strictures of history, felt the more intensely in their American contexts, where space and time had seemed so endlessly expansive only a few generations before. Their prose reflects this burden. Although in very different styles, their sentences are often constructed with a running inevitability to them, the narrative never pausing but flowing on and on, as if impervious to the events it relates, synthesizing everything as it flows toward its predetermined end. I have already noted the eschatological pressure inherent in Melquíades's narration. His phrase, "many years later," which begins the novel becomes "some years later," "a few years later," then "a few months later"; and Aureliano, approaching the end of Melquíades's parchments, accelerates his reading, even skipping pages in order to keep up with time itself as Macondo hurtles toward its end. The narrative thus reiterates cosmic process. Faulkner's narrators also embody in their narrative styles the implacable fate that they believe to be driving events forward, Miss Rosa using her Puritan vernacular of predestination, guilt, and damnation, Mr. Compson the imagery of Greek tragedy. Quentin's narration is punctuated, but never slowed, by Shreve's constant injunction to wait: "Wait, I tell you!" "*Will you wait?*" Thomas Sutpen himself is moved to finish telling his story to General Compson when he sees that time is about to overtake him. It is as if the stories of the Buendías and the Sutpens were being told in a single breathless sentence, spoken with the knowledge of the annihilating forces at work in history, and thus with the sure knowledge of the need for haste.

The apocalyptic ending of a novel is as fictional as its beginning or any other part of its fictional history. However, the novelist's choice of such an ending is important because the paradigms of apocalypse impose an ending that confers historical significance. Of course all fictional narration imposes some degree of order on the chaos of temporal reality, and the end of all stories implies the cessation, if not the termination, of the fictional world embodied therein. But the apocalyptic perspective that I have attempted to define looks back to record the entire history of a world, not simply to carve out a slice of that history from the flow of time. In *One Hundred Years of Solitude* and *Absalom, Absalom!*, the narrators' apocalyptic stance allows them to integrate memory and anticipation, past and future, into the narrative present. Such temporal integration explains Melquíades's and García Márquez's concentration of "a century of daily episodes ... in a single instant" and surely reflects as well Faulkner's conviction that "there is no such thing as *was*—only *is*. If *was* existed, there would be no grief or sorrow."[32] This inclusive narrative perspective, its comprehensive finality seeming to suspend time, underlies the transformation of history into myth which one senses with certainty in both novels. Their narrators share in the modernist thirst for myth, for explanatory masterplots which may justify their individual plots. With the loss of belief in the sacred masterplot of apocalypse, in which the secular leads to and is recuperated by the sacred, Quentin, Aureliano, and the rest are left to create their own fictions of apocalypse. There remains, after the end of the worlds they describe, the description itself, and the implicit sense that language is an antidote to past suffering, that a situation may be salvaged by being put into words. The intensity of their apocalyptic narrations underlines their yearning for the restoration of social and psychic order, and they are directed to that end.

I have suggested that the destruction of the fictional world and the narrator along with it seems to obviate a context that is external to that world, or that survives it. Of course this defies common sense, for we readers undeniably *do* survive García Márquez's biblical hurricane and Faulkner's holocaust, the novels still in our hands, ready to read again if we choose. (Surely we are able to suspend our disbelief more completely than the readers of *Moby Dick*, who, when through an error the novel was first published in England without the epilogue, asked with indignation who was left to tell the tale if everyone had gone down with *The Pequod*.[33]) In our role as survivors, we are perhaps akin to Shreve, for whom it is not history's predestined patterns but its fluidity that terrifies. That Shreve grants to Quentin (as do we, to Quentin and to Melquíades) something like total recall, however filtered through personality, represents our own desire for such a comprehensive perspective, for an end which will transform mere duration into a meaningful whole. The myth of apocalypse narrativizes history and provides for Faulkner and García Márquez a means of reclaiming in words their particular part of the American territory.

III.

Apocalypse is inextricably tied to political realities; it both responds to and imaginatively embodies social and political upheaval. The biblical apocalyptic visionary mode developed in response to political and moral crises, as I have said, and its forms have flourished when the established understanding of the history of a community is challenged. Apocalypse proposes radical changes in the organization of future world governance, in reaction to existing inadequacies and abuses. García Márquez is well known for his oppositional political stance, and he has observed (correctly, I think) that Latin American writers are, almost by definition, dissidents. He says that if he were not a Latin American, he might not feel the need to write politically charged fiction and nonfiction. However, he continues, in Latin America "underdevelopment is total, integral, it affects every part of our lives. The problems of our societies are mainly political. And the commitment of a writer is with the reality of all of society, not just with a small part of it. If not, he is as bad as the politicians who disregard a large part of our reality. That is why authors, painters, writers in Latin America get politically involved. I am surprised by the little resonance authors have in the U.S. and in Europe. Politics is made there only by the politicians."[34] If in *One Hundred Years of Solitude* hope resides in the survival of the narration itself, in *The Autumn of the Patriarch* García Márquez uses the myth of apocalypse more explicitly to protest political corruption and propose political reform.

The Autumn of the Patriarch presents the chaotic and violent ambience of a pre-apocalyptic world, a world without moral discrimination that is denied temporal coherence by the tyranny of political force. The nameless Latin American country where the novel is set is suffocating under the domination of an aging dictator, a political Antichrist; the wasteland that he creates with his brutality corresponds to the period just before the end of the world described in biblical Apocalypse. In Revelation, this transitional time does not properly belong to either the old world or the new, but is an interregnum which has its figural embodiment in the three and one-half year reign of the beast.[35] John describes the beast: He is "like unto a leopard, and his feet were as the feet of a bear, and his mouth as the mouth of a lion" (Rev. 13:2). He is specifically a political scourge. Commentators agree that he is meant to represent the state, with its seven heads symbolizing the seven Roman emperors who had been given divine honors and were thus guilty of blasphemy.[36] The mood of the transitional period is that of nightmare. The dislocation of personal and public relationships, the confusion of reality and appearance, fear of the future are its features. The general of García Márquez's novel is at home here.

The chaos of the general's realm is everywhere apparent. Each of the six chapters begins with a description of the "fabulous disarray" of the palace after the general's death, related by the collective narrative voice of the people who have survived the general and have timorously entered the "rubble pits of the vast lair of power." The disorder of the government house is rendered from many points of view. An American ambassador, in his "banned memoirs," describes the "dungheap of paper scraps and animal shit and the remains of the meals of dogs who slept in the halls," and "the reception room where hens were pecking at the illusory wheat fields on the tapestry and a cow was pulling down the canvas with the portrait of an archbishop so she could eat it...."[37] Even the general's own comments are punctuated with the phrase, "What a mess!" In apocalyptic narration, the physical realm figures moral realities. In Revelation, John describes the poisoning of the water, the drying up of the sea during the period of transition. The general here actually sells the sea to the Americans to pay off the national debt. Nautical engineers carry it off to Arizona in numbered pieces, and the country is left a flickering inferno, reminiscent of Satan's realm in *Paradise Lost*. And lest we imagine that the contrary of political disorder is order, or that the moral degeneration of the general's world is reversible, García Márquez introduces José Ignacio Sáenz de la Barra. The diabolical political terrorist establishes order in the form of a remarkably efficient organization, the better to torture and murder. He describes his activities as "peace within order" and "progress within order," and justifies his cruelty in terms of that order. So complete is the moral and political corruption of the dictator's world that it subverts and destroys the very conception of order.

The general is in absolute control of the lives of his subjects: he controls the country's resources, its weather, even the time of day. He is often described in terms of divinity (either as God's enemy or his replacement), and his activities are an ironic parody of Christ's. He is "besieged by mobs of lepers, blind people and cripples who begged for the salt of health from his hands, and lettered politicians and dauntless adulators who proclaimed him the corrector of earthquakes, eclipses, leap years and other errors of God ..." (8). When his boat enters the rural settlements, the people receive him with Easter drums, thinking that the "times of glory" have arrived. The general is the Antichrist who orchestrates the last days, and he is ruthless in exercising his authority. With the slightest hint of insubordination—and often without it—the general wreaks reprisal. He rapes a woman and then has her husband cut into small pieces because he would be an enemy if allowed to live. When a faithful underling is suspected of treason, the general has him roasted, stuffed with pine nuts and aromatic herbs, steeped with spices, garnished with cauliflower and laurel leaves and a sprig of parsley in his mouth, and served to his comrades for dinner.

It is obvious from these examples that *The Autumn of the Patriarch* is a novel of hyperbolic extremes. With its outlandish images and exaggerated horrors, García Márquez's magic realism employs strategies akin to those of biblical apocalyptic symbolism. The naturalistic setting and causal sequences of *One Hundred Years of Solitude* are abandoned in *The Autumn of the Patriarch* for a more expressionist aesthetic. Repeated patterns of poetic association, fantastic imagery and grotesque gesture replace the discursive movement of Melquíades's manuscript. For example, a series of metonyms portrays the general: the gloved hands, the huge "graveyard feet," the buzzing ears, the herniated testicle, the sound of the single gold spur. These partial descriptions suggest the paranoia of the general (he never stands fully in view of the people), his insidious and stealthy exercise of power, and the veiled nature of evil itself. Although the general is more specifically described than the beasts and monsters of Revelation, like them, he becomes a universal symbol of political repression and hence, inversely, of human suffering. García Márquez shares the apocalyptist's intuition that only through grotesquely exaggerated and fantastical imagery can the political evils of his time be fully apprehended and embodied.

As in *One Hundred Years of Solitude*, García Márquez's apocalyptic vision in *The Autumn of the Patriarch* allows him to explore individual and communal ends. The general is terrified by time's passing, and his obsessive concern is how not to die, how to prolong his era. Biblical apocalypse posits time as the medium for the fulfillment of divine purpose, and temporal progression as necessary for the ultimate destruction of evil: García Márquez's general knows that for him, time is not a redemptive force but a destructive one. Time becomes his personal enemy, the only opposition that has ever threatened his absolute power, the only assassin who will inevitably succeed. The general's reign will end, the "last frozen leaves of his autumn" will fall. Nevertheless, for decades and even centuries, the general attempts to deny that fact. When he asks what time it is, he receives the answer, "whatever you command general sir ..." (88). Indeed, for when the general decides to rearrange time, he does so. In one elaborate temporal maneuver, the insomniac general orders the clocks advanced from three to eight in the morning: "it's eight o'clock, God damn it, eight o'clock, I said, God's order" (68). Night and day are reversed at the general's whim, and cookie-paper stars and silver-plated moons are hung in the windows to attest to his power over time, but they serve rather to reveal the extent of his self-deception.

As the general imagines he can deny the reality of present time, so he attempts to deny both past and future. Like the absolute dictator in Carlos Fuentes's novel, *Terra Nostra*, the general substitutes for facts a grotesque fiction of his own making. He revises history to obscure his illegitimate beginnings and conduct, employing "the artifices of national history" to entangle and destroy "the threads of reality." In order to deny the responsibility for the death of 2,000 children, he simply denies their existence. So inclusive is his self-delusion that he writes his own graffiti on the walls of his bathroom, "long live the general, long live the general, God damn it ...," and surrounds himself with adulators who proclaim him "undoer of dawn, commander of time, repository of light," "general of the universe," with "a rank higher than that of death." As he grows increasingly terrified, he begins to insist that his sycophants call him "the eternal one," and their shouts of "long live the general" are taken in the most literal sense. When his double dies and everyone thinks that it is the general, he reappears and kills his cabinet members for the crime of imagining that they had survived him.

The general attempts to read his future in cards, coffee grounds, his palm, and basins of water, for he is desperate to know his future. He finds a fortune teller who can tell him the circumstances of his death, and then strangles her because he wants no one to know that he is mortal.

The general's attempts to transcend time are cast in ironic light by the structure of the novel. Each chapter opens with an account of the general's death—so, in fact, he seems to die not once but six times. On the first page of the novel, the general's survivors freely enter his palace, stirring up the "stagnant time," the "lethargy of the centuries" created by the general's fear of the future. This structural irony is reinforced by the general's own sense of the futility of his efforts to deny his end. In a final fleeting moment, the general does grudgingly accept his temporal condition, and thus briefly becomes a human being rather than a monster. In this moment, he faces the full extent of his self-deception and understands that he is a victim of his own sect of emperor worship, that he has believed his followers with their placards and slogans. He understands that his desire to reign "until the end of time ... was an endless vice the satiety of which generated its own appetite until the end of all times general sir ..." (267). In short, the general understands the temporal reality of his human condition, but it is, of course, too late. He is indeed time's victim.

The people too have been misled by their own placards and slogans. Even when the general's death appears to be irrefutable, they cannot believe that he has in fact died. They are unable to fathom that the general's seemingly infinite autumn has ended. For decades, centuries, they have experienced what Frank Kermode describes as the "intemporal agony" of the period of transition, which becomes an age in itself as crisis succeeds crisis. The people have accepted the notion that their stage of transition is endless, that they live, as Kermode puts it, "in no intelligible relation to the past, and no predictable relation to the future."[38] When they finally realize that the general's oppressive reign is over, they ecstatically celebrate "the good news that the uncountable time of eternity has come to an end" (269).

With these words the novel ends, the emphasis not on the final annihilating cataclysm, as in *One Hundred Years of Solitude*, or on the individual death, as in *Chronicle of a Death Foretold*, but on the better future which will succeed the general's death. As in biblical apocalypse, *The Autumn of the Patriarch* suggests that virtue can outlast persecution, that new worlds can supplant old ones. The people, to their surprise, live to celebrate the demise of their persecutor; end and ending do not coincide, time does not cease but moves forward in the hands of the survivors. And having survived, the people understand their temporal condition. They know that life is "arduous and ephemeral," and that if time's movement from past to present to future is a human contrivance, it is a contrivance that responds to a basic human need and is not to be carelessly abused. García Márquez, leftist journalist and social activist as well as apocalyptic novelist, endows the end of this novel with a future, as he does not with the other novels I have discussed here. In *The Autumn of the Patriarch*, the survivors know who they are (unlike the general, "who is left never knowing forever"), and we are given to understand that they will use that knowledge to the good. On the contrary, in *One Hundred Years of Solitude* and *Chronicle of a Death Foretold*, the fated ends and emphatically final endings seem to obviate such historical potential. Though we may rejoice that the *records* of those ends remain, we must also lament Santiago's murder, and the obliteration of Macondo in a hurricane of years, days, hours, minutes. In these two novels, García Márquez explicitly poses the permanence of narration against the terrible transience of human life. Words, he suggests, may almost overcome the temporal loss that they so poignantly describe.

It is the "almost" in the preceding sentence which García Márquez's 1982 Nobel Prize acceptance speech seems to cancel. The Nobel speech is often the occasion of a strange mix of genres, as García Márquez recognized when he said of his speech before it was written that he wanted it to be "a political speech presented as literature."[39] As if to dispel the idea that his most famous novel reflects a view of a doomed future, García Márquez used the forum provided by the Nobel speech to address the issue of his own literary apocalypticism and the apocalyptic nature of our time. He begins his speech by invoking the utopian visions and fantastic images inspired by the discovery of the New World: El Dorado, the fountain of eternal youth, a giant in Patagonia described by a sailor on Magellan's voyage. With familiar temporal sweep, the author moves immediately from such beginnings to a consideration of ends, quoting a statement made by William Faulkner when he received the 1949 Nobel Prize for Literature:

> On a day like today, my master William Faulkner said, "I decline to accept the end of man." I would feel unworthy of standing in this place that was his if I were not fully aware that the colossal tragedy he refused to recognize thirty-two years ago is now, for the first time since the beginning of humanity, nothing more than a simple scientific possibility.[40]

But even as he contemplates the end of humanity by nuclear holocaust, García Márquez oscillates back to envision its opposite, asserting that it is not too late to undertake the creation of "a new and leveling utopia of life where no one can decide the form of another person's death." Here we witness a marked shift in emphasis from the negative to the positive side of the apocalyptic myth, and a shift as well in García Márquez's relation to the Latin American literary tradition of historical idealism.

García Márquez's Nobel statement is decidedly more optimistic than anything that has yet been embodied in his fiction (as was that delivered by Faulkner, when he accepted the prize in 1949). In *One Hundred Years of Solitude* and *Chronicle of a Death Foretold*, it is the survival of the narration, not of Macondo or Santiago, that suggests temporal continuance and serves as saving counterbalance to communal and individual annihilation; and in *The Autumn of the Patriarch*, the future hardly holds out the extravagant promise of "a new and leveling utopia." The Nobel speech, however, offers a resounding affirmation of historical and human potentiality: "Neither floods nor plagues nor famine nor cataclysm nor even the eternal wars throughout centuries and centuries have managed to reduce the tenacious advantage of life over death." The emphasis has shifted, but García Márquez's speech, with its dialectic of cataclysm and millennium, remains a part of the apocalyptic tradition as I have described it. It is precisely his expressed hope that historical renewal—even utopia—may yet be possible, despite enumerated past disruptions and present dangers, that is most characteristic of apocalyptic dicta.

García Márquez ends his speech with a playful yet profound revision of the concluding sentence of *One Hundred Years of Solitude*, invoking not the historical cataclysm of his novel's ending, but historical renewal instead. In his speech, he describes a utopia where "races condemned to one hundred years of solitude will have at last and forever a second opportunity on earth." Here García Márquez dismisses the very idea of irrevocability, in history and in fiction. Nothing need be irremediable, to use a word that often appears in his novels. By proposing in his Nobel speech this new version of the apocalyptic conclusion of his masterpiece, García Márquez enacts the renovating activity he describes, calling into question the nature of finality itself, be it the finality of biblical hurricane, nuclear holocaust, or novelistic structure.

NOTES

1. Alfred J. MacAdam, *Modern Latin American Narratives: The Dreams of Reason* (Chicago: University of Chicago Press, 1977), p. 87.

2. Frank Kermode, *The Sense of an Ending: Studies in the Theory of Fiction* (New York: Oxford University Press, 1967), p. 167. See my reference to Arendt's discussion in Note 3 of Chapter 1.

3. By this assertion, I do not mean to minimize the extent to which García Márquez's fiction is grounded in, and specifically addresses, Colombian history and politics. In this regard, see Stephen Minta, *García Márquez: Writer of Colombia* (New York: Harper and

Row, 1987), and Lucila Inés Mena, *"Cien años de soledad*: Novela de 'La violencia,' *Hispamérica*, V, No. 1 (1976), 3–23.

4. Gregory Rabassa, "Beyond Magic Realism: Thoughts on the Art of Gabriel García Márquez," *Books America*, 47 (1973), p. 450.

5. Gabriel García Márquez, *One Hundred Years of Solitude*, trans. Gregory Rabassa (1967; New York: Avon Books, 1971), pp. 382–3. Subsequent references are cited parenthetically in the text.

6. Discussions of the cyclical elements of *One Hundred Years of Solitude* abound. See, for example, Carmen Arnau, *El mundo mítico de Gabriel García Márquez* (Barcelona: Editorial Península, 1971), pp. 129, 131–2; Ricardo Gullón, *García Márquez o el olvidado arte de contar* (Madrid: Editorial Taurus, 1979), p. 27; G. D. Carillo, "Lo cíclico en *Cien años de soledad*," *Razón y Fábula*, 23 (1973), 18–32; Roberto Paoli, "Carnavalesco y tiempo cíclico en *Cien años de soledad*," *Revista Iberoamericana*, Nos. 128–9 (1984), 979–98. Michael Palencia-Roth discusses the apocalyptic archetypes in the novel, contrasting, as I do, the linear to the cyclical, in *Gabriel García Márquez: La línea, el círculo y las metamórphoses del mito* (Madrid: Gredos, 1983).

7. Mikhail Bakhtin, *The Dialogic Imagination*, ed. Michael Holquist, trans. Caryl Emerson and Michael Holquist (1975; Austin: University of Texas Press, 1981), p. 248.

8. Georges Poulet, *Studies in Human Time*, trans. Elliott Coleman (1949; Baltimore: Johns Hopkins Press, 1956), p. 29. Poulet says that the modern time sense, as opposed to the romantic time sense which characterizes the Buendías, is based on the feeling that "any moment can be realized as a new moment, and that time can always be freely created from the present moment forward.... Each instant appears as the instant of a choice." The Buendías's temporal dilemma has been submitted to psychoanalytic investigation by Josefina Ludmer, *Cien años de soledad: Una interpretación* (Buenos Aires: Editorial Tiempo Contemporáneo, 1972).

9. The short story "One Day after Saturday" is, like "Big Mama's Funeral," a comic treatment of apocalyptic expectation. Father Antonio Isabel de Santísimo Sacramento del Altar, the ninety-four-year-old priest of Macondo, experiences another kind of rain, this time of dead birds, and he tries in vain to remember if there was such a plague described in Revelation. He locates the agent of the catastrophe: A peasant boy, in Macondo because he has missed his train, whom the befuddled priest labels The Wandering Jew. The plague of the dead birds reappears in *One Hundred Years of Solitude*, as does Padre Antonio Isabel, who again gives his "apocalyptic chat," inspired by The Wandering Jew (this time an old man with wings). In another early work, however, García Márquez's treatment of apocalyptic concerns is hardly comic: The epigraph of *Leaf Storm* (1955) is from *Antigone*, and its short italicized prologue describes the "whirlwind" of the U.S. banana company and the leaf storm which follows it into Macondo. (The word *hojarasca*, which is translated as leaf storm, has the connotation of a collection of useless and insubstantial items and elements—trash, rubbish, waste.) The entire novel is written in the same cataclysmic register as the final pages of *One Hundred Years of Solitude*: Whereas the biblical hurricane which ultimately sweeps Macondo away arrives only at the end of the later novel, the metaphoric leaf storm pervades the earlier novel from its opening paragraph.

10. Otto Plöger, *Theocracy and Eschatology*, trans. S. Rudman (Richmond: John Knox Press, 1964), pp. 9–10, 65. It is this apocalyptic policy that leads Martin Buber to argue that the biblical apocalyptist fails to engage the factual immediacy of human history; and it leads Robert Alter to suggest that apocalyptic thinking produces literature which withdraws from the "complexities and threats of history." The assertions would seem to ignore the radical political evolution of post-Joachimite apocalyptic thought, which I will

discuss in the context of the fiction of Walker Percy and Carlos Fuentes. And though Alter's statement is no doubt partially tenable in its suggestion that visions of apocalypse may lead to literary and political resignation, it ignores a good deal of contemporary literature that does not. We will see that contemporary visions of apocalypse in Latin America are more likely to result in fiction that is formally and thematically critical and even subversive than passively tolerant or escapist in its attitude toward historical reality. Martin Buber, "Prophecy, Apocalyptic, and the Historical Hour," in *Pointing the Way: Collected Essays*, trans. and ed. Maurice Friedman (New York: Harper, 1957), pp. 192–207; Robert Alter, "The Apocalyptic Temper," in *After the Tradition* (New York: E. P. Dutton, 1969), p. 57; see also "The New American Novel," *Commentary* 60, no. 5 (November 1975), pp. 44–51.

   11. Plöger, pp. 47–50, 100–12.

   12. Earl Rovit, "American Literature and the American Experience," *American Quarterly*, 13 (Summer 1961), pp. 118–19.

   13. Octavio Paz, *The Labyrinth of Solitude*, trans. Lysander Kemp (1950; New York: Grove Press, 1961), p. 208.

   14. Gabriel García Márquez and Mario Vargas Llosa, *La Novela en América Latina: Diálogo* (Lima: Carlos Milla Batres/Ediciones Universidad Nacional de Ingenieria, 1968), p. 53. In Luis Harss and Barbara Dohmann, *Into the Mainstream* (1966; New York: Harper Colophon, 1969), García Márquez says, "When I first read Faulkner, I thought: 'I must become a writer.'" Harss and Dohman conclude: "The chaotic materials that went into Faulknerian art, he says, were much like the raw stuff of life in Colombia. Faulkner showed him how this elemental turbulence could be manipulated and transformed" (pp. 322–3); in *La Novela en América Latina: Diálogo*, cited above, García Márquez says, "I believe that the greatest debt that we Latin American novelists have is to Faulkner ... Faulkner is present in all Latin American fiction; I believe that ... the great difference between our grandfathers ... and us is Faulkner; he was the only thing that happened between the two generations" (p. 52, my translation); see also Mario Vargas Llosa, "García Márquez: De Aracataca a Macondo," in *Nueve Asedios a García Márquez* (Santiago de Chile: Editorial Universitaria, 1972), p. 140; Armando Durán, "Conversaciones con Gabriel García Márquez," in *Sobre García Márquez*, ed. Pedro Simón Martínez (Montevideo: Biblioteca de Marca, 1971), p. 34.

   15. Roberto González Echevarría argues that, among Latin American writers, it is Carpentier who has had the greatest influence on contemporary Latin American fiction; he names García Márquez and Fuentes as among those most influenced by Carpentier. "Historia y alegoría en la narrativa de Carpentier," *Cuadernos Americanos*, No. 228 (1980), 200–20.

   16. Carlos Fuentes to Christopher Sharp in *W*, a supplement to *Women's Wear Daily*, 29 October 1976, p. 9.

   17. Jonathan Tittler, "Interview with Carlos Fuentes," *Diacritics*, 10, iii (1980), 52.

   18. For a more general treatment of the reception of Faulkner in Latin America, see Arnold Chapman, *The Spanish American, Reception of United States Fiction, 1920–1940* (Berkeley: University of California Press, 1966).

   19. García Márquez has said that *Absalom, Absalom!* is the novel by Faulkner that has most interested him. See William Kennedy, "The Yellow Trolley Car in Barcelona and Other Visions," *The Atlantic Monthly*, Jan. 1973, p. 57.

   20. Hayden White, "The Value of Narrativity in the Representation of Reality," *Critical Inquiry*, 7, i (1980), p. 5. See also by Hayden White, *Metahistory: The Historical Imagination in Nineteenth-Century Europe* (Baltimore: Johns Hopkins University Press,

1973), and *Tropics of Discourse: Essays in Cultural Criticism* (Baltimore: Johns Hopkins University Press, 1978).

21. Peter Brooks, "Fictions of the Wolfman: Freud and Narrative Understanding," *Diacritics*, 9, i (1979), 72–81. See also Brooks's article, "Incredulous Narration: *Absalom, Absalom!*," *Comparative Literature*, 34, iii (1982), 247–68, in which Quentin's narrative attempts to connect past to present are seen in psychological terms as his need to establish his relationship to his father(s), terms suggestive of another similarity between *Absalom, Absalom!* and *One Hundred Years of Solitude*.

22. William Faulkner, *Absalom, Absalom!* (New York: Modern Library, 1936), pp. 8, 38. Subsequent quotations from this novel are cited parenthetically in the text. Yoknapatawpha is not, of course, unsettled territory when Sutpen arrives; in *The Bear*, Faulkner looks back further to a time when the land was yet undefiled by European usurpers, when the primitive world of nature and its Chickasaw inhabitants existed in a state of equilibrium.

23. The Puritan uses of the myth of apocalypse have been much commented upon: See, for example, Sacvan Bercovitch, *The American Jeremiad* (Madison, Wisconsin: University of Wisconsin Press, 1978); James W. Davidson, *The Logic of Millennial Thought: Eighteenth-Century New England* (New Haven: Yale University Press, 1977); Ernest R. Sandeen, *The Roots of Fundamentalism: British and American Millenarianism, 1800–1930* (Chicago: University of Chicago Press, 1970). See also the chapter, "A Puritan Tragedy: *Absalom, Absalom!*," in Peter Swiggart, *The Art of Faulkner's Novels* (Austin, Texas: University of Texas Press, 1962).

24. There have been numerous critical examinations of *Absalom, Absalom!* in terms of tragedy. See Cleanth Brooks, "*Absalom, Absalom!* The Definition of Innocence," *Sewanee Review*, 59 (Autumn, 1951), 543–58; Walter L. Sullivan, "The Tragic Design of *Absalom, Absalom!*," *South Atlantic Quarterly*, 50 (October, 1954), 552–66.

John Paterson denies the tragic nature of the novel in "Hardy, Faulkner, and the Prosaics of Tragedy," *Centennial Review*, V (1961), 160–75. Comparing *Absalom, Absalom!* to *The Mayor of Casterbridge*, Paterson writes, "With the grisly death of Thomas Sutpen, however, the light goes out as if forever. Succeeded not by the Farfraes and Elizabeths, those pledges of a peaceful and pious future, but by a totally demoralized Quentin Compson, Sutpen passes on not a new and better world born out of the violence and ashes of the old, but a ruined universe incapable of regeneration."

See Kermode, pp. 25ff., for a discussion of the relative natures of tragedy and apocalypse.

25. Shreve participates, of course, in Quentin's narrativizing of history, but he is beyond the scope of my discussion because he is not exiled from the world he describes, nor does he have any real moral stake in it. He is not, in short, an apocalyptic narrator in the way that Quentin, Miss Rosa, and Mr. Compson decidedly are.

For specific treatments of Shreve's narration, see Terence Doody, *Confession and Community in the Novel* (Baton Rouge: Louisiana State University Press, 1980), pp. 173–84, and Lynn G. Levins, "The Four Narrative Perspectives in Faulkner's *Absalom, Absalom!*," *PMLA*, 86 (January 1970), 35–47.

26. Several critics have dwelt on Sutpen's history as a paradigm for the history of the South: Examples are Donald M. Kartiganer, "Faulkner's *Absalom, Absalom!*: The Discovery of Values," *American Literature*, 37 (November, 1965), 291; F. Garvin Davenport, Jr., *The Myth of Southern History: Historical Consciousness in Twentieth-Century Literature* (Nashville: Vanderbilt University Press, 1970).

27. In Marta Gallo, "El futuro perfecto de Macondo," *Revista Hispánica Moderna*, 38 (1974–1975), 115–35, the author analyzes the grammatical structure of the first sentence

of *One Hundred Years of Solitude* and finds its future perfect tense to contain a paradigm of the novel.

28. During Melquíades's days of feverish scribbling, we are told that the only words distinguishable in the "rocky paragraphs" are "equinox" and the name of Alexander von Humboldt. The first may suggest the temporal balance implied by Aureliano Babilonia's assertion that Melquíades has concentrated a century of daily episodes in one instant. The second, a German naturalist and traveller (1769–1859), was a great observer and namer of the South American New World. His *Kosmos* is not only a graphic description but also an imaginative conception of the physical world that prefigures Melquíades's narrative intention (and García Márquez's achievement).
For an exhaustive treatment of the implications of Melquíades's Sanskrit parchments, see Victor Farías, *Los manuscritos de Melquíades: Cien años de soledad, burguesía latinoamericana y dialéctica de la reproducción ampliada de negación* (Frankfurt/Main: Verlag Klaus Dieter Vervuert, 1981).

29. Roland Barthes, *Mythologies*, trans. Annette Lavers (1957; New York: Hill and Wang, 1972), p. 125.

30. It has been suggested that Aureliano Babilonia is Melquíades's alter ego of perhaps García Márquez's ideal reader. See George R. McMurray, *Gabriel García Márquez* (New York: Frederick Ungar Publishing Co., 1977), p. 87: "the 'speaking mirror,' into which [Aurelianol gazes upon reaching the last page, implies his perfect communication with his double, Melquíades."

31. I have discussed this novel in detail in "Ends and Endings in García Márquez's *Crónica de una muerte anunciada*," *Latin American Literary Review*, 13, No. 25 (1985), 104–16.

32. Quoted in *Writers at Work: The Paris Review Interviews* (New York: The Viking Press, 1958), p. 141.

33. Hershel Parker and Henry Binder, "Exigencies of Composition and Publication: *Billy Budd, Sailor* and *Pudd'nhead Wilson*," *Nineteenth–Century Fiction*, 30, i (1978), 131–43.

34. Marlise Simmons, "A Talk with Gabriel García Márquez," *New York Times Book Review*, 5 Dec. 1982, p. 7.

35. Kermode, p. 12. Kermode discusses in detail the defining of the myth of transition by Joachim of Fiore in the twelfth century; the Sibylline emperor cults enlarged the concept of the transitional period with their belief that the period would see not only the coming of the Antichrist but also the coming of a "knight faithful and true," the last emperor of the earth. I will return to Joachim and the Sibylline cults in my discussion of Walker Percy and Carlos Fuentes.

36. Two beasts appear during the period of transition described in Revelation. The first reigns for forty-two months—three and a half years; the second, the duration of whose reign is not stated, probably represents the priesthood of the imperial cult. John describes the second beast: "And I beheld another beast coming up out of the earth; and he had two horns like a lamb, and he spake as a dragon. And he exerciseth all the power of the first beast before him, and causeth the earth and them which dwell therein to worship the first beast ..." (Rev. 13:11–12). *The Interpreter's Bible* (New York: Abingdon Press, 1957), pp. 12, 460–4.

37. García Márquez, *The Autumn of the Patriarch*, trans. Gregory Rabassa (New York: Harper and Row, 1975), p. 86. Subsequent references are cited in the text.

38. Kermode, pp. 101–2.

39. Marlise Simmons, "A Talk with García Márquez," p. 7.

40. García Márquez, Nobel Prize Acceptance Speech, *Proceso*, No. 319 (13 diciembre de 1982), p. 46. Translated by Marina Castañeda, *The New York Times*, 6 Feb. 1983, sec. 4, p. 17.

Chronology

1928	Gabriel José García Márquez is born on March 6 in Aracataca, Colombia, to Gabriel Eligio García and Luisa Santiaga Márquez Iguarán. Spends the first eight years of his childhood with his maternal grandparents.
1936–1940	When he is eight years old, his grandfather dies, and he goes to live with his parents in Sucre. He is sent to boarding school in Barranquilla.
1940	Wins a scholarship to the Liceo Nacional de Zipaquirá, near Bogotá.
1947	Enters the Universidad Nacional in Bogotá to study law. Publishes his first short story "La tercera resignación" ("The Third Resignation") in *El Espectador*, a Bogotá newspaper.
1948	Liberal Presidential candidate Jorge Eliécer Gaintán is assassinated; civil war erupts in Columbia, known as *la violencia*. Moves to Cartagena on the coast. Continues law studies and writes a column for the newspaper, *El Universal*.
1950	Quits law school. Moves to Barranquilla and writes a column for the newspaper *El Heraldo*.
1953	Quits journalism temporarily and travels around Colombia working various jobs.
1954	Returns to Bogotá. Writes articles and film reviews for *El Espectador*.

1955	Wins a national prize for a short story, and publishes his first novel, *La hojarasca* (*Leaf Storm*). Writes account of Luis Alejandro Velasco's survival at sea for *El Espectador.* Travels to Geneva as a correspondent. The government closes down *El Espectador* and García Márquez stays in Europe.
1956	Lives in Paris and works on manuscripts for two novels, *La mala hora* (*In Evil Hour*) and *El coronel no tiene quien la escriba* (*No One Writes to the Colonel*).
1957	Finishes *No One Writes to the Colonel*. Travels to East Germany, Czechoslovakia, Poland, Russia, and Hungary. Moves to Caracas to work for the newspaper *Momento*.
1958	Marries Mercedes Barcha. Writes almost all of the stories in the collection *Los funerales de la Mama Grande* (*Big Mama's Funeral*).
1959–1961	Cuban Revolution. Works for Cuba's Prensa Latina in Bogotá, Cuba, and New York. His first child, Rodrigo, is born.
1961	Resigns from Prensa Latina. Makes "Homage to Faulkner" bus trip across the Deep South to Mexico City, where he is an editor for magazines. Awarded the Colombian Esso Literary Prize for *In Evil Hour*.
1962	Publishes *Big Mama's Funeral* and *No One Writes to the Colonel*. A censored *In Evil Hour* is published in Spain. His second son, Gonzalo, is born.
1963	Works for advertising agency and writes films.
1965	Goes into seclusion to write *Cien años de soledad* (*One Hundred Years of Solitude*).
1966	Authorized version of *In Evil Hour* is published in Mexico.
1967	*One Hundred Years of Solitude* is published in Buenos Aires. Moves to Barcelona, Spain.
1968	*No One Writes to the Colonel* published in the U.S.
1969	*One Hundred Years of Solitude* wins the Chianchiano Prize in Italy and is named the Best Foreign Book in France.
1970	*One Hundred Years of Solitude* is published in English and chosen as one of twelve best books of the year by U.S. critics.
1971	Peruvian novelist Mario Vargas Llosa publishes the first book-length study of García Márquez's life and work, *Gabriel García Márquez: Historia de un deicidio*. García

	Márquez receives an honorary Doctorate of Letters from Columbia University.
1972	Awarded Rómulo Gallegos Prize. Publishes *La increíble y triste de la cándida Eréndira y de su abuela desalmada* (*The Incredible and Sad Tale of Innocent Eréndira and Her Heartless Grandmother*). Awarded *Books Abroad*/Neustadt Prize. *Leaf Storm and Other Stories* published in New York.
1974	Founds *Alternativa*, a leftist magazine, in Bogotá.
1975	Publishes *El otoño del patriarca* (*The Autumn of the Patriarch*). Leaves Spain and returns to Mexico.
1976	*The Autumn of the Patriarch* is published in New York.
1977	Publishes *Operación Carlota* (*Operation Carlota*), essays on Cuba's role in Africa.
1978	*Innocent Eréndira and Other Stories* published in the U.S.
1979	English translation of *In Evil Hour* published in the U.S.
1981	Publishes *Crónica de una muerta anunciada* (*Chronicle of a Death Foretold*). Awarded the French Legion of Honor Medal. When he returns to Colombia from Cuba, the government accuses him of financing a guerrilla group; he flees and seeks political asylum in Mexico. *Obra periodística*, four volumes of his journalistic pieces, edited by Jacques Gilard, is published.
1982	Awarded Nobel Prize for Literature. Publishes *El olor de la guayaba* (*The Fragrance of Guava*), conversations with Plinio Apuleyo Mendoza. Writes *Viva Sandino*, a screenplay about the Nicaraguan revolution.
1983	Returns to Colombia from his exile in Mexico. *Chronicle of a Death Foretold* published in the U.S.
1984	*Collected Stories* is published in the U.S.
1985	Publishes *El amor en los tiempos del cólera* (*Love in the Time of Cholera*), a novel. The English translation is released in the U.S. in 1988.
1986	*La adventura de Miguel Littín, clandestino en Chile*, a work of nonfiction, published. *The Story of a Shipwrecked Sailor*, his tale of Luis Alejandro Velasco's survival, published in the U.S.
1987	*Clandestine in Chile: The Adventures of Miguel Littín* published in the U.S.

1989   The novel *El general en su labertino* (*The General in His Labyrinth*) is published in Argentina, Colombia, Mexico and Spain. A year later the English translation is published in the U.S.

1992   *Doce cuentos peregrinos* (*Strange Pilgrims: Twelve Stories*) published in Madrid. A year later, English translation published in the U.S.

1994   *Del amor y otros demonios* (*Of Love and Other Demons*) published in Barcelona. A year later, the English translation published in the U.S.

1996   *Noticia de un secuestro* (*News of Kidnapping*) published. A year later, the English translation is published.

1998   He is a guest of Fidel Castro's during the historic visit of Pope John Paul II to Colombia.

1999   Purchases *Cambio*, a Colombian newsmagazine. In June he is hospitalized for fatigue; in September he goes to Los Angeles to undergo treatment for lymphatic cancer.

2001   Publishes first volume of memoirs, called *Vivir para contarla* (*Living to Tell the Tale*).

2003   *Living to Tell the Tale* is published in the U.S.

2005   The novella *Memories of My Melancholy Whores* is published in the U.S.

Contributors

HAROLD BLOOM is Sterling Professor of the Humanities at Yale University. He is the author of 30 books, including *Shelley's Mythmaking* (1959), *The Visionary Company* (1961), *Blake's Apocalypse* (1963), *Yeats* (1970), *A Map of Misreading* (1975), *Kabbalah and Criticism* (1975), *Agon: Toward a Theory of Revisionism* (1982), *The American Religion* (1992), *The Western Canon* (1994), and *Omens of Millennium: The Gnosis of Angels, Dreams, and Resurrection* (1996). *The Anxiety of Influence* (1973) sets forth Professor Bloom's provocative theory of the literary relationships between the great writers and their predecessors. His most recent books include *Shakespeare: The Invention of the Human* (1998), a 1998 National Book Award finalist, *How to Read and Why* (2000), *Genius: A Mosaic of One Hundred Exemplary Creative Minds* (2002), *Hamlet: Poem Unlimited* (2003), *Where Shall Wisdom Be Found?* (2004), and *Jesus and Yahweh: The Names Divine* (2005). In 1999, Professor Bloom received the prestigious American Academy of Arts and Letters Gold Medal for Criticism. He has also received the International Prize of Catalonia, the Alfonso Reyes Prize of Mexico, and the Hans Christian Andersen Bicentennial Prize of Denmark.

RITA GUIBERT is the author of *Seven Voices: Seven Lain American Writers Talk to Rita Guibert*.

GENE H. BELL-VILLADA is the author of *García Márquez: The Man and His Work, One Hundred Years of Solitude: A Casebook,* and *Conversations with Gabriel García Márquez* (2005). Bell-Villada's other books include *Art for*

Art's Sake & Literary Life: How Politics and Markets Helped Shape the Ideology & Culture of Aestheticism 1790-1990 (1996), a finalist for the National Book Critics' Circle Award, and his memoir *Overseas American: Growing Up Gringo in the Tropics* (2005).

HARLEY D. OBERHELMAN is the author of many scholarly articles, *The Presence of Faulkner in the Writings of García Márquez,* and *The Presence of Hemingway in the Short Fiction of García Márquez.*

VERA M. KUTZINSKI joined Vanderbilt University in 2004 as the Center for America's first director and the first Martha Rivers Ingram Professor of English. Kutzinski is a literary scholar and cultural historian whose research has focused on the United States, Caribbean, and Latin America during the nineteenth and twentieth centuries. Along with scores of articles, Kutzinski has authored three books in her field: *Against the American Grain: Myth and History in Williams Carlos Williams, Jay Wright, and Nicolás Guillén* (1987), and *Sugar's Secrets: Race and the Erotics of Cuban Nationalism* (1993).

STEPHEN M. HART is the author of *Gabriel García Márquez: crónica de una muerte anunciada* and *A Companion to Spanish-American Literature,* and is co-editor of *Companion to Magical Realism.*

STEVEN BOLDY is a university senior lecturer in the Department of Spanish and Portuguese at the University of Cambridge. He is the author of (among other works) *The Novels of Julio Cortázar, Memoria Mexicana,* and many articles on the authors Cortázar, Rulfo, Carpentier, and Carlos Fuentes. His latest book is entitled *The Narrative of Carlos Fuentes.*

A Fullbright and ACLS fellow, DIANE E. MARTING has edited several reference works on Spanish-American women writers and Clarice Lispector. She has written many articles on Latin-American literature and is the author of *The Sexual Woman in Latin American Fiction.*

RAYMOND L. WILLIAMS, professor of Spanish at the University of California, Riverside, is a specialist in Latin American narrative and Colombian literature. He is an internationally recognized scholar of the Colombian novel and the writings of Carlos Fuentes, Mario Vargas Llosa, and Gabriel García Márquez. He is the author of several books, and currently has a new book in press: *The Twentieth Century Spanish American Novel: A Critical History* (University of Texas Press).

JO LABANYI is professor of languages at Southampton, and has specialized in 19th and 20th century Spanish culture, including literature and film. She has also published on Latin American culture, particularly women's writing, and is the author of *Gender and Modernization in the Spanish Realist Novel*. She is currently writing a book on 1940s Spanish cinema, and editing the collective volumes *Reconfigurations of Empire: Cultural Perspectives on the War in the Caribbean and the Philippines* (with Alistair Hennessy and Sebastian Balfour) and *Cultures of Remembrance/Culture as Remembrance*. In 2005 she was elected a Fellow of the British Academy.

ISABEL ALVAREZ-BORLAND is professor of Spanish at the College of the Holy Cross. She is the author of *Cuban-American Narratives of Exile: From Person to Persona*.

ROBIN FIDDIAN is the author of *Postcolonial Perspectives on Latin American and Lusophone Cultures* and *The Novels of Fernando Del Paso*. He teaches Spanish at Oxford University in England.

LOIS PARKINSON ZAMORA teaches at the University of Houston in the departments of English, history, and art. Zamora's main area of specialization is contemporary fiction in the Americas and her many publications include *Writing the Apocalypse: Historical Vision in Contemporary U.S and Latin American Fiction* (1989), *Image and Memory: Photography from Latin America 1866-1994* (1998), and *The Usable Past: The Imagination of History in Recent Fiction of the Americas* (1997), and she co-edited with Wendy B. Faris *Magical Realism: Theory, History, Community* (1995).

Bibliography

Alèthea 13 (Spring–Summer 1984). *Gabriel García Márquez: The Man and the Magic of His Writings.* Ed. Ricardo Pastor.

Alvarez-Borland, Isabel. "From Mystery to Parody: (Re)Readings of García Márquez's Crónica de una Muerte Anunciada." *Symposium* 38, no. 4 (Winter 1984–85).

Anderson, Jon Lee. "The Power of García Márquez." *New Yorker* (September 27, 1999): 56–66, 68–71.

Bell, Michael. *Gabriel García Márquez: Solitude and Solidarity.* New York: St. Martin's Press, 1993.

Bell-Villada, Gene H. *García Márquez: The Man and His Work.* Chapel Hill: The University of North Carolina Press, 1990.

———. *One Hundred Years of Solitude: A Casebook.* New York: Oxford University Press, 2002.

Boldy, Steven. "*One Hundred Years of Solitude* by Gabriel García Márquez." In *The Cambridge Companion to the Latin American Novel.* Ed. Efraín Kristal. Cambridge: Cambridge University Press, 2005. 258–69.

Brushwood, John S. "Reality and Imagination in the Novels of García Márquez." *Latin American Literary Review* 25 (1985): 9–14.

Davis, Mary E. "The Town That Was an Open Wound." *Comparative Literature Studies* 23, no. 1 (Spring 1986): 24–43.

Donoso, José. *The Boom in Spanish American Literature: A Personal History.* Trans. Gregory Kolovakos. New York: Columbia University Press, 1977.

Earle, Pete G., ed. *Gabriel García Márquez*. Madrid: Taurus, 1981.

Fau, Margaret Eustella. *Gabriel García Márquez: An Annotated Bibliography, 1947–1979*. Westport, CT: Greenwood Press, 1980.

Fau, Margaret Eustella and Nelly Sefir de González, ed. *Bibliographic Guide to Gabriel García Márquez, 1979–1985*. Westport, CT: Greenwood Press, 1986.

Fiddian, Robin, ed. *García Márquez*. New York: Longman, 1995.

Fuentes, Carlos. "Gabriel García Márquez: la segunda lectura." in *La nueva novela hispanoamericana*. Mexico City: Joaquín Mortiz, 1969: 58–67.

———.*Gabriel García Márquez and the Invention of America*. Liverpool, England: Liverpool University Press, 1987.

Goldman, Francisco. "In the Shadow of the Patriarch." *New York Times Magazine*. November 2, 2003: 38+.

Guibert, Rita. "Gabriel García Márquez." In *Seven Voices: Seven Latin American Writers Talk to Rita Guibert*. Trans. Frances Partridge. New York: Knopf, 1973: 305–37.

Hart, Stephen M. *Gabriel García Márquez: crónica de una Muerte Anunciada*. London: Grant & Cutler, 2005.

———. "Magical Realism in the Americas: Politicised Ghosts in *One Hundred Years of Solitude, The House of Spirits*, and *Beloved*." *Tesserae: Journal of Iberian and Latin American Studies* 9, no. 2 (December 2003): 115–23.

Janes, Regina. *Gabriel García Márquez: Revolution in Wonderland*. Columbia: University of Missouri Press, 1981.

Kerr, R.A. "Patterns of Place and Visual-Spatial Imagery in García Márquez's *Del amor y otros demonios*." *Hispania* 79, no. 4 (December 1996): 772–80.

Kutzinski, Vera M. "The Logic of Wings: Gabriel García Márquez and Afro-American Literature." *The Latin American Literary Review* 13, no. 25 (January–June 1985).

Latin American Literary Review 13 (January–June 1985). *Special Issue: Gabriel García Márquez*. Eds. Yvette E. Miller and Charles Rossman.

Marting, Diane E. "The End of Eréndira's Prostitution." *Hispanic Review* 69, no. 2 (Spring 2001): 175–90.

McGuirk, Bernard and Richard Cardwell, ed. *Gabriel García Márquez: New Readings*. New York: Cambridge University Press, 1987.

McMurray, George R. *Gabriel García Márquez*. New York: Ungar, 1977.

McNerney, Kathleen. *Understanding Gabriel García Márquez*. South Carolina: University of South Carolina, 1989.

Mellen, Joan, ed. *Literary Masters: Gabriel García Márquez.* Vol. 5. Detroit: Gale Group, 2000.

Minta, Stephen. *Gabriel García Márquez: Writer of Colombia.* London: Jonathan Cape, 1987.

Oberhelman, Harley D. *The Presence of Faulkner in the Writings of García Márquez.* Lubbock: Texas Tech Press, 1980.

———. *The Presence of Hemingway in the Short Fiction of García Márquez.* Fredericton, N.B., Canada: York Press Ltd, 1994.

Pelayo, Ruben. *Gabriel García Márquez: A Critical Companion.* Westport, CT: Greenwood Press, 2001.

PEN America: A Journal for Writers and Readers 3, no 6. (2005). "Gabriel García Márquez: Everyday Magic."

Rodman, Selden. "Gabriel García Márquez." *Tongues of Fallen Angels: Conversations.* New York: New Directions, 1974. 113–133.

Santos-Phillips, Eva. "Power of the Body in the Novella The Incredible and Sad Tale of Innocent Eréndira and of Her Heartless Grandmother and the Film *Eréndira.*" *Literature Film Quarterly* 31, no. 2 (2003): 118–23.

Shaw, Bradley A. and Nora Vera-Goodwin, eds. *Critical Perspectives on Gabriel García Márquez.* Lincoln, Nebraska: Society of Spanish and Spanish-American Studies, 1986.

Stone, Peter. "Gabriel García Márquez." In *Writers At Work: The Paris Review Interviews—Sixth Series.* Ed. George Plimpton. New York: Viking, 1984. 313–39.

Vargas Llosa, Mario. *Gabriel García Márquez: historia de un deicidio.* Barcelona: Barral Editores, 1971.

Williams, Raymond. *Gabriel García Márquez.* Boston: Twayne, 1984.

Wood, Michael. *Gabriel García Márquez: One Hundred Years of Solitude.* Cambridge & New York: Cambridge University Press, 1990.

Zamora, Lois Parkinson. "Apocalypse and Human Time in The Fiction of Gabriel García Márquez." In *Writing of the Apocalypse.* Cambridge: Cambridge University Press, 1989.

Acknowledgments

"Interview with Gabriel García Márquez" by Rita Guibert. *Seven Voices: Seven Latin American Writers Talk to Rita Guibert.* © 1973 by Alfred A. Knopf, Inc. Reprinted by permission.

"The Writer's Life" by Gene H. Bell-Villada. *García Márquez: The Man and His Work.* © 1990 by The University of North Carolina Press. Used by permission of the publisher.

"Hemingway's Presence in the Early Short Fiction (1950–55)" by Harley D. Oberhelman. *The Presence of Hemingway in the Short Fiction of Gabriel García Márquez.* © 1994 York Press, Ltd. Reprinted by permission.

"The Logic of Wings: Gabriel García Márquez and Afro-American Literature" by Vera M. Kutzinski. *García Márquez*, ed. Robin Fiddian. © 1995 by Longman Group Limited. Originally from *Latin American Literary Review* 13, no. 25 (1985): 133–146. Reprinted by permission.

"Magical Realism in the Americas: Politicised Ghosts in *One Hundred Years of Solitude, The House of Spirits*, and *Beloved*" by Stephen M. Hart. From *Journal of Iberian and Latin American Studies* Vol. 9, No. 2 (December 2003): 115–124. © 2003 by Taylor and Francis, Ltd. Reprinted by permission.

"*One Hundred Years of Solitude* by Gabriel García Márquez" by Steven Boldy. *The Cambridge Companion to The Latin American Novel*, ed. Efraín Kristal. ©

2005 by Cambridge University Press. Reprinted with permission of the Cambridge University Press.

"The End of Eréndira's Prostitution" by Diane E. Marting. From *Hispanic Review* Vol. 69, No. 2 (Spring 2001): 175–190. © 2001 by Hispanic Review. Reprinted by permission of the University of Pennsylvania Press.

"*The Autumn of the Patriarch* (1975)" by Raymond L. Williams. From *Gabriel García Márquez* by Raymond L. Williams, Twayne Publishers, copyright © 1984, Twayne Publishers. Reprinted by permission of The Gale Group.

"Language and Power in *The Autumn of the Patriarch*" by Jo Labanyi. From *Gabriel García Márquez: New Readings*, ed. Bernard McGuirk and Richard Cardwell, pp. 135–149. © 1987 by Cambridge University Press. Reprinted with permission of Cambridge University Press.

"From Mystery to Parody: (Re)readings of García Márquez's Crónica de una Muerte Anunciada" by Isabel Alvarez-Borland. From *Symposium* Vol. 38, No. 4 (Winter 1984–85): 278–286. © 1985 by the Helen Dwight Reid Educational Foundation. Reprinted by permission.

"A prospective post-script: apropos of *Love in the Times of Cholera*" by Robin Fiddian. *Gabriel García Márquez: New Readings*, ed. Bernard McGuirk and Richard Cardwell. © 1987 by Cambridge University Press. Reprinted with permission of Cambridge University Press.

"Apocalypse and Human Time in The Fiction of Gabriel García Márquez" by Lois Parkinson Zamora. From *Writing the Apocalypse: Historical Vision in Contemporary U.S. and Latin American Fiction* pp. 25–51 © 1989 by Cambridge University Press. Reprinted with permission of Cambridge University Press.

Every effort has been made to contact the owners of copyrighted material and secure copyright permission. Articles appearing in this volume generally appear much as they did in their original publication with few or no editorial changes. Those interested in locating the original source will find bibliographic information in the bibliography and acknowledgments sections of this volume.

Index

Absalom, Absalom! (Faulkner)
  Chronicle of a Death Foretold and, 201–2
  history as myth in, 203–204
  incest in, 103, 194
  man's taming of wilderness in, 193–195
  narrator as decipherer/mediator in, 199–201
  narrators of, 195–197
  One Hundred Years of Solitude and, 192–193
  promised land/New World in, 194
  prose style of, 101–203
Afro-American culture, 67–81
  Caribbean setting and, 67–69
  García Márquez on, 69
  santería element, 70–73
"All God's Chillun Had Wings," 71–72
Allende, Isabel, 87–88
Americanism, 175
ancestry, 69
Antigone (Sophocles), 103
apocalypse
  comic versions of, 188, 211
  in García Márquez's perspective, 183–184
  as giving structure to narrative

  history, 193
  language and, 198–199, 211
  in narrative stance, 195–199
  patterns of, 184, 211, 212
Apuleyo Mendoza, Plinio, 43
Aracataca, 33, 34, 98–99
Arendt, Hannah, 184
Ariel, 16
Arnau, Carmen, 185
Asturias, Miguel Angel, 30
Autocrítica, 60
The Autumn of the Patriarch, 44, 51
  anecdotal nature of, 125
  apocalyptic symbolism of, 206–207
  characterization in, 137–139, 143–144, 151–152
  characters of, 125–126
  comet imagery in, 151
  decadence in, 146
  as exposé of political corruption, 205–207
  illiteracy in, 148–149
  language and power in, 145–157
  location of, 124–125
  narrative focus in, 132–137
  narrative style of, 152–157
  nightmare quality of, 205–206
  as novel of the dictator, 123
  poetry in, 148